S p l a s h !

Splash!

Great Writing About Swimming

Edited and with an Introduction
by Laurel Blossom

Preface by
George Plimpton

THE ECCO PRESS

for my coach,

Mr. Godfrey,

and for my dad

THE ECCO PRESS
100 West Broad Street
Hopewell, New Jersey 08525

Published simultaneously in Canada by
Penguin Books Canada Ltd., Ontario
Printed in the United States of America

Library of Congress Cataloging-in-Publication Data

Splash! : great writing about swimming / edited with an introduction
by Laurel Blossom ; preface by George Plimpton. — 1st ed.
p.   cm. — (Ecco companions series)
Includes bibliographical references.
ISBN 0-88001-449-0 (paper)
1. Swimming — Miscellanea.   I. Blossom, Laurel.   II. Series: Ecco
companions.
GV837.S818   1996
797.2'1 — dc20   95-46562

Pages 251 to 254 constitute an extension of this copyright page.

Designed by Richard Oriolo

The text of this book is set in Electra

9 8 7 6 5 4 3 2 1

FIRST EDITION

Contents

George Plimpton

Preface

Years ago, not long out of college, I dated a young Floridian who had been a high school swimming champion. She kept her trophies in her room—dozens of tiny dime-sized medals hanging from thin ribbons. At the time, I was struck with how minuscule the rewards were for such an exacting sport—the innumerable hours spent training, lap after lap, in that strange, surreal, chlorine-scented world with little to see except the tile patterns below. I once asked her if she'd ever discovered anything on the bottom. She said she had—a shoe, a pie plate, plastic spoons, and once, a sodden rag doll—but not enough to make up for the monotony.

I never thought to compete against her. It would have been embarrassing. It was enough to watch her glide through the water, so thin and graceful she hardly seemed to displace the surface. In my odd career as a participatory journalist (football with the Detroit Lions, hockey with the Boston Bruins, basketball with the Boston Celtics) it never occurred to me to try her world of swimming—to enter a diving competition, say, or stand on a pedestal at the end of an Olympic pool, shaking my muscles loose, among a line of Olympic champions doing the same.

Then one day in the late 1960s, while I was at Yale University giving a speech, the students, without my knowledge, arranged an informal race—me against Don Schollander, the freestyle champion in the Tokyo Olympics in 1964. I resisted. I said I didn't have a bathing suit. I said I was allergic to chlorine. None of this worked. The students said I was duty-bound as a participatory journalist to expand my horizons by including competitive swimming. Besides, they had persuaded one of history's greatest swimmers to be my competitor. How could I turn down this opportunity?

I met Schollander in the shower before the race. I told him that at Harvard we showered only after leaving the pool, not before. I doubt that's so, but I thought it might throw him a bit. He looked puzzled. He said that at Yale the athletes showered before *and* after. "Oh yes," I said.

I was supplied a brief pair of swimming trunks. Out at poolside Schollander suggested I start off first; when he thought the handicap was sufficient, he'd come after me. How decent of him, I thought. Quite a crowd of students were in the stands. I jumped in and lazied down the lane, intending to go into full gear when I heard Schollander's body hit the water. That didn't happen for quite awhile, not until I was almost halfway down the length of the pool. To this day I can hear the odd thumping sound, not unlike the whump-whump of a motor yacht's propeller thrashing the water, as he came up and passed me within a yard or so of the end of the pool. He grinned as he looked over, the water glistening on his otter-sleek hair. The only mild compensation for what I'd endured was that Schollander's coach leaned over and praised him for his sprint speed—"Very nice, very nice." He nodded down at me: I could pride myself on being a first-rate trial horse.

Schollander was the first of a number of renowned swimmers I eventually got to know. Indeed, there was one vaguely in the family: my aunt by marriage had a distant cousin who was a famous long-distance swimmer, Diana Nyad. She once tried to swim to Cuba, towed through the seas in a cage to protect her from sharks. Endlessly she sang "Row, row, row your boat." She was forced to give up because of rough seas that battered her around in her cage. She told me she had estimated the number of times she sang the verses before they pulled her out—a staggering number, a hundred thousand or so, the exact count I have since forgotten. On one occasion she swam around the island of Manhattan. From my living-room windows that look out on the East River, I watched her go by—a diminutive figure in the currents. I wanted to say to someone, "Hey, that's a distant cousin of mine by marriage out there in the river," but there wasn't anyone in the apartment at the time.

Four years after Mark Spitz won seven Olympic gold medals in Munich, I interviewed him in his condominium complex in Marina del Rey, California. He had some interesting observations about competitive swimming that made me think back on my Florida friend: "What a price I paid for all that work," Spitz said. "There is something very depressing about becoming the best in the world at something. I was programmed for all those years. I swam two-and-a-half hours in the morning and two in the evening, maybe seven miles a day for six years, and during all those hours I'd think about getting out of the pool at the end of the session and how pleasant that was going to be. I *loved* to think about getting out."

He justified all of the labor in defining this triumphant moment: "When I got off the awards stand after the seventh gold medal," he said, "my teammates picked me up and carried me on their shoulders. I'd gained their respect."

Was that what it was all for, I wanted to know—gaining the respect of his fellow athletes?

"And self-recognition," he said. "Swimming is the only sport where before an athlete competes he stands on a pedestal, is introduced and applauded. He hasn't even done anything. Instant recognition. That's so much of what an athlete wants. Then he gets rewarded immediately afterwards. It would be terrible if he got the award the next day. He might forget what he got it for."

Spitz then added a curious comment: "The great thing about being a competitive swimmer is that you know it's going to end quickly. When you're 23, you quit."

He went on to say that in the four years since Munich he had pretty much kept to his work, truly avoiding the medium that had made him so famous. Once in awhile he did a lap or two in his in-laws' swimming pool.

Later I ran into a friend who had been at a party the year before at which Spitz had been persuaded to go swim.

"He went home to get his swimsuit. It's a small pool. He can cross it in several strokes. But it's big enough so you can see how good he is. I went in with him. He passed me using his legs only, cruising by with his arms out of the water! I couldn't stand it. I jumped out of the pool. I loved it. It really turned me on to see anybody that good. That's what he ought to do until he gets too old to float—cruise up and down pools so that people can see what an incredible sight that is."

Finally, I had the opportunity to talk to some swimmers during the 1984 Olympics in Los Angeles—in particular John Nabor, the winner of four gold medals in Montreal in 1976. We were sitting in the stands. The women divers were collected on the various levels of the diving platforms, chatting amongst themselves. "Very gregarious bunch, divers," Nabor said. "Far more social than swimmers."

"Why is that?" I asked.

"Swimmers don't have anyone to commune with except themselves," Nabor told me. "Nothing but the rush of water in their ears, hour after hour in practice. Many of them sing to themselves to pass the time. I used to sing 'Smoke on the Water'."

I mentioned my distant cousin by marriage singing "Row, row, row your boat." I remembered my Florida friend and couldn't resist asking: "Ever find anything in the bottom of the pool?"

He said he had once discovered $4.79 in change in his high school's pool, down by one of the drains.

When I asked him how he figured the money got there, he said that a question like that was worth dozens and dozens of pool-length laps to think about, even if one never came up with an answer.

"You were talking about the divers," I said. "I interrupted."

"They're different from the swimmers who spend all their time in the water. Divers stand around in the open air. They preen a lot, very conscious of their bodies because they're judged on form, how they look. They're like high-fashion models. They spend a lot of time jabbering to each other in Jacuzzis."

We watched them on the platform, elegant and lovely, like egrets in a rookery.

A number of years ago I was up there on one of those platforms—thirty feet up—persuaded by a television producer to leap off as a penalty for losing an exhibition tennis match to Bobby Riggs. If memory serves, it was on the Mike Douglas Show and the venue was the Fountainbleu Hotel in Miami. The producer asked me to jump at noon, three hours before our match was scheduled. "The light's just right for the cameras," he explained.

"Hey, we haven't played yet," I complained.

"Riggs'll win. He always does. Your jump into the pool will be very filmic," the producer said. "Great conclusion to the show."

I asked if Riggs was willing to jump from the tower if he lost.

"No," the producer replied, "Riggs is scared of heights."

He finally persuaded me. Eventually, rather gloomily, I climbed the tower. Riggs was up there, capering about.

"Hey," I said. "I thought you were scared of heights."

He looked puzzled. "What?"

So I went off the edge...the pool far below, about the size of a thumbnail if an arm were held out at full length. I entered it full blast—with a cannonball dive, as I recall. The producer was right. Three hours later I lost the match. Riggs played the last game handicapping himself with a pair of Wellington boots and a dachshund on a leash.

But enough of this! What follows is a wonderful mélange of stories, reminiscences, and accounts by various folk—some champions, some not—sporting, competing, whatever, in swimming pools, lakes, bays, oceans. Mankind is supposed to have emerged from the seas in primeval times. By the time readers finish this collection, they'll feel they have returned to that primal state; they'll be completely water logged. But why not? Come on in. The water's fine!

Laurel Blossom

Introduction

I

Two extraordinary events occurred at the turn of the twentieth century that helped determine the starting point of the present anthology: the founding of the modern Olympic Games in 1896 and the introduction of the Australian crawl to Europe and America in 1902. Together, I have learned, these developments revolutionized the sport of swimming and gradually changed public attitudes toward health, decency, and morality.

The modern Olympic movement was founded in 1896 by Baron Pierre de Coubertin. De Coubertin perceived a weakness in the character of his French compatriots, debilitated by the Franco-Prussian War, that he believed athletic competition could overcome. England's experience with swimming convinced him that the body, the mind, and the spirit are enhanced by participation in sports; win or lose, he believed, athletic activity could build both self-esteem and respect for others. By building individual character, furthermore, a modern Olympic movement could promote a more peaceful world; in ancient Greece war was suspended for the duration of all Olympic contests.

When the Olympics were revived (as in ancient times, for men only) in Athens in 1896, swimming was included for the first time. The preferred strokes were the breaststroke and the newly introduced trudgen stroke, a double overarm stroke combined with the traditional scissors kick. In 1900, backstroke events were instituted. Richard Cavill introduced the flutter kick, overarm Australian crawl to England in 1902 by swimming 100 yards in 58.6 seconds, a speed no breast- or trudgen stroker could hope to match. In 1904, therefore, the breaststroke and the crawl were made separate Olympic events. Diving was introduced in 1908, and in 1912, women joined Olympic competition.

The introduction of the crawl soon turned swimming enthusiasm from endurance to speed. Throughout the second half of the nineteenth century, while swimming in England and the United States had become increasingly popular, the emphasis was on distance and the focus was the English Channel. When Captain Matthew Webb succeeded in swimming from Dover to Cap Gris-Nez on August 24, 1875, he became famous throughout the world for accomplishing what had been thought an impossible feat; not satisfied with the Channel record, he tried to swim the rapids above Niagara Falls in 1883

and died in the attempt. It wasn't until 1911, thirty-six years after Webb's crossing, that another man succeeded in swimming the Channel. Gertrude Ederle
revived public interest in distance swimming when, in 1926, she became the
first woman to cross the Channel; since then, interest has continued to grow.
Today a worldwide professional circuit exists for open-water swimming competition.

Recreational swimming was traditional for boys and men in England and
the United States throughout the nineteenth century. Even nude swimming
was considered a natural activity until swimming began to attract women
and girls in the second half of the century. Female swimming quickly came
under attack by Victorian moralists and did not regain respectability until after
World War I; swimming was alleged to affect the womb and to make it difficult
for a woman to conceive or to carry a baby to term. In the early years of the
twentieth century, several pioneer women swimmers were arrested at the
beach for swimming without stockings or unencumbered by the heavy skirts
then in fashion. Exposed female flesh was a scandal, raising fears of unbridled
sexuality.

However, certain lonely voices continued to promote the benefits of swimming for health and safety. The YMCA movement sought to teach children
and adults to swim, in fulfillment of its *mens sana in corpore sano* ideal. Glam-
orous swimming exhibitions by famous swimmers such as Annette Kellerman
and Johnny Weissmuller, bare skinned and beautiful, began to open people's
eyes to swimming's wider possibilities. By the twenties and thirties, swimming—and especially, the swimming pool—had become positive symbols of
status and sexuality, epitomized by the movie-star culture of Hollywood that the
United States was exporting to the rest of the world. The New York World's Fair
of 1939, which predicted the suburban American lifestyle of the second half of
the century, included promises of backyard swimming pools. One of its most
popular attractions was impresario Billy Rose's spectacular Aquacade, in which
Eleanor Holm, a backstroke champion who had been thrown off the 1936
Olympic team for drinking champagne on board ship, delighted audiences
with her glittering aquatic displays. It was only a step—a virtuous step—from
there to the movies of Esther Williams, who created the athletic–romantic
ideal of womanhood with which I and many other young men and women in
the late forties and early fifties grew up. Meanwhile, swimming pools had pro-
liferated to such a degree that Ned Merrill, the protagonist of John Cheever's
story "The Swimmer," could conceive of them as a river winding across
Westchester County.

Today, swimming is enjoyed by millions of people every year, at the beach,
in lakes or rivers, at the Y, in public or private pools, and at clubhouses around
the world. Its popularity suggested the present anthology.

I I

"Swimming cultivates imagination," wrote Annette Kellerman in *How to Swim*. When we swim we shed our higher consciousness, the complex, reasoning human organism, and remember, deep inside ourselves, the first oceanic living cell; we almost become our origins. Whether in lake, ocean, or pool, there comes that moment when the world of our ordinary preoccupations washes away and we sink into a meditative state in which the instinctual, intuitive, subconscious mind can tell us what we need to know.

The question is always the same: Who am I? The answer is in each swimmer's—and each writer's—imagination.

The writers presented here, some of whom are swimmers themselves, turn the tables on Kellerman's insight or carry it one step further. They use their imaginative powers to reinvent on the page the experience swimmers have in the water: from a daughter's first lesson to swimming the Hellespont; from myth and science fiction to the neighborhood pool; from the hallucinations of the long-distance swimmer to the drama of Olympic competition.

The literature of swimming is rich and varied, and like all good literature it does not confine itself to its primary subject, but delves deep into human experience. In the world of water, we become aware of our skin, of the body's limits and definitions, while we are simultaneously wrapped in an element so familiar, so delightful, so sensual that we feel we have come home. Because life seeks both merger and separation, swimming is a perfect correlative for its mystery.

The experience of swimming is both sexual and spiritual. The sensation of water flowing over the body is dynamic, erotic, enlivening, and yet it awakens, at every moment, our consciousness of the fragility of our breath. No wonder religions all over the world see water as holy. We are washed clean both by its action on our bodies and by the act of faith we make when we lay ourselves upon it, believing it will hold us up. The miracle is, of course, that it does.

Swimming is redemptive, a holy act, a healing ritual. But it is more than that: Swimming is creative. Paul Valéry wrote in his journal, "To plunge into water, to move one's whole body, from head to toe, in its wild and graceful beauty; to twist about in its pure depths, this is for me a delight only comparable to love." In that pause away from the desk or the lab, the shop counter or the factory floor, some of our most profound connections are made.

I became particularly aware of the similarities between swimming and the creative process while considering the work that appears here. I realized that both swimming and writing engender and allow the trancelike state in which the imagination flourishes without censor or restraint. Water is an ancient metaphor for the subconscious; swimmers choose, as writers do, to immerse themselves in it. Scott Fitzgerald, in "The Crack Up," describes "all good writing" as "swimming underwater and holding your breath." This immersion isolates swimmers and writers. It involves them, as Charles Sprawson wrote in his illuminating history of swimming, *Haunts of the Black Masseur,* "in a mental world of their own" that leads others, sometimes, to accuse them of narcissism and self-absorption. It isn't that. It's absorption in the worlds they enter, so different from ordinary life or land.

There are physical similarities, too, between swimming and writing. Swimmers do laps; poets do lines. Both of them count, syllables, lengths, beats. Swimmers strike out across immeasurable bodies of water, the dangers, frustrations, and ends of which are unknown; novelists do the same. Picking up a pen is like stepping onto a diving board; beginning to write is like jumping into deep, cold water. But, despite ourselves, we hold our breath and dive in. After a page or two we warm to the task. The temperature equalizes inside and out. We feel comfortable; we forget the unnaturalness of breathing to one side; the movement of our arms, the kicking of our feet, the stroke of our pen become unconscious, a means of pushing us forward into the unknown that awaits us with the next word we write or over the crest of the next wave.

I I I

This book grew out of a love for swimming and a love for writing and reading. The choices I have made are necessarily personal, informed by my own experience and literary preferences. Nevertheless, I have tried to make the book as representative of the experience of swimming as possible. Unfortunately, not every fine piece of writing could be included in the limited space of a single volume. F. Scott Fitzgerald's story "The Swimmers" is included in his *Collected Stories.* Greg Louganis has told his story in an autobiography, *Breaking the Surface.* Roald Dahl's mordant story "A Dip in the Pool" can be found in his book *Someone Like You.* Somerset Maugham's long story "The Pool" is in his *Collected Stories.* Mary Roberts Rinehart's novel *The Swimming Pool* evokes the vanished lifestyle of the upper middle class. Michael Blumenthal has written a book-length poem called *Laps.* A number of swimming poems by Susan Ludvigson appear in her book *The Swimmer.* All of these, and others, had to be left out for reasons of space, variety, or emphasis.

I want to thank Daniel Halpern and Ellen Foos for their editorial expertise and generosity; Leonard Todd, Connie Berry, and Jason Shinder for their close reading of the manuscript; Steven Haas for his research assistance; Fred Courtright for obtaining permissions; Preston and Rita Levi of the Henning Library at the International Swimming Hall of Fame for their kindness in helping me find my way through their invaluable resources; Jennifer Moyer for her interest and advice; Buck Dawson for lunch, twice; and all those who sent me work or gave me leads to work I wouldn't otherwise have known about. They have all been my coaches and companions in this wonderful, long-distance endeavor.

The experience of swimming is elusive; it cannot be captured by a single voice at any one time because it is always changing. That is one of its allures. It is my hope that *Splash!* tells the story, from many points of view, of its shifting facets.

"The sea is my memory, my awesome memory,"

thought the swimmer heading out from the shore.

—Edmond Jabès, "The Book"

Carol Anshaw

October 1968,
Mexico City

*F*or a few supersaturated moments, Jesse feels and sees and smells and hears everything. The crushing heat, the Mexican sky white with a flat sun, pressing like an iron against the roll of her shoulders. The rising scent of chlorine and baby oil and something that's not sweat exactly, but an aquatic analog, something swimmers give off in the last few minutes before an event, a jazzy mix of excitement and fear and wanting. The crowd, riled up as though they are going to swim this race themselves.

Except for her godmother, who sits in the stands, unruffled, unflapped—a midwestern Buddha, here by way of two days and a long night on a Trailways bus from Missouri. With her is Jesse's brother, bouncing a little in his seat, twiddling his hands like a haywire backup singer, a Temptation gone kaflooey. There's so much else going on, though, that for once he draws no particular attention.

Down at pool level with Jesse is Bud Freeman, coach of the American women's team, a crew-cut fireplug several inches shorter than Jesse, at the moment casually peppering her arm with light jabs of his thick finger, reminding her that Marty Finch is a splash-out-and-die girl, not to worry about her in the first fifty meters. His mouth is so close to Jesse's face she can smell his breath, which is like oranges. She nods and tongues the insides of her goggles and looks over his shoulder at Marty, who is doing leg stretches against the next starting block, not looking at Jesse. Which is smart. Jesse shouldn't be looking at her either, not now.

Jesse stands next to the Lane 4 starting block. She's still nodding at whatever Bud is saying, although she has stopped listening, doesn't really need to. She has swum this race in her head every day since she was fourteen. For most of those three years' worth of days, her body has been through fifteen thousand meters, so it will know on its own precisely how to take these hundred. Today she will really just be going along with herself for the ride.

It's time to take to the blocks. In this instant, the wave she was riding—absorbing everything at once—crashes onto the shore of her self, and she whites out into a space at her dead center. She loses Bud, the crowd, the sun. All there is is her and the water stretching out in front of her, to be gotten through. Fifty meters up. Flip. Fifty meters back. A quick trip.

She stretches the strap of her goggles around the back of her head, lets it snap. Fiddles with the eye cups, tugs at the strap ends until she's sure she has a seal. She crouches and swings her arms behind her, then forward, just short of losing her balance. She's ready. She doesn't even need to see the starter to know he's raising the pistol. She can feel the event approaching, feel herself moving into it.

"Swimmers, take your marks." The metallic command comes through the public address horns, taking the event out of the dimension of not-happening, onto the plane of about-to-happen.

She hyperventilates to expand her lungs, flattens her soles against the roughed surface of the block. Now comes the critical moment, the one in which she needs to leave even herself behind and become purely what she can do, translate matter into energy, become velocity. In the hundreds of events she has swum on the way to this one, this split second in which she can see the race ahead completely, and see herself winning it, has given her an edge.

This time, though, the power of belief slips away, just a little. Just for the microslice of the second it takes for her to look over at Marty. Who does, for a flash instant, look back. But, through her goggles and then Marty's, and with the sun behind her blacking her out, Jesse can't read her face. She is still trying to decipher it, to pull some important message off it. . . . While she is temporarily lost in this constellation of fear and exhilaration and squeezed hope, the starter's pistol, which she is supposed to respond to instinctively, as though it's inside her, goes off in some very faraway place. Taking her completely by surprise.

And so Jesse Austin leaps out, hangs suspended for a freeze-frame moment, and enters Olympic waters one tenth of a second later than she should. She can't curse the lapse. There's no time. The next minute is an aquamarine blur.

The color shattered into a million wavy panes as the water prisms the sunlight that hits the pool bottom. Aquamarine and the deep blue of the wide stripe she follows down the center of the lane, tucking into her flip turn where the stripe dead-ends in a T. The touch of painted concrete against the balls of her feet as she pushes off. And then the last fifty. She knows she's swimming fast, maybe faster than she ever has. She feels an infinitesimal difference. It's as though the water has given in, is letting her through.

And then, there's the slick slap of tile on the palm of her hand as she finishes where she started. She comes up fast and flushed and eating air. She corkscrews out of the water, ripping off her goggles, looking around wildly for signs. To her left, in Lane 5, Marty has also touched. She's pulling off her cap with a rubbery squeak, bending back, her hair catching the water like white seagrass. Jesse watches this for a moment; it's a part of the too much happening all at once. She's still looking for the word to come down.

Then Bud is crouching on the rim of the pool just above her, shaking his head, holding up two fingers. She has come in second, taken the silver. Won something, but it's the loss that hits her first. She feels as though great weights are dragging her under. She looks over and watches Marty catch the good news from Ian Travers, the Australian coach. She has taken the gold. She's tossing her cap and goggles into the air and smiling with her whole body. And then she looks around and reaches outside the perimeter of her victory, over the lane markers to wrap an arm around Jesse's shoulders. It's a cross-chest carry of sorts, a gesture to bring Jesse up with her.

Amazingly, it works. Jesse can feel her spirit grabbing onto Marty's, and for this moment at least believes *they've* won, that together they've beat out the competition, that the two of them are laughing together in the hilarious ozone just above the plane of regular mortals. They go under, somersault, come up, and shoot out of the water, trailing arcs of spray behind them.

Jesse feels they have attained a great height, as though glory is a wide, flat place they will inhabit forever, rather than a sharp peak that will eventually slide them down another side, to ground level. But she isn't looking down now, only out, toward the limitless possibilities implicit in having attained this one.

She can feel their breezes rushing over her, lightly.

Philip Booth

First Lesson

Lie back, daughter, let your head
be tipped back in the cup of my hand.
Gently, and I will hold you. Spread
your arms wide, lie out on the stream
and look high at the gulls. A dead-
man's-float is face down. You will dive
and swim soon enough where this tidewater
ebbs to the sea. Daughter, believe
me, when you tire on the long thrash
to your island, lie up, and survive.
As you float now, where I held you
and let go, remember when fear
cramps your heart what I told you:
lie gently and wide to the light-year
stars, lie back, and the sea will hold you.

Ray Bradbury

The Women

*I*t was as if a light came on in a green room.

The ocean burned. A white phosphorescence stirred like a breath of steam through the autumn morning sea, rising. Bubbles rose from the throat of some hidden sea ravine.

Like lightning in the reversed green sky of the sea it was aware. It was old and beautiful. Out of the deeps it came, indolently. A shell, a wisp, a bubble, a weed, a glitter, a whisper, a gill. Suspended in its depths were brainlike trees of frosted coral, eyelike pips of yellow kelp, hairlike fluids of weed. Growing with the tides, growing with the ages, collecting and hoarding and saving unto itself identities and ancient dusts, octopus-inks and all the trivia of the sea.

Until now—it was aware.

It was a shining green intelligence, breathing in the autumn sea. Eyeless but seeing, earless but hearing, bodyless but feeling. It was of the sea. And being of the sea it was—feminine.

It in no way resembled man or woman. But it had a woman's ways, the silken, sly, and hidden ways. It moved with a woman's grace. It was all the evil things of vain women.

Dark waters flowed through and by and mingled with strange memory on its way to the gulf streams. In the water were carnival caps, horns, serpentine, confetti. They passed through this blossoming mass of long green hair like wind through an ancient tree. Orange peels, napkins, papers, eggshells, and burnt kindling from night fires on the beaches; all the flotsam of the gaunt high people who stalked on the lone sands of the continental islands, people from brick cities, people who shrieked in metal demons down concrete highways, gone.

It rose softly, shimmering, foaming, into cool morning airs.

The green hair rose softly, shimmering, foaming, into cool morning airs. It lay in the swell after the long time of forming through darkness.

It perceived the shore.

The man was there.

He was a sun-darkened man with strong legs and a cow body.

Each day he should have come down to the water, to bathe, to swim. But he had never moved. There was a woman on the sand with him, a woman in a black bathing suit who lay next to him talking quietly, laughing. Sometimes they held hands, sometimes they listened to a little sounding machine that they dialed and out of which music came.

The phosphorescence hung quietly in the waves. It was the end of the season. September. Things were shutting down.

Any day now he might go away and never return.

Today he must come in the water.

They lay on the sand with the heat in them. The radio played softly and the woman in the black bathing suit stirred fitfully, eyes closed.

The man did not lift his head from where he cushioned it on his muscled left arm. He drank the sun with his face, his open mouth, his nostrils. "What's wrong?" he asked.

"A bad dream," said the woman in the black suit.

"Dreams in the daytime?"

"Don't *you* ever dream in the afternoon?"

"I *never* dream. I've never had a dream in my life."

She lay there, fingers twitching. "God, I had a horrible dream."

"What about?"

"I don't know," she said, as if she really didn't. It was so bad she had forgotten. Now, eyes shut, she tried to remember.

"It was about me," he said, lazily, stretching.

"No," she said.

"Yes," he said, smiling to himself. "I was off with another woman, that's what."

"No."

"I insist," he said. "There I was, off with another woman, and you discovered us, and somehow, in all the mix-up, I got shot or something."

She winced involuntarily. "Don't talk that way."

"Let's see now," he said. "What sort of woman was I with? Gentlemen prefer blondes, don't they?"

"Please don't joke," she said. "I don't feel well."

He opened his eyes. "Did it affect you that much?"

She nodded. "Whenever I dream in the daytime this way, it depresses me something terrible."

"I'm sorry." He took her hand. "Anything I can get you?"

"No."

"Ice-cream cone? Eskimo pie? A Coke?"

"You're a dear, but no. I'll be all right. It's just that, the last four days haven't been right. This isn't like it used to be early in the summer. Something's happened."

"Not between us," he said.

"Oh, no, of course not," she said quickly. "But don't you feel that sometimes *places* change? Even a thing like a pier changes, and the merry-go-rounds, and all that. Even the hot dogs taste different this week."

"How do you mean?"

"They taste old. It's hard to explain, but I've lost my appetite, and I wish this vacation were over. Really, what I want to do most of all is go home."

"Tomorrow's our last day. You know how much this extra week means to me."

"I'll try," she said. "If only this place didn't feel so funny and changed. I don't know. But all of a sudden I just had a feeling I wanted to get up and run."

"Because of your dream? Me and my blonde and me dead all of a sudden."

"Don't," she said. "Don't talk about dying that way!"

She lay there very close to him. "If I only knew what it was."

"There." He stroked her. "I'll protect you."

"It's not me, it's you," her breath whispered in his ear. "I had the feeling that you were tired of me and went away."

"I wouldn't do that; I love you."

"I'm silly." She forced a laugh. "God, what a silly thing I am."

They lay quietly, the sun and sky over them like a lid.

"You know," he said, thoughtfully, "I get a little of that feeling you're talking about. This place has changed. There *is* something different."

"I'm glad you feel it, too."

He shook his head, drowsily, smiling softly, shutting his eyes, drinking the sun. "Both crazy. Both crazy." Murmuring. "Both."

The sea came in on the shore three times, softly.

The afternoon came on. The sun struck the skies a grazing blow. The yachts bobbed hot and shining white in the harbor swells. The smells of fried meat and burnt onion filled the wind. The sand whispered and stirred like an image in a vast, melting mirror.

The radio at their elbow murmured discreetly. They lay like dark arrows on the white sand. They did not move. Only their eyelids flickered with awareness, only their ears were alert. Now and again the tongues might slide along their baking lips. Sly prickles of moisture appeared on their brows to be burned away by the sun.

He lifted his head, blindly, listening to the heat.

The radio sighed.

He put his head down for a minute.

She felt him lift himself again. She opened one eye and he rested on one elbow looking around, at the pier, at the sky, at the water, at the sand.

"What's wrong?" she asked.

"Nothing," he said, lying down again.

"Something," she said.

"I thought I heard something."

"The radio."

"No, not the radio. Something else."

"Somebody *else's* radio."

He didn't answer. She felt his arm tense and relax, tense and relax. "Dammit," he said. "There it is, again."

They both lay listening.

"I don't hear anything—"

"Shh!" he cried. "For God's sake—"

The waves broke on the shore, silent mirrors, heaps of melting, whispering glass.

"Somebody singing."

"What?"

"I'd swear it was someone singing."

"Nonsense."

"No, listen."

They did that for a while.

"I don't hear a thing," she said, turning very cold.

He was on his feet. There was nothing in the sky, nothing on the pier, nothing on the sand, nothing in the hot-dog stands. There was a staring silence, the wind blowing over his ears, the wind preening along the light, blowing hairs of his arms and legs.

He took a step toward the sea.

"Don't!" she said.

He looked down at her, oddly, as if she were not there. He was still listening.

She turned the portable radio up full, loud. It exploded words and rhythm and melody:

"—I found a million-dollar baby—"

He made a wry face, raising his open palm violently. "Turn it off."

"No, I like it!" She turned it louder. She snapped her fingers, rocking her body vaguely, trying to smile.

It was two o'clock.

The sun steamed the waters. The ancient pier expanded with a loud groan in the heat. The birds were held in the hot sky, unable to move. The sun struck through the green liquors that poured about the pier; struck, caught and burnished an idle whiteness that drifted in the offshore ripples.

The white foam, the frosted coral brain, the kelp pip, the tide dust lay in the water, spreading.

The dark man still lay on the sand, the woman in the black suit beside him.

Music drifted up like mist from the water. It was a whispering music of deep tides and passed years, of salt and travel, of accepted and familiar strangenesses. The music sounded not unlike water on the shore, rain falling, the turn of soft limbs in the depths. It was a singing of a time-lost voice in a caverned seashell. The hissing and sighing of tides in deserted holds of treasure ships. The sound the wind makes in an empty skull thrown out on the baked sand.

But the radio on the blanket on the beach played louder.

The phosphorescence, light as a woman, sank down, tired, from sight. Only a few more hours. They might leave at any time. If only he would come in, for an instant, just an instant. The mists stirred silently, aware of his face and his body in the water, deep under. Aware of him caught, held, as they sank ten fathoms down, on a sluice that bore them twisting and turning in frantic gesticulations, to the depths of a hidden gulf in the sea.

The heat of his body, the water taking fire from his warmth, and the frosted coral brain, the jeweled dusts, the salted mists feeding on his hot breath from his open lips.

The waves moved the soft and changing thoughts into the shallows which were tepid as bath waters from the two o'clock sun.

He mustn't go away. If he goes now, he'll not return.

Now. The cold coral brain drifted, drifted. *Now.* Calling across the hot spaces of windless air in the early afternoon. *Come down to the water. Now,* said the music. *Now.*

The woman in the black bathing suit twisted the radio dial.

"Attention!" cried the radio. "Now, today, you can buy a new car at—"

"Jesus!" The man reached over and tuned the scream down. "Must you have it so loud!"

"I like it loud," said the woman in the black bathing suit, looking over her shoulder at the sea.

It was three o'clock. The sky was all sun.

Sweating, he stood up. "I'm going in," he said.

"Get me a hot dog first?" she said.

"Can't you wait until I come out?"

"Please." She pouted. "*Now.*"

"Everything on it?"

"Yes, and bring *three* of them."

"Three? God, what an appetite!" He ran off to the small café.

She waited until he was gone. Then she turned the radio off. She lay listening a long time. She heard nothing. She looked at the water until the glints and shatters of sun stabbed through her eyes like needles.

The sea had quieted. There was only a faint, far and fine net of ripples giving off sunlight in infinite repetition. She squinted again and again at the water, scowling.

He bounded back. "Damn, but the sand's hot; burns my feet off!" He flung himself on the blanket. "Eat 'em up!"

She took the three hot dogs and fed quietly on one of them. When she finished it, she handed him the remaining two. "Here, you finish them. My eyes are bigger than my stomach."

He swallowed the hot dogs in silence. "Next time," he said, finishing, "don't order more than you can use. Helluva waste."

"Here," she said, unscrewing a thermos, "you must be thirsty. Finish our lemonade."

"Thanks." He drank. Then he slapped his hands together and said, "Well, I'll go jump in the water now." He looked anxiously at the bright sea.

"Just one more thing," she said, just remembering it. "Will you buy me a bottle of suntan oil? I'm all out."

"Haven't you some in your purse?"

"I used it all."

"I wish you'd told me when I was up there buying the hot dogs," he said. "But, okay." He ran back, loping steadily.

When he was gone, she took the suntan bottle from her purse, half full, unscrewed the cap, and poured the liquid into the sand, covering it over surreptitiously, looking out at the sea, and smiling. She rose then and went down to the edge of the sea and looked out, searching the innumerable small and insignificant waves.

You can't have him, she thought. Whoever or whatever you are, he's mine, and you can't have him. I don't know what's going on; I don't know anything, really. All I know is we're going on a train tonight at seven. And we won't be here tomorrow. So you can just stay here and wait, ocean, sea, or whatever it is that's wrong here today.

Do your damnedest; you're no match for me, she thought. She picked up a stone and threw it at the sea.

"There!" she cried. "You."

He was standing beside her.

"Oh?" She jumped back.

"Hey, what gives? You standing here, muttering?"

"Was I?" She was surprised at herself. "Where's the suntan oil? Will you put it on my back?"

He poured a yellow twine of oil and massaged it onto her golden back. She looked out at the water from time to time, eyes sly, nodding at the water as if to say, "Look! You see? Ah-ha!" She purred like a kitten.

"There." He gave her the bottle.

He was half into the water before she yelled.

"Where are you going! Come here!"

He turned as if she were someone he didn't know. "For God's sake, what's wrong?"

"Why, you just finished your hot dogs and lemonade—you can't go in the water now and get cramps!"

He scoffed. "Old wives' tales."

"Just the same, you come back up on the sand and wait an hour before you go in, do you hear? I won't have you getting a cramp and drowning."

"Ah," he said, disgusted.

"Come along." She turned, and he followed, looking back at the sea.

·

Three o'clock. Four.

The change came at four ten. Lying on the sand, the woman in the black suit saw it coming and relaxed. The clouds had been forming since three. Now, with a sudden rush, the fog came in from off the bay. Where it had been warm, now it was cold. A wind blew up out of nothing. Darker clouds moved in.

"It's going to rain," she said.

"You sound absolutely pleased," he observed, sitting with arms folded. "Maybe our last day, and you sound pleased because it's clouding up."

"The weatherman," she confided, "said there'd be thunder showers all to-night and tomorrow. It might be a good idea to leave tonight."

"We'll stay, just in case it clears. I want to get one more day of swimming in, anyway," he said. "I haven't been in the water yet today."

"We've had so much fun talking and eating, time passes."

"Yeah," he said, looking at his hands.

The fog flailed across the sand in soft strips.

"There," she said. "That was a raindrop on my nose!" She laughed ridiculously at it. Her eyes were bright and young again. She was almost triumphant. "Good old rain."

"Why are you so pleased? You're an odd duck."

"Come on, rain!" she said. "Well, help me with these blankets. We'd better run!"

He picked up the blankets slowly, preoccupied. "Not even one last swim, dammit. I've a mind to take just one dive." He smiled at her. "Only a minute!"

"No." Her face paled. "You'll catch cold, and I'll have to nurse you!"

"Okay, okay." He turned away from the sea. Gentle rain began to fall.

Marching ahead of him, she headed for the hotel. She was singing softly to herself.

"Hold on!" he said.

She halted. She did not turn. She only listened to his voice far away.

"There's someone out in the water!" he cried. "Drowning!"

She couldn't move. She heard his feet running.

"Wait here!" he shouted. "I'll be right back! There's someone there! A woman, I think!"

"Let the lifeguards get her!"

"Aren't any! Off duty; late!" He ran down to the shore, the sea, the waves.

"Come back!" she screamed. "There's no one out there! Don't, oh, don't!"

"Don't worry, I'll be right back!" he called. "She's drowning out there, see?"

The fog came in, the rain pattered down, a white flashing light raised in the waves. He ran, and the woman in the black suit ran after him, scattering beach implements behind her, crying, tears rushing from her eyes. "Don't!" She put out her hands.

He leaped into an onrushing dark wave.

The woman in the black bathing suit waited in the rain.

At six o'clock the sun set somewhere behind black clouds. The rain rattled softly on the water, a distant drum snare.

Under the sea, a move of illuminant white.

The soft shape, the foam, the weed, the long strands of strange green hair lay in the shallows. Among the stirring glitter, deep under, was the man.

Fragile. The foam bubbled and broke. The frosted coral brain rang against a pebble with thought, as quickly lost as found. Men. Fragile. Like dolls, they break. Nothing, nothing to them. A minute under water and they're sick and pay no attention and they vomit out and kick and then, suddenly, just lie there, doing nothing. Doing nothing at all. Strange. Disappointing, after all the days of waiting.

What to do with him now? His head lolls, his mouth opens, his eyelids loosen, his eyes stare, his skin pales. Silly man, wake up! Wake up!

The water surged about him.

The man hung limply, loosely, mouth agape.

The phosphorescence, the green hair weed withdrew.

He was released. A wave carried him back to the silent shore. Back to his wife, who was waiting for him there in the cold rain.

The rain poured over the black waters.

Distantly, under the leaden skies, from the twilight shore, a woman screamed.

Ah—the ancient dusts stirred sluggishly in the water—isn't that *like* a woman? Now, *she* doesn't want him, *either!*

At seven o'clock the rain fell thick. It was night and very cold and the hotels all along the sea had to turn on the heat.

Daniel Chambliss

The Mundanity of Excellence

*T*he champion athlete does not simply do more of the same drills and sets as other swimmers; he or she also does things *better*. That's what counts. Very small differences, consistently practiced, will produce results. In swimming it could be doing all turns legally, or swimming one extra set of repeats after practice every day, or wearing gloves on your hands to keep them warm at a meet. American historian John Morton Blum reportedly has said that to be successful a writer need produce only three pages a day—every single day. Often the trick is doing little things (like good turns) correctly, all the time, every time. Championship training consists of doing more and more of these little things—and they are, finally, innumerable—each one consistently, so that each one produces a result.

The results of such quality training inevitably add up. Swimming is swimming, we can say—in practice, or in meets, it's all the same. If you swim sloppily for 364 days a year, nothing great is going to happen on the day of that one big meet, no matter how excited you get. Nowadays top-level swimmers tend to treat workouts as meets, where every swim counts; they have to win each repeat, always do great starts and turns. Steve Lundquist, for example, decided early in his career to try to win every swim in every practice, and eventually he did that. Many Mission Viejo swimmers took time every day to psych up for workouts, which they treated as intense competitions. It was not uncommon to see swimmers at Mission Viejo swimming within seconds of their lifetime bests in practices, going all out every day. When they eventually got to a meet, there was nothing new to be overcome, and the conclusion was all but foregone: For all the closeness of the times at Nationals, the same people often do win, year after year.

When Rowdy Gaines studied the starter in the Olympic Games, that was not a new "trick" he invented that day. He always checked the starter, as do many swimmers, because he knows that sometimes it makes a difference. He wasn't "cheating" to win that day. He was simply attending to details that other people didn't, and he had the good luck that the officials didn't recall the start. Mike Heath and Mark Stockwell and the five other swimmers in that race could have anticipated the gun, too, perhaps with good results, but they didn't. Gaines did.

These little things matter not so much because of their physical impact but because psychologically they separate the champion from everyone else. Having done the little things, the champion can say, "I have done what no one else has done, and I know it; and they know it, too." The little things, the details, then can be important for their testimonial value, their symbolic value, in setting one apart as someone special or different—someone to be watched and to be paid attention to. "This guy takes this seriously (and we don't); he really does deserve to win." "Why should I hurt myself in this race when Christine wants it that bad?" The little things, far from being an aggravation for top-level athletes, are the part they most enjoy: the polished points that mark the craftsmen of sport.

One result of this we call "confidence." Some people believe that confidence is "mental" or is "all in your head," as if you could just, one day, decide to have it. Or they believe that you get "confidence" when you buy a cassette tape that tells you to *relax, think positively, visualize your races,* and so on. They believe that confidence is a mental trick, like hypnosis, that can take one to incredible feats. But the confidence of the champion is not some trick learned by listening to an inspiring lecture. Confidence is not the cause of championship; it is the result of setting up difficult tasks and then doing them. As one coach put it, "Mental preparation is something you do in the water every day."

Our usual view of champions tells us the opposite. We think they are special people, larger than life: unusually good-looking, successful, happy all the time, patriotic, and self-confident. Failures don't get much TV coverage. For the sake of drama, reasonably enough, storytellers enhance some parts of the story and downplay others. And we think reasonably: *My God, this guy is nothing like me, I could never do what he does.*

But there is no magic that separates Olympians from everyday people, despite the fact that the title suggests Greek gods. No one is born to make the

Olympic finals; potential doesn't win a gold medal. Doing it is the only thing that counts. The truth is simple: Most swimmers choose every day not to do the little things. They choose, in effect, not to win. They say, "I could do this workout if I wanted to," or "I could have rolled with the start," or "I would have won if I had been healthy." In some sense, everyone "could" win in the Olympic Games, but "could" doesn't count. The gold medal is reserved for those who *do*.

The *doing*—this alone makes champions different. The excitement they feel comes from the raw physical and emotional reality they face every morning as they swim six miles, paying attention to all the details. Certainly the Olympic Games represent a rare opportunity to demonstrate publicly one's heroic capabilities. But champions do not wait four years to find their heroic opportunities; they create those opportunities, every day.

John Cheever

The Swimmer

*I*t was one of those midsummer Sundays when everyone sits around saying, "I
drank too much last night." You might have heard it whispered by the parish-
ioners leaving church, heard it from the lips of the priest himself, struggling
with his cassock in the *vestiarium*, heard it from the golf links and the tennis
courts, heard it from the wildlife preserve where the leader of the Audubon
group was suffering from a terrible hangover. "I *drank* too much," said Donald
Westerhazy. "We all *drank* too much," said Lucinda Merrill. "It must have been
the wine," said Helen Westerhazy. "I *drank* too much of that claret."

This was at the edge of the Westerhazys' pool. The pool, fed by an artesian
well with a high iron content, was a pale shade of green. It was a fine day. In the
west there was a massive stand of cumulus cloud so like a city seen from a distance—from the bow of an approaching ship—that it might have had a name.
Lisbon. Hackensack. The sun was hot. Neddy Merrill sat by the green water,
one hand in it, one around a glass of gin. He was a slender man—he seemed to
have the especial slenderness of youth—and while he was far from young he
had slid down his banister that morning and given the bronze backside of
Aphrodite on the hall table a smack as he jogged toward the smell of coffee in
his dining room. He might have been compared to a summer's day, particularly
the last hours of one, and while he lacked a tennis racket or a sail bag the im-

pression was definitely one of youth, sport, and clement weather. He had been swimming and now he was breathing deeply, stertorously, as if he could gulp into his lungs the components of that moment, the heat of the sun, the intenseness of his pleasure. It all seemed to flow into his chest. His own house stood in Bullet Park, eight miles to the south, where his four beautiful daughters would have had their lunch and might be playing tennis. Then it occurred to him that by taking a dogleg to the southwest he could reach his home by water.

His life was not confining and the delight he took in this observation could not be explained by its suggestion of escape. He seemed to see, with a cartographer's eye, that string of swimming pools, that quasi-subterranean stream that curved across the county. He had made a discovery, a contribution to modern geography; he would name the stream Lucinda after his wife. He was not a practical joker nor was he a fool but he was determinedly original and had a vague and modest idea of himself as a legendary figure. The day was beautiful and it seemed to him that a long swim might enlarge and celebrate its beauty.

He took off a sweater that was hung over his shoulders and dove in. He had an inexplicable contempt for men who did not hurl themselves into pools. He swam a choppy crawl, breathing either with every stroke or every fourth stroke and counting somewhere well in the back of his mind the one-two one-two of a flutter kick. It was not a serviceable stroke for long distances but the domestication of swimming had saddled the sport with some customs and in his part of the world a crawl was customary. To be embraced and sustained by the light green water was less a pleasure, it seemed, than the resumption of a natural condition, and he would have liked to swim without trunks, but this was not possible, considering his project. He hoisted himself up on the far curb—he never used the ladder—and started across the lawn. When Lucinda asked where he was going he said he was going to swim home.

The only maps and charts he had to go by were remembered or imaginary but these were clear enough. First there were the Grahams, the Hammers, the Lears, the Howlands, and the Crosscups. He would cross Ditmar Street to the Bunkers and come, after a short portage, to the Levys, the Welchers, and the public pool in Lancaster. Then there were the Hallorans, the Sachses, the Biswangers, Shirley Adams, the Gilmartins, and the Clydes. The day was lovely, and that he lived in a world so generously supplied with water seemed like a clemency, a beneficence. His heart was high and he ran across the grass. Making his way home by an uncommon route gave him the feeling that he was a pilgrim, an explorer, a man with a destiny, and he knew that he would find friends all along the way; friends would line the banks of the Lucinda River.

He went through a hedge that separated the Westerhazys' land from the Grahams', walked under some flowering apple trees, passed the shed that housed their pump and filter, and came out at the Grahams' pool. "Why,

Neddy," Mrs. Graham said, "what a marvelous surprise. I've been trying to get you on the phone all morning. Here, let me get you a drink." He saw then, like any explorer, that the hospitable customs and traditions of the natives would have to be handled with diplomacy if he was ever going to reach his destination. He did not want to mystify or seem rude to the Grahams nor did he have the time to linger there. He swam the length of their pool and joined them in the sun and was rescued, a few minutes later, by the arrival of two carloads of friends from Connecticut. During the uproarious reunions he was able to slip away. He went down by the front of the Grahams' house, stepped over a thorny hedge, and crossed a vacant lot to the Hammers'. Mrs. Hammer, looking up from her roses, saw him swim by although she wasn't quite sure who it was. The Lears heard him splashing past the open windows of their living room. The Howlands and the Crosscups were away. After leaving the Howlands' he crossed Ditmar Street and started for the Bunkers', where he could hear, even at that distance, the noise of a party.

The water refracted the sound of voices and laughter and seemed to suspend it in midair. The Bunkers' pool was on a rise and he climbed some stairs to a terrace where twenty-five or thirty men and women were drinking. The only person in the water was Rusty Towers, who floated there on a rubber raft. Oh, how bonny and lush were the banks of the Lucinda River! Prosperous men and women gathered by the sapphire-colored waters while caterer's men in white coats passed them cold gin. Overhead a red de Haviland trainer was circling around and around and around in the sky with something like the glee of a child in a swing. Ned felt a passing affection for the scene, a tenderness for the gathering, as if it was something he might touch. In the distance he heard thunder. As soon as Enid Bunker saw him she began to scream: "Oh, look who's here! What a marvelous surprise! When Lucinda said that you couldn't come I thought I'd *die*." She made her way to him through the crowd, and when they had finished kissing she led him to the bar, a progress that was slowed by the fact that he stopped to kiss eight or ten other women and shake the hands of as many men. A smiling bartender he had seen at a hundred parties gave him a gin and tonic and he stood by the bar for a moment, anxious not to get stuck in any conversation that would delay his voyage. When he seemed about to be surrounded he dove in and swam close to the side to avoid colliding with Rusty's raft. At the far end of the pool he bypassed the Tomlinsons with a broad smile and jogged up the garden path. The gravel cut his feet but this was the only unpleasantness. The party was confined to the pool, and as he went toward the house he heard the brilliant, watery sound of voices fade, heard the noise of a radio from the Bunkers' kitchen, where someone was listening to a ball game. Sunday afternoon. He made his way through the parked cars and down the grassy border of their driveway to Alewives Lane. He did not want to be seen on the road in his bathing trunks but there was no traffic and he made the short distance to the Levys' driveway, marked with a PRIVATE PROPERTY sign and a green tube for *The New York Times*. All the doors and windows of the big house were open but there were no signs of life; not even a dog barked. He went around the side of the house to the pool and saw that the Levys had only recently left. Glasses and bottles and dishes of nuts were on a table at the deep end, where there was a bathhouse or gazebo, hung with Japanese lanterns. After swimming the pool he got himself a glass and poured a drink. It was his fourth or fifth drink and he had swum nearly half the length of the Lucinda River. He felt tired, clean, and pleased at that moment to be alone; pleased with everything.

It would storm. The stand of cumulus cloud—that city—had risen and darkened, and while he sat there he heard the percussiveness of thunder again. The de Haviland trainer was still circling overhead and it seemed to Ned that he could almost hear the pilot laugh with pleasure in the afternoon; but when there was another peal of thunder he took off for home. A train whistle blew and he wondered what time it had gotten to be. Four? Five? He thought of the provincial station at that hour, where a waiter, his tuxedo concealed by a raincoat, a dwarf with some flowers wrapped in newspaper, and a woman who had been crying would be waiting for the local. It was suddenly growing dark; it was that moment when the pin-headed birds seem to organize their song into some acute and knowledgeable recognition of the storm's approach. Then there was a fine noise of rushing water from the crown of an oak at his back, as if a spigot there had been turned. Then the noise of fountains came from the crowns of all the tall trees. Why did he love storms, what was the meaning of his excitement when the door sprang open and the rain wind fled rudely up the stairs, why had the simple task of shutting the windows of an old house seemed fitting and urgent, why did the first watery notes of a storm wind have for him the unmistakable sound of good news, cheer, glad tidings? Then there was an explosion, a smell of cordite, and rain lashed the Japanese lanterns that Mrs. Levy had bought in Kyoto the year before last, or was it the year before that?

He stayed in the Levys' gazebo until the storm had passed. The rain had cooled the air and he shivered. The force of the wind had stripped a maple of its red and yellow leaves and scattered them over the grass and the water. Since it was midsummer the tree must be blighted, and yet he felt a peculiar sadness at this sign of autumn. He braced his shoulders, emptied his glass, and started for the Welchers' pool. This meant crossing the Lindleys' riding ring and he was surprised to find it overgrown with grass and all the jumps dismantled. He wondered if the Lindleys had sold their horses or gone away for the summer and put them out to board. He seemed to remember having heard something about the Lindleys and their horses but the memory was unclear. On he went, barefoot through the wet grass, to the Welchers', where he found their pool was dry.

This breach in his chain of water disappointed him absurdly, and he felt like some explorer who seeks a torrential headwater and finds a dead stream. He was disappointed and mystified. It was common enough to go away for the summer but no one ever drained his pool. The Welchers had definitely gone away. The pool furniture was folded, stacked, and covered with a tarpaulin. The bathhouse was locked. All the windows of the house were shut, and when he went around to the driveway in front he saw a FOR SALE sign nailed to a tree. When had he last heard from the Welchers—when, that is, had he and Lucinda last regretted an invitation to dine with them? It seemed only a week or so ago. Was his memory failing or had he so disciplined it in the repression of unpleasant facts that he had damaged his sense of the truth? Then in the distance he heard the sound of a tennis game. This cheered him, cleared away all his apprehensions and let him regard the overcast sky and the cold air with indifference. This was the day that Neddy Merrill swam across the county. That was the day! He started off then for his most difficult portage.

·

Had you gone for a Sunday afternoon ride that day you might have seen him, close to naked, standing on the shoulders of Route 424, waiting for a chance to cross. You might have wondered if he was the victim of foul play, had his car broken down, or was he merely a fool. Standing barefoot in the deposits of the highway—beer cans, rags, and blowout patches—exposed to all kinds of ridicule, he seemed pitiful. He had known when he started that this was a part of his journey—it had been on his maps—but confronted with the lines of traffic, worming through the summery light, he found himself unprepared. He was laughed at, jeered at, a beer can was thrown at him, and he had no dignity or humor to bring to the situation. He could have gone back, back to the Westerhazys', where Lucinda would still be sitting in the sun. He had signed nothing, vowed nothing, pledged nothing, not even to himself. Why, believing as he did, that all human obduracy was susceptible to common sense, was he unable to turn back? Why was he determined to complete his journey even if it meant putting his life in danger? At what point had this prank, this joke, this piece of horseplay become serious? He could not go back, he could not even recall with any clearness the green water at the Westerhazys', the sense of inhaling the day's components, the friendly and relaxed voices saying that they had *drunk* too much. In the space of an hour, more or less, he had covered a distance that made his return impossible.

An old man, tooling down the highway at fifteen miles an hour, let him get to the middle of the road, where there was a grass divider. Here he was exposed to the ridicule of the northbound traffic, but after ten or fifteen minutes he was able to cross. From here he had only a short walk to the Recreation Center at the edge of the village of Lancaster, where there were some handball courts and a public pool.

The effect of the water on voices, the illusion of brilliance and suspense, was the same here as it had been at the Bunkers' but the sounds here were louder, harsher, and more shrill, and as soon as he entered the crowded enclosure he was confronted with regimentation. "ALL SWIMMERS MUST TAKE A SHOWER BEFORE USING THE POOL. ALL SWIMMERS MUST USE THE FOOT-BATH. ALL SWIMMERS MUST WEAR THEIR IDENTIFICATION DISKS." He took a shower, washed his feet in a cloudy and bitter solution, and made his way to the edge of the water. It stank of chlorine and looked to him like a sink. A pair of lifeguards in a pair of towers blew police whistles at what seemed to be regular intervals and abused the swimmers through a public address system. Neddy remembered the sapphire water at the Bunkers' with longing and thought that he might contaminate himself—damage his own prosperousness and charm—by swimming in this murk, but he reminded himself that he was an explorer, a pilgrim, and that this was merely a stagnant bend in the Lucinda River. He dove, scowling with distaste, into the chlorine and had to swim with his head above water to avoid collisions, but even so he was bumped into, splashed, and jostled. When he got to the shallow end both lifeguards were shouting at him: "Hey, you, you without the identification disk, get outta the water." He did, but they had no way of pursuing him and he went through the reek of suntan oil and chlorine out through the hurricane fence and passed the handball courts. By crossing the road he entered the wooded part of the Halloran estate. The woods were not cleared and the footing was treacherous and difficult until he reached the lawn and the clipped beech hedge that encircled their pool.

The Hallorans were friends, an elderly couple of enormous wealth who seemed to bask in the suspicion that they might be Communists. They were zealous reformers but they were not Communists, and yet when they were accused, as they sometimes were, of subversion, it seemed to gratify and excite them. Their beech hedge was yellow and he guessed this had been blighted like the Levys' maple. He called hullo, hullo, to warn the Hallorans of his approach, to palliate his invasion of their privacy. The Hallorans, for reasons that had never been explained to him, did not wear bathing suits. No explanations were in order, really. Their nakedness was a detail in their uncompromising zeal for reform and he stepped politely out of his trunks before he went through the opening in the hedge.

Mrs. Halloran, a stout woman with white hair and a serene face, was reading the *Times*. Mr. Halloran was taking beech leaves out of the water with a scoop. They seemed not surprised or displeased to see him. Their pool was perhaps the oldest in the county, a fieldstone rectangle, fed by a brook. It had no filter or pump and its waters were the opaque gold of the stream.

"I'm swimming across the county," Ned said.

"Why, I didn't know one could," exclaimed Mrs. Halloran.

"Well, I've made it from the Westerhazys'," Ned said. "That must be about four miles."

He left his trunks at the deep end, walked to the shallow end, and swam this stretch. As he was pulling himself out of the water he heard Mrs. Halloran say, "We've been *terribly* sorry to hear about all your misfortunes, Neddy."

"My misfortunes?" Ned asked. "I don't know what you mean."

"Why, we heard that you'd sold the house and that your poor children . . . "

"I don't recall having sold the house," Ned said, "and the girls are at home."

"Yes," Mrs. Halloran sighed. "Yes . . . " Her voice filled the air with an unseasonable melancholy and Ned spoke briskly. "Thank you for the swim."

"Well, have a nice trip," said Mrs. Halloran.

Beyond the hedge he pulled on his trunks and fastened them. They were loose and he wondered if, during the space of an afternoon, he could have lost some weight. He was cold and he was tired and the naked Hallorans and their dark water had depressed him. The swim was too much for his strength but how could he have guessed this, sliding down the banister that morning and sitting in the Westerhazys' sun? His arms were lame. His legs felt rubbery and ached at the joints. The worst of it was the cold in his bones and the feeling that he might never be warm again. Leaves were falling down around him and he smelled wood smoke in the wind. Who would be burning wood at this time of year?

He needed a drink. Whiskey would warm him, pick him up, carry him through the last of his journey, refresh his feeling that it was original and valorous to swim across the county. Channel swimmers took brandy. He needed a stimulant. He crossed the lawn in front of the Hallorans' house and went down a little path to where they had built a house for their only daughter, Helen, and her husband, Eric Sachs. The Sachses' pool was small and he found Helen and her husband there.

"Oh, *Neddy*," Helen said. "Did you lunch at Mother's?"

"Not *really*," Ned said. "I *did* stop to see your parents." This seemed to be explanation enough. "I'm terribly sorry to break in on you like this but I've taken a chill and I wonder if you'd give me a drink."

"Why, I'd *love* to," Helen said, "but there hasn't been anything in this house to drink since Eric's operation. That was three years ago."

Was he losing his memory, had his gift for concealing painful facts let him forget that he had sold his house, that his children were in trouble, and that his friend had been ill? His eyes slipped from Eric's face to his abdomen, where he saw three pale, sutured scars, two of them at least a foot long. Gone was his navel, and what, Neddy thought, would the roving hand, bed-checking one's gifts at 3 A.M., make of a belly with no navel, to link to birth, this breach in the succession?

"I'm sure you can get a drink at the Biswangers'," Helen said. "They're having an enormous do. You can hear it from here. Listen!"

She raised her head and from across the road, the lawns, the gardens, the woods, the fields, he heard again the brilliant noise of voices over water. "Well, I'll get wet," he said, still feeling that he had no freedom of choice about this means of travel. He dove into the Sachses' cold water and, gasping, close to drowning, made his way from one end of the pool to the other. "Lucinda and I want *terribly* to see you," he said over his shoulder, his face set toward the Biswangers'. "We're sorry it's been so long and we'll call you *very* soon."

He crossed some fields to the Biswangers' and the sounds of revelry there. They would be honored to give him a drink, they would be happy to give him a drink. The Biswangers invited him and Lucinda for dinner four times a year, six weeks in advance. They were always rebuffed and yet they continued to send out their invitations, unwilling to comprehend the rigid and undemocratic realities of their society. They were the sort of people who discussed the price of things at cocktails, exchanged market tips during dinner, and after dinner told dirty stories to mixed company. They did not belong to Neddy's set—they were not even on Lucinda's Christmas-card list. He went toward their pool with feelings of indifference, charity, and some unease, since it seemed to be getting dark and these were the longest days of the year. The party when he joined it was noisy and large. Grace Biswanger was the kind of hostess who asked the optometrist, the veterinarian, the real-estate dealer, and the dentist. No one was swimming and the twilight, reflected on the water of the pool, had a wintry gleam. There was a bar and he started for this. When Grace Biswanger saw him she came toward him, not affectionately as he had every right to expect, but bellicosely.

"Why, this party has everything," she said loudly, "including a gate crasher."

She could not deal him a social blow—there was no question about this and he did not flinch. "As a gate crasher," he asked politely, "do I rate a drink?"

"Suit yourself," she said. "You don't seem to pay much attention to invitations."

She turned her back on him and joined some guests, and he went to the bar and ordered a whiskey. The bartender served him but he served him rudely. His was a world in which the caterer's men kept the social score, and to be rebuffed by a part-time barkeep meant that he had suffered some loss of social esteem. Or perhaps the man was new and uninformed. Then he heard Grace at his back say: "They went for broke overnight—nothing but income—and he showed up drunk one Sunday and asked us to loan him five thousand dollars. . . . " She was always talking about money. It was worse than eating your peas off a knife. He dove into the pool, swam its length and went away.

The next pool on his list, the last but two, belonged to his old mistress, Shirley Adams. If he had suffered any injuries at the Biswangers' they would be cured here. Love—sexual roughhouse in fact—was the supreme elixir, the pain killer, the brightly colored pill that would put the spring back into his step, the joy of life in his heart. They had had an affair last week, last month, last year. He couldn't remember. It was he who had broken it off, his was the upper hand, and he stepped through the gate of the wall that surrounded her pool with nothing so considered as self-confidence. It seemed in a way to be his pool, as the lover, particularly the illicit lover, enjoys the possessions of his mistress with an authority unknown to holy matrimony. She was there, her hair the color of brass, but her figure, at the edge of the lighted, cerulean water, excited in him no profound memories. It had been, he thought, a lighthearted affair, although she had wept when he broke it off. She seemed confused to see him and he wondered if she was still wounded. Would she, God forbid, weep again?

"What do you want?" she asked.

"I'm swimming across the county."

"Good Christ. Will you ever grow up?"

"What's the matter?"

"If you've come here for money," she said, "I won't give you another cent."

"You could give me a drink."

"I could but I won't. I'm not alone."

"Well, I'm on my way."

He dove in and swam the pool, but when he tried to haul himself up onto the curb he found that the strength in his arms and shoulders had gone, and he paddled to the ladder and climbed out. Looking over his shoulder he saw, in the lighted bathhouse, a young man. Going out onto the dark lawn he smelled chrysanthemums or marigolds—some stubborn autumnal fragrance—on the night air, strong as gas. Looking overhead he saw that the stars had come out, but why should he seem to see Andromeda, Cepheus, and Cassiopeia? What had become of the constellations of midsummer? He began to cry.

It was probably the first time in his adult life that he had ever cried, certainly the first time in his life that he had ever felt so miserable, cold, tired, and bewildered. He could not understand the rudeness of the caterer's barkeep or the rudeness of a mistress who had come to him on her knees and showered his trousers with tears. He had swum too long, he had been immersed too long, and his nose and his throat were sore from the water. What he needed then was a drink, some company, and some clean, dry clothes, and while he could have cut directly across the road to his home he went on to the Gilmartins' pool. Here, for the first time in his life, he did not dive but went down the steps into the icy water and swam a hobbled sidestroke that he might have learned as a youth. He staggered with fatigue on his way to the Clydes' and paddled the length of their pool, stopping again and again with his hand on the curb to rest. He climbed up the ladder and wondered if he had the strength to get home. He had done what he wanted, he had swum the county, but he was so stupefied with exhaustion that his triumph seemed vague. Stooped, holding on to the gateposts for support, he turned up the driveway of his own house.

The place was dark. Was it so late that they had all gone to bed? Had Lucinda stayed at the Westerhazys' for supper? Had the girls joined her there or gone someplace else? Hadn't they agreed, as they usually did on Sunday, to regret all their invitations and stay at home? He tried the garage doors to see what cars were in but the doors were locked and rust came off the handles onto his hands. Going toward the house, he saw that the force of the thunderstorm had knocked one of the rain gutters loose. It hung down over the front door like an umbrella rib, but it could be fixed in the morning. The house was locked, and he thought that the stupid cook or the stupid maid must have locked the place up until he remembered that it had been some time since they had employed a maid or a cook. He shouted, pounded on the door, tried to force it with his shoulder, and then, looking in at the windows, saw that the place was empty.

John Ciardi

On Being Much Better Than Most and Yet Not Quite Good Enough

There was a great swimmer named Jack
Who swam ten miles out—and nine back.

*L*ucy was a born swimmer: she had been in the water as an infant and swam without water wings by the time she was three. At five, she was swimming underwater with ease and began to practice diving when she was six.

Her family lived in St. Paul and spent the summers in a cedar-shingled house at Stone Boy Lake. A set of steps led from the house to the dock. The lake was a mile long, ringed by dense, moss-sided firs and overshadowed by hills of timber. It was almost gothically dark, except at high noon when the sun cut straight down onto the water like the beam of a klieg light. It was so quiet that if you swam early in the morning all you would hear was the sound of your own splashing. At Stone Boy Lake, you swam to your friends, and it was not uncommon for Lucy to swim several miles a day. The summer people kept towels waiting on their docks.

In the winter, Lucy swam in the pool of Mallard Academy in St. Paul. In the East, at college, she swam through the seasons, through exams, through love affairs. She was in the water the morning of her marriage to Carl Wilmott, keeping her scarfed head up so as not to ruin her wedding hairdo.

Carl and Lucy had met in Boston, and were married three years later in the summer house on Stone Boy Lake. They lived in a light, sparse apartment in

Cambridge. The wooden floors were highly polished and the furniture was so trim and modern that it looked as if it would skim across the room if pushed. Lucy worked for the law review, and Carl had an assistantship in the history department, but when he was offered a position in Chicago, they decided to take it, packed, and were ready to move within a week. Neither went in much for heavy baggage or personal artifacts. They liked what could be easily carried. Their only decorations were a Peruvian wall rug, two Appalachian quilts, a watercolor of Boston Common in the 1880's, and a soapstone seal, carved by Eskimos. Three days after New Year's, they flew to Chicago and were settled the next day.

.

Lucy was middle-sized and lean. Her features were small, but craggy, as if they had been reduced to human scale from some large, rough-hewn monument. When she smiled, her eyes almost disappeared behind her cheekbones and her skin was so translucently white you could see the veins beneath it.

Carl, who was ruddy and large, was often stricken at the thought of her fragility, and he was constantly amazed by her ruggedness. His sports were handball and squash—he liked to sweat and strain—and he watched with wonder as his delicate wife dove from boulders into mountain pools so cold they shocked his entire body if he put so much as a foot in. She raced into the ocean at Maine in October while he sat shivering on the beach wearing double sweaters. He watched her slide down waterfalls in Vermont, her hair tangled by white water.

The first day in Chicago, Carl went to a faculty meeting, while Lucy unpacked the last two cartons and then called University Information to find out where she could swim. There was a pool, she was told, at McWerter Hall, nine blocks away.

It was below freezing. She could feel the cold through her boots. It had been ten years since she had lived in this kind of weather, and her body had forgotten. The inside of her nose was stiff. By the time she reached McWerter Hall her feet felt like stones.

The guard pointed the way to the ladies' locker room, where she filled out forms for an official pass and was given a temporary card stamped "new faculty." The pool was empty except for two girls who sat on the side in dry bathing suits, dangling their feet in the water. Their voices murmured and echoed. When they laughed, it sounded like distant gun shot.

Lucy dove off the high board and swam a lap under water. When she surfaced, she was alone, and she swam by herself for two hours. In the locker room, she combed her lank hair in front of the foggy mirror, and by the time she got home, even with a hat and scarf, the front of her hair was frozen.

In February, it snowed, and then got colder. Coal trucks unloaded in the streets, turning the ice black, and children coming home from school skated on jet-colored humps that formed in the middle of the streets. They played with their heads down and walked backward against the wind. People passed each other with their eyes streaming. When the wind let up, they brushed the tears off with their gloves, as if suffering from secret heartbreak.

Carl hated the cold, but he and Lucy liked Chicago. Their new apartment was very much like the one they had had in Cambridge—light and sparse. A small set of people they had known at college formed the beginning of their social life. Carl was making friends in the department, and Lucy, who was job hunting, explored the neighborhood.

After his two o'clock class, Carl usually had coffee with Johnny Esterhazy, who had gone to high school and college with him. They were both New Yorkers and the cold exhausted them.

"I saw Lucy on the street yesterday," Johnny said. "I thought I was coming down with terminal frostbite, but she looked like the breath of spring."

"She's the old original polar bear," said Carl. "She grew up in St. Paul, which is the arctic circle, as far as I'm concerned."

"Well, I admire her," said Johnny. "Her bangs were frozen."

"You admire her because her bangs were frozen?"

"What I mean is, it takes real fortitude to swim in this kind of weather. It takes courage to even *walk* in this kind of weather. I told her I thought she was crazy, but she said she'd been in the pool almost every day since you came here."

Carl drank his coffee in silence and watched a group of girls go by, so swaddled in their layers of clothing they could hardly walk. He knew Lucy loved to swim: she swam all summer, but it surprised him to know she swam in the winter, too. The fact that she had gone swimming every day since they had come to Chicago and had never said a word about it left him speechless. He had no idea where the university pool was, and thought of asking Johnny, but it seemed to him that asking was an admission of some terrible ignorance. How could he not know such an elementary fact about his own wife?

Walking home, he decided to confront her, but he could not arrange a question that was neither accusatory nor whimpering, and he could not articulate the source of his pain. Was it that she swam, or that she didn't tell him? Lucy had been swimming all her life: it was a perfectly natural thing for her to do, but he was suffering nonetheless.

She was in the kitchen when he came in. Her hair wasn't wet. It didn't smell of chlorine. Her face was cool when she kissed him, as it always was.

They sat down to a large, cheering dinner, after which they stretched out on the sofa and read. It was normal life. At midnight, they yawned, and with their arms around each other, went to bed.

.

In March, the cold began to crack and the black ice softened, forming deep, muddy puddles. When it snowed, the snow was light and fine. Then it sleeted, and by April it only rained. Tiny green swells began to appear on the stunted hedges.

Finally, it was clear, cold prairie spring. Lucy walked toward Lake Michigan. The grass in the park was brown and scorched, and the bridle path was as wet as a creek. Clouds of mist embraced the Museum of Science and Industry. She walked across the bridge above the Outer Drive and onto the rocks by the lake. Under her bluejeans, sweater, and coat she was wearing a bathing suit, and in her book bag was a beach towel. Johnny Esterhazy had told her that Lake Michigan was polluted, but it was clear enough so that she could see the rocks beneath the water and the swaying beards of algae on their sides. Whatever it had in it, it did not have chlorine. She stripped to her bathing suit and the wind smacked her like a fist.

There was not a soul around. She climbed from rock to rock until she was standing in water up to her knees, and then she jumped.

.

Over dinner, Lucy and Carl talked about the casual, easy shape their life was taking. Johnny Esterhazy and his fiancée were coming to dinner on Friday. The head of the history department had invited them to a cocktail party. Lucy had an interview at the law library. Ted and Ellie Lifter, a pair of sociologists who lived downstairs, had asked them for coffee and dessert.

They reviewed the events of their day, and wondered whether to get orchestra or box seats for the Chicago symphony. But Lucy never said anything about swimming, and Carl knew that in some way he had overreacted. Swimming to Lucy was like breathing, and did she report to him that she had breathed all day?

When he looked at her across the dinner table, her pale, fair hair and skin, her pale eyes, and the vein that divided her forehead, he looked for any sign of deception, but there was nothing but openness and affection. He looked into her steady, unblinking eyes and tried to see if she was capable of duplicity, but every feature in her face was loving, straightforward, and direct.

At night, her long thighs were cool and the insides of her arms were cold. As she slept, Carl thought how fragile she appeared, and how tough she actually was. It occurred to his sleepy mind that this was a deception in itself. At times, he was overwhelmed that she was purposely shutting him out of a part of her life, and then, suddenly, it all seemed normal to him. If he asked her, she would smile her eye-diminishing smile and tell him of course she swam every day. But he did not ask, and could not. He could not bear to admit that what was second nature to her had been news to him. He fluctuated between panic and calm. If she was swimming every day in Chicago, it meant that she had done the same in Cambridge—all that time and she had never said a word, but had simply arranged a part of her life away from him and gone swimming in it.

In the summers they went to his parents in Maine, or to hers on Stone Boy Lake, and swam together. But usually they were apart for most of the day, and she spent several hours of it in secret. It seemed so deliberate, so concealed and contrived—it broke his heart to think about it. But then perhaps his vision was distorted. They had been together for five years and he knew her swimming was something she probably assumed he took for granted, but at night it looked like sabotage.

.

On the day of a heavy rainstorm, he saw her from the window of his office, walking under a golf umbrella toward McWerter Hall, and he followed her. He climbed the stairs to the bleachers and waited until she came through a door and walked to the edge of the pool. His jacket was glazed with mist and he was sweating under his collar. The roots of his hair were damp. Through the steam and haze, he saw his wife on the low board. She dove into the water like a bird and he could see the white streak of her gliding to the shallow end. He wanted to call out, but held himself back, and since she didn't look up, she never saw him. She tossed her hair out of her eyes and he could see that they were slightly unfocused by chlorine.

There was a catch in his throat as he watched her walk the perimeter of the pool, leaving delicate footprints on the tiles. She stood on the tip of the high board, and when she connected with the water it seemed to slice his heart.

She did a swan dive, then a jackknife. Stifling in his tweed, he watched ten laps of her sleek, racing crawl. Then she climbed back on the high board, framed by a window the width of the room. The sky was the color of faded ink. His clothes itched and he longed to throw them off and dive in with her. But it would have been betrayal. Instead, he watched her do a half-gainer and when she was underwater, he left by the side door.

.

After dinner, he said abruptly: "I want to go swimming with you tomorrow." He was that desperate.

Lucy smiled and her cheekbones hid her eyes. It was a truly open smile.

"Sure," she said. "That would be nice. I'm going around three thirty. Is that O.K. for you?"

"It's fine."

That was the end of the conversation: the spell was broken. They were going swimming together and everything was all right. When the dishes were done, Lucy curled up on the sofa to read, and Carl took the garbage out. When the wind hit him suddenly, he leaned against the railings and, to his own amazement, wept.

.

He was at the pool by twenty past three and she was already swimming laps. Bleak light glared through the window. When she lifted her head to the side, performing her slow, determined crawl, her eyes were albino.

Carl played in the water; did surface dives, stood on his head in the shallow end. He jackknifed from the low board and he and Lucy swam four laps of side stroke together. Then they dove from opposite sides of the pool, met in the middle, and kissed underwater. They held hands and floated. Finally Carl got out, sat on the side, and watched. She was not swimming for fun or exercise or habit. She had never joined a swimming team, not even in high school. It was like the air for her: she was amphibious.

She got out and sat beside him. Her feet were long and bladelike.

"That was refreshing," he said.

"It's really all right, for a pool."

"If it ever gets warm again, we can swim in Lake Michigan."

"That's the ticket," Lucy said. "It's wonderful in the lake. I was in a couple of weeks ago."

Whatever spell had been broken re-formed. A couple of weeks ago, it had still been winter. She had been swimming out of doors—something unusual enough to tell him about, yet she had seen fit to conceal it. The skin around her nails was grainy and her hair was flat against her head. Drops ran from her bangs to her nose and down her cheeks. He stared at their separate feet, spookily luminescent in the blue water.

.

The weather got warm and the spring air was sweet. Riders appeared on the bridle paths in Jackson Park. The ground was fuzzy with new grass.

Carl walked under a little stone bridge in the park, listening to the traffic above him. He followed a winding cement path until he came to the rocks that lined the lake. The sun was setting and when the park lights came on, there were halos of mist around them. He climbed the rock steps down to the lake and sat by the water. He had come directly from the office and was still wearing his tie and jacket. Lucy might be home, or she might be on the other side of the park, swimming while he sat. He looked down into the deep water that had contained her and saw mossy algae moving gently with the current. He took off one shoe and sock and tested the water with his toes. It was icy cold. He stretched out on the rocks and watched the sun go down.

It was dark when he got home. Lucy had left a note that she had gone to do some last-minute shopping. His bones felt light and he took a nap on the couch with the windows wide open, and dreamed that he had a fever. He was awakened by Lucy's cool hand on his forehead. In her other hand she was holding a brandy snifter full of water.

"Look," she said. "Snails." In the bottom of the glass were some small stones covered with algae. Two snails sat on the stones, and four clung to the side. The water magnified them, and when he took one out it was gray and tiny in his hand.

"I got them today," she said. "They're all over the rocks. I went snorkeling."

·

They had a quiet dinner, read the papers, and listened to the Mozart clarinet concerto. Every window was open, and the sweet air breathed in.

Late at night, the bedroom was cool. Lucy slept without a sound, but Carl was awake. He had his arm around her and he put his cheek next to her damp hair. Her sides, as always, were cold, as if under her skin her bones were cold. He watched her sleep and knew that even with his arms around her, she was dreaming in private. He kissed the top of her head, resting his chin on her hair. It gave up a heavy, slightly burned smell: she was drying. A cool lock of hair fell across his wrist and he moved closer to her. In a few weeks, it would be warm enough for them to swim together. Then it would be summer. They would go to Stone Boy Lake and swim some more. It seemed to him that he had done some fine adjusting. What had grieved him was simply a fact: every day of her life she would be at some point damp, then drying, and for one solid time, wet.

James Dickey

Coming Back to America

We descended the first night from Europe   riding the ship's sling
Into the basement.   Forty floors of home weighed on us.   We broke through
To a room, and fell to drinking madly with all those boozing, reading
The Gideon Bible in a dazzle of homecoming scripture   Assyrian armies
The scythes of chariots blazing like the windows of the city   all cast
Into our eyes in all-night squinting barbaric rays of violent unavoidable glory.
There were a "million dollars in ice cubes" outside our metal door;
The dead water clattered down hour after hour as we fought with salesmen
For the little blocks that would make whole our long savage drinks.
I took a swaying shower, and we packed the whole bathroom of towels into
Our dusty luggage, battling paid-for opulence with whatever weapon
Came to hand.   We slept; I woke up early, knowing that I was suffering
But why not. My breath would not stir, nor the room's.   I sweated
Ice in the closeness   my head hurt with the Sleep of a Thousand Lights
That the green baize drapes could not darken.   I got up, bearing
Everything   found my sharp Roman shoes   went out   following signs
That said SWIMMING POOL.   Flashing bulbs on a red-eyed panel, I passed
Through ceiling after ceiling of sleeping salesmen and whores, and came out
On the roof.   The pool water trembled with the few in their rooms
Still making love.   This was air.   A skinny girl lifeguard worked
At her nails; the dawn shone on her right leg in a healthy, twisted flame.
It made me squint   slick and lacquered with scars   with the wild smoky city
Around it   the great breath to be drawn above sleepers   the hazy
Morning towers.   We sat and talked   she said a five-car wreck
Of taxis in Bensonhurst had knocked her out and taken her kneecap
But nothing else.   I pondered this   the sun shook off a last heavy
Hotel   and she leapt and was in the fragile green pool as though
I were still sleeping it off eleven floors under her: she turned in a water
Ballet by herself   graceful   unredeemable   her tough face exactly
As beautiful and integral as the sun come out of the city.   Vulnerable,
Hurt in my country's murderous speed, she moved   and I would have taken
Her in my arms in water throbbing with the passion of travelling men,
Unkillable, both of us, at forty stories in the morning   and could have
Flown with her   our weightlessness preserved by the magic pool drawn from

Under the streets   out of that pond   passing over the meaningless
Guardrail   feeling the whole air pulse like water sleepless with desperate
Love-making   lifting us out of sleep into the city summer dawn
Of hundreds of feet of gray space spinning with pigeons now under
Us   among new panels of sun in the buildings blasting light silently
Back and forth across streets between them: could have moved with her
In all this   over the floods of glare raised up in sheets   the gauze
Distances where warehouses strove to become   over the ship I had ridden
Home in   riding gently   whitely   beneath.   Ah, lift us, green
City water, as we turn the harbor around with our legs   lazily changing
The plan of the city with motions like thistles   like the majestic swirl
Of soot   the winged seed of pigeons   and so would have held her
As I held my head   a-stammer with light   defending it against the terrible
Morning sun of drinkers   in that pain, exhalting in the blind notion
Of cradling her somewhere above ships and buses   in the air like a water
Ballet   dancing deep among the dawn buildings in a purely private
Embrace of impossibility   a love that could not have been guessed:
Woman   being   idea   temple dancer   tough girl from Bensonhurst
With a knee rebuilt out of sunlight   returned-to amazement O claspable
Symbol   the unforeseen on home ground   The thing that sustains us forever
In other places!

M. Coleman Easton

from Swimmers Beneath the Bright

*O*n a warm festival evening, marking Verdant's end and Barren's start, a wiry figure darted into shadows at the harbor's edge. Behind her, in the streets of Port Thra, the singing and parading had grown frenetic. Looking back, Pinal saw torches moving along avenues that twisted up toward the sky. The hillside city was alive with merrymakers, but she cared nothing for their celebrations. What mattered to Pinal was that the guards would be busy. None would notice a solitary swimmer.

Turning to the water, she glimpsed shapes of merchant ships at anchor, riding low, their holds filled with produce. Sleek galleys bobbed gently, dark except for lanterns at prow and stern. Perhaps a few watchmen remained on board. She wanted nothing in their keeping.

Pinal unpinned her kirtle, folded it hastily and secured the garment within a waterproof pouch at her belt. She wore nothing but the belt now, with a trident sheathed at her back and a slitter at her narrow hip. Had a guard happened by at this moment, he would have been startled by a pretty sight. Though old enough to have a daughter reaching womanhood, Pinal retained the graceful form of her youth. Her small breasts were firm, her arms smoothly muscled. And her eyes—huge orbs of turquoise—had no match in all Samothra.

Certain now that she was unobserved, Pinal slipped from the quay into the tepid ocean. She had passed her first hazard of the evening. Yet, as water covered her ears and muffled the sounds of drums and horns, she readied herself for other dangers.

In times past, once she'd escaped land, she had been free to swim where she pleased. But now there was trouble between her homeland Samothra and neighboring Rhentus. The hostile Rhentan king was sending men across the border in darkness to patrol the coast, seizing suspected poachers for his forced-labor gangs. The thought of slavery in Rhentus brought Pinal gooseflesh as she stroked silently from shore.

Carver-kings, these rulers called themselves. Now they wanted to carve up each other, and the prospect of war hovered over everyone's thoughts. But Pinal had long engaged in a private struggle that meant more to her than the fate of nations. Phelmiran, her own king, had a long-standing debt to her, and tonight she would exact another partial payment.

Dark hulls loomed above as she slipped through the harbor. Water carried to her ears the scraping of anchor chains and the slap of waves on wood. Across the harbor's mouth the Sentries, two weathered stone pillars, stood guard; she could see only hints of their jagged profiles against the sky. A swift and dangerous current ran out between these two obstacles, and boats never dared pass between them.

Pinal had no fear of the rocks. Heading for the gap, she smiled as she felt the warm current's pull. The water surged, catching her and speeding her to open sea.

When the flow eased, she paused to check her bearing with the Western Bright. Behind this fixed star, a handful of others floated dimly. Just for a moment she recalled a childhood tale. If the Bright was an eye of the gods, then what must they think of her?

Pinal pushed the thought aside. The gods had died long ago, she believed, leaving their children on Safehold to survive as best they could. If the Bright was an eye, then it was blind, its original purpose forgotten.

She listened for oars, but only faint cries of merrymakers reached her. Thank the gods, at least, for so many festivals. It was on such nights that she provided for herself and her daughter.

But what if the patrols should snare her after all? What of the others who must suffer? There was her wife Alcis, who, despite recent coolness toward her, would be shaken by the loss. And Pinal's daughter Losenne would have to content herself with one mother instead of two. How could Pinal justify the risks that she was taking?

On her last foray she had come home empty-handed, barely ahead of the dawn. She had even considered, at her brother's urging, looking for "honest" work. There were women of Pinal's slight build who made a success of stone-cutting . . . But no. The Crown owed her more than she could ever take. How else, but by stealth, might she gain repayment for that debt?

She listened again and heard nothing amiss. The Rhentans—Ekinoff's patrols—must be searching elsewhere. Or perhaps the men had slipped ashore to enjoy festivities their tyrant suppressed. The way was clear for her to swim to the Branching Reef. But she did not start—

For at that instant, the surf-change began to come over her.

Feeling her senses opening, Pinal took one deep breath, then pulled her head under to prepare for the transformation. At the onset she suffered, as always, an initial moment of giddiness, a sensation of floating at great heights. And then her awareness of other swimmers began, neither as smell nor color but as a fusion of the two.

Moments before, the water had been black. Now, below her, the depths pulsed with streamers of light—oranges, reds, silver. Some shapes carried harsh scents. Others were aromatic as rare incense. In every direction, they moved in shimmering silence.

After seasons of practice, Pinal had gained control over the sea-sense. This was not a common ability. Fearing what they did not understand, many of her friends dared bathe only in rock-enclosed pools.

But Pinal, after much daytime swimming, had learned to interpret what the sea-sense showed. Tonight she recognized the slow stirrings of a school of saltminnows—their yellow glints, their vinegary scents. She glided over them, then twitched involuntarily at the darker image of a chisel-fish. This predator was too small to menace a human swimmer, but the minnows were in danger from it. She extended her reach.

Golden candlejacks winked as she passed, but her attention was drawn elsewhere. Reef fish waved lazily in their dens; she knew them as a profusion of flowery scents. Now she could find her way without the Bright, for she was well acquainted with the patterns of life here. Underwater, the land jutted out. She followed its contour, only vaguely aware of stringy kelps that slipped past her legs.

Thick seaworms probed the bottom mud, but she paid them little heed. Her quarry, if it came, would rise through pungent waters in search of its own prey. The reef was a favorite feeding ground for the royal *gleaner* fish she sought. She had no pretensions to nobility, but she had come to hunt a prize reserved for kings.

Rational thoughts fled as the surf-change reached its final stage. Feeling the smooth flexing of her muscles, she rejoiced in her strength. Though she knew herself to be outwardly unaltered, she seemed now a creature much like those around her, a being propelled by simple needs and fears. Her weapons—the trident and the long slitter—were as dangerous as any teeth.

Pinal halted, floating near the reef with her head underwater. Caution was required now, for fish could sense a careless human swimmer and react to human emotions. She must hold in her feelings, fight the instincts that the sea-change unleashed. Until the moment came to strike . . .

She waited at the surface, lifting her face to breathe as seldom as she could manage. The waves rocked her gently; she kept herself in place by occasionally paddling. Below, the tiny reef fish nibbled at kelp.

A smell of fermented fruit arrived, along with a flash of deep violet. An ocean denizen twice her length made its slow way by. Her hand closed on the trident's shaft, but there was no need. The predator did not waver from its path.

Another scent—musty, almost choking. A bottom-walker, armored and impregnable, moved off toward the east. The seaworms fled its approach, but one was too slow.

Then, from another direction, came a message that she knew well—the odor of decay, the fetor of dead flesh. This was the scent of a gleaner, and one few swimmers could bear; she had learned to gird herself against it.

Clamping down on her rising excitement, she willed herself to hold still. To her visual sense, the fish showed a garish yellow silhouette with tapered head and elongated jaws. Though the gleaner was still far off, she could not help thinking of its quills and of the poison cloud they could spew. More than once she had come close to suffering the deadly spray.

At last her quarry approached and began feeding, poking its mouth into crevices of the reef. Pinal held back her urge to strike, waiting for its belly to fill. Its motions became more sluggish after a time; now she was ready to dive. Gripping the trident's shaft, she lifted her legs to help thrust herself down. The gleaner, wary, twitched as she sped toward it.

Too soon! shouted a voice within. The skittish creature flashed and was gone. She surfaced, alternately sucking air and cursing, then pulled her head under once more.

For the moment she could not discern her fish. Was it hiding nearby, she wondered, or was it already far out of reach? Straining her sense, she did not find it, but she did detect something else. In distant waters she noted an odd iridescence, faint but disturbing. She could give no name to what lay behind it. But she lost interest in the anomaly, for her elusive quarry reappeared. The fish had not gone far!

Soon, as she had hoped, the gleaner returned to her part of the reef. Again she throttled her impulse to close too quickly. She watched its darting motions and judged where its path must lead. Taking a last breath, she dove, aiming at a rich coral bank.

The timing must be perfect now. With powerful kicks she dove deeper, leveled out and began to rise. The gleaner changed course and she hastily made what corrections she could. The feeling of death was almost unbearable as the quarry passed overhead. Again it seemed to waver, ready to dart off.

But suddenly she shot up under the fish, thrusting her trident into its belly. Holding her arm outstretched, she hastily kicked higher, leaving the reflex-activated toxin streaming into the water behind her. Now she had to keep swimming until the death throes ended.

Did she feel a tingle against her legs? She winced, imagining the searing effect of the poison if it should touch her at full strength. The fish's spasms were threatening to loosen her grip.

At last she felt the shuddering cease. She broke the surface and filled her lungs with great gulps of air. For the moment, she forgot all caution. If Ekinoff's patrols came now, they would have to fight her for this prize.

The creature was dead; it showed nothing to her sea-sense. She paused, trod water while she pulled the slitter from its sheath. In starlight, her eyes discerned only vague outlines of the body. Still suffering from waterborne rashness, Pinal made a sudden but skillful slash to lay open the creature's side. Risking the cruel spines, any of which might still contain a lingering drop of toxin, she slipped a finger inside the fish.

The feel of a hard nugget made her grin. Here lay solid proof of victory—fifty days' wages for a stonecutter, maybe more. She rinsed the precious nodule in the waves, then popped it for safekeeping inside her cheek. The size of the metallic lump was comforting, though she knew it to be small by kings' standards.

The big fish, the gleaners that the royals took, were too fierce for Pinal to tackle. From the nuggets of those swimming treasuries, palaces were furnished, invasions financed. One day, perhaps, she would learn the secrets used to snare such huge prizes. For she sneered at the royals' claims of hereditary talents and god-granted privileges. The gleaners were just fish; why did not everyone have the right to harvest them?

Now she must dispose of the body, for should it be found it would draw more patrols to the sea. And no predator had ever been known to make a meal of gleaner flesh.

Pinal was familiar with a current that might sweep the evidence far to the west, even past the shores of Limnis. She began to two the remains, her senses reaching broadly. The hunt finished, she could afford to let her feelings of triumph touch the swimmers below. She smiled as they scattered at her passing. *Let all who might trouble Pinal be wary.*

From time to time she looked up, finding the Bright where it always hung, the pale stars having shifted behind it. She followed the beacon, touched at last the current she sought. Loosening her gutted catch with the knife's point, she allowed the stream to tug it away. Let them blame the Limnis poachers for that one, she thought gleefully. Limnis's waters, from what she knew, were thick with outlaws. She put her weapons away and headed for home.

The sound of oars, when it came, was sudden and startling. As quickly as she could turn, she scanned the outlines of approaching low-prowed boats. By the light of the soldiers' torches, she glimpsed mirthless features of tight-lipped men with shaven heads. Rhentans violating Samothran waters! These foreigners had not been celebrating, and from their expressions they meant her to pay for their unwelcome duties this night. The boats were speeding in from three directions. She could flee seaward, she thought, but even as she took her first strokes she realized that she was encircled. The soldiers were unwinding their nets.

She dove instantly, aware how quickly the weighted nets could drop. They would fall deeper than anyone could swim, and then the boats would converge.

Her next thought was to swallow the pellet. She felt the lump stick hard in her gullet, and feared for a moment that she might choke on it. But the sensation eased as the piece went down. Now all her instincts turned to seeking an escape. She must outswim the nets by descending faster and then speeding out from under them. Was that possible?

She fled the panic of fish above her as they discovered their new walls. The thrashings of a school of eels spurred her on despite the first aching in her lungs. She felt pressure rising against her ears, salt burning the insides of her nostrils. Even so, she strove to push deeper.

Suddenly her fingers were tangled in mesh. She had swum straight into the net. Might she not pull it up and swim under?

She clawed at the snarl of cords, but could find no end to them. Noticing a swarm of minnows bouncing crazily on the other side, she realized that a second curtain had dropped behind this one. It was impossible to swim deeper now; the sea was thrusting her up.

Perhaps her water-sense might save her. Everywhere she looked, the panicked fish were flitting one way and then another. Most appeared trapped, yet a few seemed to have found a way out. Far above, she saw their glinting forms following a zigzag path. A hole in the barrier? A gap between two boats?

The discovery came too late, for she had run out of air! Even if she surrendered now, aimed straight for the surface, she would drown. But she forced her feet to kick and her arms to sweep. Now the sea was her ally again, buoying her upward. Thinking of great fish that sometimes leapt from the water, she fought her burning lungs and aimed for the gap.

Coarse netting brushed against her skin as she slid through the opening. Following the fish, she quickly found the second break. Suddenly she was at the surface, hearing angry shouts behind her. She was too busy gasping and stroking to make out their words. Slipping away while the men cursed and struggled with their equipment, she found herself in open water.

She could not pause for breath. The splashing of oars urged her on as she followed the Eastern Bright.

Bypassing the reef, she made for a rocky inlet, then hugged the shoreline to let the current help her in. The steep cliffs here could not be scaled, but she remembered a small cave that might hide her. With spent muscles she pulled herself up onto its dry, gravelly floor and lay still.

Slowly Pinal roused herself from stupor, and realized that she was shaking. From the pouch, she unrolled her thin kirtle, only slightly damp, and covered herself. Then the emptiness of sensation struck her, the absence of water-sense. When the change ended, the awareness of loss was almost as great a shock as the onset.

Now she must depend on her ears for warning. A faint echoing of voices came — men hailing each other from afar. She trembled when she thought the sounds came closer. But, daring a glance out at the sky, she discovered the night was waning. The patrols must row quickly for Rhentus, or be caught outside their borders in daylight.

Pinal could not go home now. Emerging from the waves at this hour would be tantamount to admitting her guilt. At midday her appearance would draw less attention from the guards at the harbor.

Were it not for steep cliffs that bordered most of the sea, forcing her to enter and exit in public view, her risk of punishment by Samothran authorities would be slight. But she could not change the coastline, so she must remain here for a time. Already her stomach was rumbling for breakfast. In the loneliness of the cave, she longed for Alcis's embrace and for the sound of her daughter's voice.

Brushing aside gravel, she tried to sleep on the cold floor. Dawn came, light filtering into recesses where she lay. Her thoughts returned to Losenne, who by now knew that her mother had run into difficulties. This had happened twice before. Would the girl remain confident that Pinal could look after herself?

With a whole morning of enforced solitude, Pinal allowed her doubting voice to surface. This hunting of gleaners was a self-indulgence, too risky to be justified on any account. And cruel to her daughter as well as to her husband. How could she persist?

Yet it was her Carver-king whose inept captain had doomed Losenne's father. The messenger who brought news of his death had assured her he'd been sacrificed for the good of Samothra, but Pinal had uncovered the truth. To gain time for a rendezvous with a strumpet, the captain had sent his men through a treacherous pass. A rock slide buried seven. The captain climbed over the rubble and enjoyed his bawdy night anyway.

Since that day, Pinal had been combining revenge with a good livelihood. She had long relished hunting, and with it the knowledge that she was effectively stealing from Phelmiran's treasury. Now her career was threatened, not by her easygoing ruler but by another—Ekinoff, King of Rhentus. Perhaps her nights of swimming were finally over.

David Allan Evans

The Celebration

*T*here were no stars and no moon over Crystal Lake. It was early in May, after swimming hours. We were the Central High School relay team—which earlier that day had broken two twenty-five-year-old records at the Holstein Relays, the last meet of our senior year—sitting on the edge of the dock about fifteen yards from shore, with our feet cut off at the ankles by the cold, black water. We were celebrating, working on our third beer.

"Okay," said Max, "we all get one dive, and then we have to tell the others what it was like down there."

"Scary," said Leroy.

"You first, Maxie," said Jim.

Max was short and stocky, the fastest out of the blocks, and so the lead-off runner. He eased his hips over the tires that bolstered the dock's sides, and slid into the water.

A minute and a half later he burst out next to the dock just beyond Jim's feet. He blew water out of his nose, climbed the two-step aluminum ladder, sat back down in his spot, and picked up his beer.

He was excited, breathing hard, as if he'd just finished his leg of a race.

"You wouldn't believe it," he said.

"Believe what?" said Jim.

Max rubbed his hair with his towel. "You can't see anything. It's like being in a cave, being blindfolded in a cave." He paused, still excited.

"I'm not sure I want to do this," said Leroy, speaking through his towel over his head.

"No," said Max, "it's great. You've got to feel your way around; you might as well not have eyes. Like those fish at the bottom of the ocean."

"It's that dark?" said Jim.

"Unbelievable," said Max.

"Okay," I said. "Let's drink to Max." We all held up our cans high and took a long drink.

Jim was next. He was the second runner, the slowest, but the surest with the handoff, had never dropped a baton in four years. He put down his beer and pointed his toes at the water and slid off the dock like a knife—both hands palm-down on his hips.

He came up about a minute later, holding onto the dock with one hand.

"Goddamn, you're right, Max," he said. "But the mud . . . " He took a couple of deep breaths.

"You hit bottom?" asked Leroy.

"Not me," said Max.

"Yeah," said Jim, "it's only about ten feet deep. I went down fast and then I hit the mud. It was so slimy and deep; I thought I'd just keep going through it and never get back up, but I must've hit the bottom of the mud; it was up to my knees, almost."

"The bottom of the bottom," said Leroy.

"That mud—goddamn," said Jim. "That was something else. Dark too." He was breathing evenly now and he moved hand over hand to the ladder, climbed up and got his towel and sat down in his spot next to his beer, and wiped off his head and face.

"This is to Jim and his muddy dive," I said, and we all toasted and took a drink.

I was next. Number three, the second slowest, the best diver. I stood up on the dock.

"Watch this," I said.

"Hey, look—the diver," said Jim.

I put my hands together in front of my face as if starting to pray, and stood knock-kneed.

"Thithy," said Leroy in a high voice. "Here's the thithy going head first."

I shuffled awkwardly to the edge, stood there, eased my toes until I could grip the very edge, pretended to teeter, then let myself tip over into the water like a praying statue, tucking up tight into a cannonball just after the shock of the cold, then let myself fall deeper and deeper, turning over completely and passing through a sudden and very cold current; then I hit the mud and opened up. I had my eyes closed. At first I fought against the sucking slime, but the more I struggled the deeper I went. Then I relaxed again, stopped kicking, moved my hands and arms vigorously, and rose. It was soundless. I yelled as loud as I could, but heard only a small, tight noise inside my skull, as if from inside a bank vault. I let myself fall again and this time when I got to the bottom I picked up a handful of mud and held it close to my face, and then I opened my eyes wide for about three seconds, but saw nothing, not even my hand. The mud dissolved or was swept away quickly, and I imagined my hands getting cleaner and cleaner by the second. I pulled upward and my hand hit the underside of the dock. Where was I, under the very middle of the dock? I felt a mossy, empty barrel and rapped on it several times with my knuckles, but heard nothing. I kicked and swam forward, touched a cable, grabbed it, using it to pull myself quickly away—far enough, I figured, to get clear of the dock. I reached upward; nothing. I swam another few seconds and, just before I emerged, opened my eyes one more time. Open or closed, even near the surface, the darkness was the same. Then I busted out, almost out of breath.

I was about ten yards from the dock, in deep water, facing the center of the lake. I turned around and looked back at the others.

I heard Max's girlish voice "Over here, thithy."

I swam quickly to the dock, found the ladder, climbed up and stood above my spot. It had been a good, quick workout; my heart was ticking fast, but I was in good shape. I wiped off my face with my towel and hung it over my shoulders, and picked up my beer.

"Your turn, Thomas," said Jim.

"The mud is so soft you wonder how it holds together," I said. "And there's no noise at all. Did you hear me yelling?"

"Not me," said Max.

"I thought maybe I felt something underneath me," said Jim.

"I was right under you, knocking on the barrel," I said. "And the current was so cold. You guys feel a current?"

"Not me," said Jim. "It was all cold."

"Current? Crystal Lake is no river," said Max.

I wiped off my hands. "It's hard to describe," I said, trying to think of more words, and just then a thought came to me, and I wondered if the others had it too: we were all diving into the same spot in the same lake, but every one of us had a different dive, a different story to tell. What I brought back up out of that private, cold, and muddy darkness was mine alone, and nobody else would ever understand it completely. Even friends are strangers.

"I was just thinking," I said. "It's great, but it's hard to put into words."

"That's right," said Jim. "It's a strange feeling down there."

Leroy held up his beer. "To Thomas and his dive," he said.

We all drank to me, my dive.

"Oh shit," said Leroy. "I'm not sure I want to do this." He was the anchor man, the fastest by far: conference champion in the hundred, the best swimmer—city champion in the butterfly and backstroke.

"You of all people," I said.

"Here goes nothing," he said, and dropped off the dock, clothespinning his nose with his fingers.

About thirty seconds later, Jim suddenly yelled and rolled backward on the dock, holding his beer upright. "What the hell!" he said, and then Leroy came up right under where he'd been sitting.

"What the hell?" said Jim, pointing down at Leroy.

Leroy, Max, and I laughed, and then Leroy climbed up on the dock and sat down. We were all looking at Jim and laughing. Finally, I said:

"The last story of the evening."

"Yeah, what was it like, you bastard?" said Jim.

"Nothing," said Leroy.

"Nothing?" said Max.

Leroy wiped off his face.

"Except for one thing," he said.

"One thing," I said.

"The monster," said Leroy.

"Oh yeah," said Max. "The monster."

"Tell us about it, asshole," said Jim.

"The slimy monster of the deep," said Leroy. The mon-ster of the mud.

"Get real," said Max.

"The cold, slimy monster of Crystal Lake," said Leroy.

"That's it," I said. "Let's drink to the Cold, Slimy Monster of Crystal Lake."

Now we were all laughing, holding up our beers—the relay team with two brand-new records—drinking to Leroy, to the Monster, to all of us, good friends and strangers, about to start on the fourth and final beer.

John Fox

from The Boys on the Rock

*O*ther than some girl timekeepers at this end of the pool, Al was the only one there so far, sitting aways down in the top back row of the bleachers under our gold-on-blue HOGAN banner, leaning forward with his forearms on his thighs and his hands clasped, looking across the pool at the huge saggy white-on-maroon MOUNT ST. MATTHEW banner with tassels and things on it. This was Saturday night, the big Bronx–Westchester invitational at the Mount that I've mentioned a million times but I don't know if I really feel like going into it because it was a huge drag.

There were six other banners scattered around, among them Kathy's—FARRELL—which is the lamest team on earth because they've only had boys in that school for a couple of years although they do have really attractive swimsuits with orange and yellow diagonal stripes. Every now and then Al would scratch his face or sit back and fold his arms or cross his legs. I figured he must have felt pretty weird sitting there behind the Hogan bench. After all, he swam on the Mount team and everything, so I bopped out from the locker room in just my swimsuit past those timekeepers, some of whose eyes followed me over to Al. He sat up straight and scanned my body, sort of like browsing, and like he was overcome by the experience, shook his head once and said, "Whew," as I plopped down next to him and said, "Hi."

"Hey, hotstuff," he whispered huskily, touching my arm with an elbow. "Excited about the meet?"

"Yeah." I was more excited about being with him later at his house.

He said, "I can't wait till later."

"Me neither."

He glanced around, scratching his neck, his mouth in an O. Back to me, a pucker and an airy kiss. I returned it.

He examined the palm of his hand. "Nice legs you got there, handsome."

"Quit it, will ya?" I pulled my legs together. "Shit."

He leaned back, laughing, his feet off the floor. If I had pulled down my suit I would have BOIINNGGGed straight out of it, in other words. And most of those timekeepers were watching us now, pencils or stopwatches in their hands.

"What am I gonna do?" I said, amused but getting worried. He responded with a laugh and I clipped him on the arm. He laughed harder and then so did I.

I stood and faced the wall and, pretending to be adjusting the Hogan banner, tried to think about Brother Laughlin drawing geometry all over a blackboard, but the left-hand gold vertical stripe of my suit was now pulsating, getting the stretch test of its life. "What the fuck am I gonna do? I have to go right by those girls."

"Dive in the pool," Al said. Which did the trick. I surfaced and boosted myself out and as I strolled past those girls I snapped the seat of my suit and said hi and a few of them smiled or giggled or said hi and one of them mumbled something about "snot nose." Before entering the locker room I tossed one last glance at Al and he beamed, a white flash. In a while the place got noisy with relatives and friends and students and so forth and there was Al alone among them.

·

"Judges and timers read-yy. Swimmers take your mark!"

It was my event, the 100-breast—a cinch. I stood on the block in lane four. Al was leaning on his hand, his elbow on his knee, watching me, happy and proud. He winked. The Kathy in lane five giggled. I don't know if he caught the wink or not, but Al had been doing it all night, each time I'd glance over to him, which was quite often.

The Iona Preppy in lane three false-started so we had to do it over. Al was now waving or signaling to someone across the pool, which threw me slightly as the gun went off, but I dove perfectly. I pumped and breathed and went and went and turning on their slippery wall was no problem. Turning again, into the third lap, I had a good lead. Then I looked. Which is one of the mortal sins of swimming. Looking. Ordinarily this means glancing to your right or left to see where the other swimmers are, and that slight split-second lapse can cost you the event, so it's something you *don't do.* But I not only looked, I looked *up* and *out* to the right into the bleachers for Al and he wasn't even there. So I fell behind and, looking out to the left for a split-second, saw him squeezing in next to some guy behind the Mount bench, the guy with his hand out for a shake. By now I must have dropped three seconds, completely blowing my lead. Mr. Bieniwicz was running alongside the pool yelling things at me. I was all pissed off and shaken up right there in the pool. I tried to make up for the lost time with the strength you use to punch a wall when you're mad. I surged and reached and stretched and forgot about their goddamn tile walls and slipped as I pushed off and in the end got touched out by the guy in lane five, who at that moment for some reason I thought was a Mountie. As I boosted myself out I couldn't look at anybody and then I remembered that it was that Kathy who was in lane five, not a Mountie, and there he was gloating in his orange-and-yellow suit, flexing his thighs over the fact that he came in *third*—Mount first and me *fourth.*

Mr. Bieniwicz ran over and hustled me over to the side. "What the hell were you looking at?" he said with this intense whisper which was more shock than anger. We were attracting a crowd, the rest of the Hogan team.

I was staring at my feet, thinking. Then I looked at him. "Nothing," I said.

His whistle was all jittery. "I don't understand."

"I shouldn't have looked, I know, I'm sorry, I shouldn't have been looking." I pulled away from him and broke between a couple of teammates and looked across the pool at Al—standing behind the Mount team—staring at me confusedly, his hands in his back pockets.

Then who bops over to me, blocking my sight line, but the Kathy who touched me out. "Hey, queer," he says, and giggles in this high-pitched manner.

"*What?*" I said.

He goes, "I hear you don't like girls, and you suck everybody off in the shower, that you—OOOMPH—" He doubled over, my fist in his stomach. I guess he wasn't expecting this from a faggot. Then I got grabbed and held from behind and so did he and he's yelling Faggot and Queer and Fuckin' homo and things like that and this big Hogan vs. Farrell shouting match erupted and all the coaches were keeping the two teams separated, trying to cool everyone down. Evan and Kevin surrounded me against a wall, saying things like, "Okay, relax, cool it," and stuff like that, their hands gripping my biceps. Mr. Bieniwicz ran over and Kevin said, "He's okay." I was looking at his chipped tooth.

I didn't get disqualified or anything. In the other events I used that fist-through-the-wall energy and we won the 100-medley and something else, I don't remember what. Winning that 100-breast meant more to me than I thought it could. If I hadn't looked I would have won and *then* seen that Al wasn't on the Hogan side, seen him on the Mount side reminiscing or some shit with some jerk ex-classmate. So it all would have turned out the same anyway but at least I would have won the 100-breast.

Dawn Fraser with Harry Gordon

The Night of the Big, Big Minute

An Olympic 100-meter free-style championship takes around one minute to decide. In the space of that minute you can thrash your way into history. You can realize the only ambition you ever cherished. You can fulfill all the hopes and prayers of your family and your friends. You can justify years of personal dedication and years of patient coaching and polishing. It can be the biggest, the loveliest, the most memorable minute of your life. Or it can be a pretty unhappy minute. For seven out of the eight people who line up at the start, it has to be a minute of failure. Some of them will remember it always with pride and affection, surely; but for all seven losers it has to mean that all the dedication and all the polishing have not been fully rewarded. It has to mean that they are the not-quite people of sport.

I want to tell you about my biggest minute. I had three really big minutes at three successive Olympic Games, and they were all beautiful minutes. When I'm old, I know that I will caress the three of them in my memory. And there have been other minutes to remember always—minutes that seemed massive at the time. But the biggest of all came on Saturday, December 1, 1956. That was the night I won my first gold medal. My mother and father and I always used to call it Don's gold medal, because it was my dead brother Don who started me swimming. I was still very inexperienced, and it was the first really big milestone in my career. In Tokyo eight years later, after I'd become the first person ever to win a swimming championship three times in a row, I felt just wonderful. It was the climax, the culmination. But I was 27 years old then and less susceptible to excitement. The contentment was sweet; I felt that I had come to the end of a fairly hard road, and that knowledge was warm and relaxing. But for the sheer bubbling thrill of success, nothing could ever match that first night in Melbourne, when I was 19 and so very nervous.

I used to have an awful dream before a big event. It recurred a lot through my career, but in the later years it didn't bother me so much. Early, though, I would wake up actually trembling with fright, my heart pounding, unable to go back to sleep for a long time. I had it the night before that race of the first gold medal. I'd gone to bed early, and I had prayed for the strength to win. Then I thought about the race for a long time . . . about the turn I'd do, about how important it would be to stay motionless on the block, about keeping a little power in reserve for the last 15 yards. Then I dozed off, and sometime I started to dream.

The gun went off, but I had honey on my feet and it was hard to pull them away from the starting block. I finally fought free and dived high. I floated up steeply and wafted down. It seemed a long time before I hit the water, and the water wasn't water; it was spaghetti. I fought with it and kept going up and down in the one place, like a yo-yo. The spaghetti strands tangled and tied my feet, and I was swimming with my arms alone. Of course I fouled up the turn and took a few mouthfuls, and I woke up gasping and fighting in a sea of spaghetti.

I had a squirt of adrenalin from my asthma spray, and this only made my heart beat faster. It took a long time to get back to sleep. I've learned to live with dreams like that now, but they still sometimes manage to make me panic in my half-sleep and flutter like a frightened bird.

On the day of an Olympic final you feel like something delicate—a wedding cake, maybe, or a spring hat—that shouldn't be touched. You lie around on your back for most of the day, and you feel that the blanket around you should be cotton wool or even tissue paper. The other athletes leave you alone a lot, unless you say you want to talk. The atmosphere is hushed and the care is special, as if you're in a hospital ward. Because their fitness is so vital, Olympic athletes suffer from occupational hypochondria. They always feel that something is going to go wrong—that their muscles will seize up or that they'll cave in with a chill. On that last day, when you know that you have the ability to do well, you don't want to take a single risk. You walk slowly to the mess hall and you eat things that can't possibly affect your tummy. You talk with the other girls and boys, but the conversation is always a little unreal. You have an important appointment that night, possibly with a gold medal, and it dances in the mist of your mind all the time. You can talk about other things, but you can't stop thinking about the moments to come on the starting block. You maybe write a note to your parents and tell them you'll add a P.S. after the race, and sometimes you try to read a paperback. Sometime during the day, maybe even twice, I pull on a tracksuit and go for a swim. Not a training swim. No amount of training on this day is going to be of the slightest benefit. But a soothing swim . . . a swim for the nerves. I get more relaxation from an easy swim than from anything in the world. It sounds silly, but being in the water is like being with an old friend.

I don't think I'm a hypochondriac, but for some reason I've gone down with an illness before each Olympic Games in which I've competed. That first time in 1956 I was admitted to the Village hospital about 10 days before my first event. I had an earache, an eye infection and bad headaches, and I had to have penicillin injections every day for a week. In Rome I suffered a shocking attack of gastroenteritis, lost a lot of weight and went into the Games a lot weaker than I should have. And even in Tokyo, a week before I was due to race, I got myself a virus infection. In 1958, at the Cardiff Empire Games, I contracted pneumonia and spent six days in the Village hospital.

Anyway, on that day of the 1956 final, I went to the Olympic Pool and I walked around it. I really feel that you can get to know a pool and that knowing it can be a big aid in a race. I know it's all water—sure. But it isn't a case of "if you've seen one, you've seen 'em all." I feel that in Melbourne we Australian girls had a big advantage in having trained for weeks in the Olympic Pool. One big thing for me was that I had my spots marked out. That probably sounds crazy, and I don't know whether other topline swimmers do what I do. But I always pick certain spots—places where I'll swim very fast or where I'll slacken off maybe 5 per cent. The problem is this: over 100 meters you can't swim flat-out all the way. Even a man can't do it. You can swim at maybe 95 per cent all the way, but I don't know anyone who can sustain a flat-out effort for the whole distance. There was a lad in Sydney a few years ago, a boy called Charlie Staples, who could do it for a while. He could go through the first 50 meters at full throttle, and he would reach the halfway mark in about 24 seconds—maybe three yards ahead of the opposition. But then he would die. He would keep swimming, but he wouldn't be getting anywhere, and the others would pass him.

To me, the solution to this problem has always been to choose a few spots around the pool and use them in the expenditure of my energy. At one of them I'll slacken just a little; at another I'll try to hit my second wind for a 100-percent finish. Sometimes I use a pipe at the side of the pool, sometimes a hole where the water comes bubbling through, sometimes a mark on the guttering that skirts the water. I've even used people standing close to the edge.

I had my marks, I knew without lifting my head out of the water exactly where the 25-meter mark was, and I knew the amount of turbulence I could expect in the water. That's another thing you get to know: just how rough it's going to be. I was in one of the center lanes that night. They're awarded to the fastest of the qualifiers for the final, and I wished I didn't get one so often. The turbulence is usually worst in the center, while a lane a little nearer the side, maybe number six, is usually a lot calmer. You get the turbulence on the second half of the 100-meter, after you've turned; and it's obvious that the amount of body waves from the wake of all the other swimmers that come at you will be worst in the dead center of the pool. Maybe you've always thought of a championship pool as a dead-calm place, a sheet of water with a surface smooth as ice. That's how it is before eight swimmers hit it and churn it with their arms and feet. But at the halfway mark, as you come out of your turn, for a moment it's like swimming in the surf. At the sides of the pool it's a lot calmer, because the gutters remove a lot of the roughness; but a lot of people don't like swimming right beside the wall. It gives them a cramped feeling . . . maybe something like the discomfort golfers experience when they're playing across water. In both cases it's only a mental hazard. The swimmer beside the wall, like the golfer playing across the creek, should just use his ordinary stroke. In both cases, they sometimes don't.

I had a light meal that night and put on my togs and tracksuit at the Village. In the bus I sat next to John Marshall, and felt as if I was on my way to an accident. John talked about other things, but I was shaking with nerves and apprehension and excitement. It was a delicious, awful feeling. I was a bit confident, a bit afraid. At the pool there were crowds waiting beside the bus stop, and I looked round to see who they were waiting for. Then I realized that we were the people they wanted to see. A cheer went up as I went down the steps, and somebody yelled out, "Good on you, Dawnie." I said thanks automatically when people wished me luck, but all I wanted to do was to get into that pool and dive into the water and get rid of all the strange, discomforting emotions that were inside me.

I parked the bag in which I'd brought along a towel, a dressing gown and a second swimsuit, and I found Harry Gallagher beside the pool.

"How do you feel, champ?" he asked.

"Awful," I said.

"Go get yourself a warm-up," he told me. "You'll be all right. And give yourself a very hard fifty meters."

Harry was chirpy and confident. Jon Henricks had won the men's 100-meter free style the previous night, and Harry was expecting to win the double.

I took a very long warm-up swim, and it calmed me down, as it always did. I could feel the tension flowing out of me as I hit the water. Underneath I opened my eyes and began to feel good. It was cool and glassy, and I was in familiar territory. My tummy had stopped somersaulting even as I surfaced, and the more I cut into the water, the better I felt. I swam a very fast 50-meter dash—around 29 seconds. But in that burst I somehow felt that I couldn't get going.

After I hauled myself out, I went to the locker room and put on a dry swimsuit and then zipped my tracksuit over it and wound my green towel round my neck. There were other girls there, and they were all pretty edgy. The Australian girls were very strained and talking all the time about how terrible they felt. I finally couldn't stand it and left the room. I have trouble sharing tension with other girls. I figure that it's hard enough to cope with my own emotions without trying to calm other people down.

I went down the side of the pool looking for Harry Gallagher. He was at the diving end with a stop watch round his neck.

There were a couple of races to go before mine, and Harry and I sat on the edge of the deep diving pool.

"I feel as if I'm waiting for an execution," I told him. "My own execution."

"You'll be all right," he said. "You'll kill 'em. Just remember to keep very still on the blocks. I know you'll win it. And your mum and dad know you'll do it."

My parents were somewhere up there in the dark. It was the first time they'd visited Melbourne, and I had queued up for a long time to get their seats. Even then, I was lucky; the swimming was sold out early, and I'd got cancellations.

Harry talked about the race then. He told me to go hard early, to keep with the leaders, to take a look at how I was going as I was coming out of the turn. "You'll have the look on Lorraine on the way back," he said. "She's the worry. But if you can be with her halfway back, you can win it. Just make sure you keep something in reserve for those last 10 yards. Do that, and you'll finish stronger than Lorraine."

I nodded. The last 10 yards seem to take longer to swim than any other part of the race. In fact, the whole of the second leg is tougher than the first. I listened to Harry's advice. But I wasn't calm enough either to absorb or to follow it . . . and this I knew. I decided that I would probably swim my own race, and that's what I did.

I went to the changing room and joined a tight, taut little group of girls, all in tracksuits, all with towels. Somebody checked our names off and said, "Right, girls . . . on your way." We marched, in single file in the order of our lane numbers, alongside the pool and around behind the starting blocks. A couple of girls asked the referee if they could dive in, and he told them they could. I swung my arms round and did a few knee bends behind my block. There was plenty of noise about now, but once, as I waited behind my block, I distinctly heard my father's voice: "Come on, Dawnie. You can do it, love."

· The quick dip before the race is designed to settle down boys and girls who are either very nervous or very warm in their tracksuits. It's sometimes used for other purposes, though. Some people will get permission to take a plunge simply because it means a delay and they know that any extra waiting will upset some opponents. I've done it myself if I've known that I'm up against someone who's highly nervous. In Honolulu in 1957 I took a long, leisurely swim before I raced against Chris von Saltza. I wanted to make her cook a little, and I did. Another method of adding to the ordeal of a rival who's overtense is to take a long time getting undressed. I've often been accused of doing this—with some justification. Almost invariably, I'm the last of the field to get unzipped and stripped down to my swimsuit before a start. But, to be quite fair to myself, I should point out that it isn't all gamesmanship; I like to keep warm as long as possible, and I hate standing round in the cold.

The most dangerous form of starting-block gamesmanship that I know is the intentional false start. This involves "breaking," or beating the gun, purposely. The idea, again, is to rattle someone who's already nervous. I've done that, too. I've had a go at just about everything at some time. But doing a false start by design is really hazardous, and I wouldn't recommend it to anyone. In swimming you're disqualified if you make two false starts. If you do it once, then somebody else does it, you're still out of the race if you make a second false start.

The point about all these devices is that they make capital out of the tension of the other swimmers. But, really, everybody in a big race should be very tense at the start. The adrenalin glands have been working overtime, and your heart is really bumping. I always figure that if my opponents aren't as nervous as I am, then they're far too confident anyway. But sometimes I know that if I rattle them a bit it will help settle my own nerves. And this knowledge has helped me win races.

On the night of my big minute I took as long as I could to peel off my tracksuit and sandals. A whistle blast was the signal to undress. Then another whistle blast meant that we were to stand behind our blocks. I wasn't showing much nervousness outwardly—I never do—but my tummy was turning over and I was trembling inside.

Then we were out of the referee's hands and in the starter's. He told us to mount our blocks. This, for the swimmer, is the moment of truth. Until then, there is a low, steady murmur from the crowd; but as you climb onto that block there comes the strange sound of thousands and thousands of people being absolutely silent. You can almost hear a gigantic intake of breath. You look out at the blueness and the stillness of the water and you realize that this is your minute of history. Within seconds, now, that lovely surface is going to get all roughed up by eight highly charged young women. Afterward, their hair will be mussed and dripping and they'll be breathless. Somebody will have earned a gold medal, and you hope it's going to be you.

Between the whistle blast which tells you to mount your blocks and the explosion of the starter's pistol there usually elapses something between three and five seconds. At times, if some of the contestants are rocking and wobbling, the gap can be as much as 10 seconds. The starter is waiting and watching . . . and mainly he's watching eight pairs of feet. All the heels have to be down flat, and he isn't going to fire that gun until they are.

This is a time of intense concentration. Herb Elliott once likened his concentration before running a mile to adding up huge columns of figures. I know what he meant. You have to be totally absorbed in the business before you — which in my case is to get from one end of a pool to the other and back in the shortest possible time. You must deliberately exclude everything else from your mind.

I take a few long, easy deep breaths at this point, filling my lungs completely, exhaling slowly. I grip the edge of the block with my toes and I bend my knees. Since I have to stay quite immobile for anything up to 10 seconds, I jam my heels down hard and try to transfer all my weight to the dead center of my feet. (At the sound of the gun I'll get all the force of my lunge at the water from the balls of my feet.) I pull back my arms, and I'm coiled, ready to go. Some swimmers keep their arms in front; there's no set rule, but I feel that I save winding-up time by doing it my way.

As the gun sounded that night, I lost my nerves. I hit the water fast and flat and surfaced quickly; my legs started to beat the moment they were wet. A lot of swimmers start to kick as they leave the blocks; I feel that this is of no benefit, though — that, in fact, these swimmers are losing some of the power of their dive. The whole idea of the racing dive is to plop into the water like a torpedo. You should be perfectly flat and still as you hit, as you start stroking and your hands push up to the surface.

I covered the first 15 meters before I took a gulp of air. Under the water I could vaguely see Lorraine's shape blurring along in the next lane. But I'd forgotten whatever Harry Gallagher had told me about tactics. This wasn't any time for being crafty; the important thing was to swim hard and judge the turn that was coming. Even the preparation for the turn was done instinctively, without thought; my mind was one large, determined blank. I did a reasonably good tumble turn, but Lorraine's was better; I hit the halfway a touch ahead, but she came out of her turn a little ahead. I'd say that she got a yard better push-away than I did.

I should tell you here something about the mechanics of the tumble turn. The rule is that you have to hit the end of the pool with one of your hands before you turn about.* For the tumble, you go down almost to the bottom of the pool. You touch inches from the base, then flip your legs over and push your feet to the wall. At that stage, at the push-off, you should be half turned on one side; you've dropped the opposite shoulder from the hand with which you touched. It's an underwater flip, and the reason why it's so often favored is that under the water there's no turbulence and no outside movement. Your body moves in full flow, like a fish's. It's a very fast turn, but a hard one to do: for two full seconds out of the race you're not breathing. Sometimes people have asked me how to do it and I've shown them; they've tried, and they've come up gasping for air. So it isn't surprising that in the middle of an effort that's close to 100 per cent it's a tough one.

Personally, I don't trust the tumble turn. I just feel that it's risky, that there's always the chance that something will go wrong. I used to use it a lot, but for a few years now I've relied almost exclusively on the ordinary turn that beginners do, which simply involves touching above the surface and pushing away from the wall with the feet. I've sharpened that up to such a degree that it's usually just about as fast as a good tumble. Not always, though. In Tokyo, against the American girl, Sharon Stouder, I went into my ordinary turn with a handy lead; she tumbled magnificently, and I've been told she actually came out of the turn ahead.

Coming out of that 1956 turn, I tapered down to maybe a 90-per-cent effort on the first half of the home stretch. I stole a glance across at Lorraine as I took a breath 25 meters from the finish and I could see that she was dead level. She was a terrific fighter, Lorraine . . . and she was experienced in a tight finish. I gave it everything, but over the last 10 meters I felt I was fading just a little; I'd swum the first leg too fast. We were stroke for stroke over the last few yards, and it seemed to me that we hit together. Neither of us knew then who was the winner, but a moment after we touched we were both watching the tremendous battle for third placing between Faith Leech and the American girl, Joan Rosazza. Faith just made it, to give Australia a one–two–three clean sweep.

Afterward we just lay on our backs and hung onto the cork ropes and floated. I had a lovely sense of relaxation, even though I didn't know whether I'd won. Then an official winked at me and held up one finger. I'd made it. I was the champion of the world. Lorraine and I embraced in the water. We didn't talk. We were both still numb. But outside the pool there seemed to be pandemonium. The crowd was roaring wildly, and timekeepers were jumping about. One of them came across to the poolside and whispered hoarsely, "It looks like a world record."

---

*This rule has been changed. Swimmers must touch the wall, but they no longer have to touch it with their hands. Most swimmers flip some distance from the wall and touch with their feet as they push off.

Lorraine grinned and said, "It makes our relay team look pretty good." It was something of an understatement.

It was all very confused—the kisses, the congratulations, the conversations in the water. We didn't know for certain that it was a world record; they were still working out an average from the five official times taken. We lazed and splashed around until a whistle blast told us that we could get out and towel ourselves.

It *was* a world record. I was timed at 62.0 seconds and Lorraine was clocked at 62.3 seconds, so we had both cut Lorraine's world time of 62.4 seconds. Some idea of the massive improvement that had taken place in women's swimming can be gauged from the fact that my time would have won the Australian *men's* 100-meter championship just a few years earlier. Of the eight 1956 finalists, five had bettered the previous Olympic record.

Afterward I was up on the victory dais with a gold medal hanging from a ribbon looped round my neck. It was a moment of sweet satisfaction. I had never swum in international competition before; I had been taken seriously as a swimmer for maybe a year. They played the national anthem, and Lorraine, Faith and I were laughing and crying together. The previous night Jon Henricks, John Devitt and Gary Chapman had given Australia a one–two– three result in the men's 100-meter free style. The two results were the greatest that Australia had ever had in Olympic competition, and they just about ensured that we had a mortgage on the two relays.

I ran across later to some television crewmen and asked if I could use their ladder. They said I could, and I propped it against the balcony close to where my mother and father were sitting. They were sitting just a few feet from the rail, and I climbed across to them. Mum was crying, Dad was crying, I was crying. The three of us were always sentimental slobs; all the Frasers were, I guess. It was the only time either of my parents ever saw me win an Olympic medal, and I think it was the happiest moment we ever shared. We all had Don in our minds: his name used to crop up whenever we talked about the Olympics. Dad told me, "I knew you could do it, love."

Jewelle Gomez

A Swimming Lesson

At nine years old I didn't realize that my grandmother, Lydia, and I were doing an extraordinary thing by packing a picnic and riding the elevated train from Roxbury to Revere Beach. It seemed part of the natural rhythm of summer to me. I didn't notice until much later how the subway cars slowly emptied most of their Black passengers as the train left Boston's urban center and made its way into the Italian and Irish suburban neighborhoods to the north. It didn't seem odd that all of the Black families sorted themselves out in one section of the beach and never ventured onto the boardwalk to the concession stands or the rides, except in groups.

I do remember Black women perched cautiously on their blankets, tugging desperately at bathing suits rising too high in the rear and complaining about their hair "going back." Not my grandmother, though. She glowed with unembarrassed athleticism as she waded out, just inside the reach of the waves, and moved along the riptide parallel to the shore. Once submerged, she would load me onto her back and begin her tireless, long strokes. With the waves partially covering us, I followed her rhythm, my short, chubby arms taking my cue from the power in her back muscles. We did this over and over until I'd fall off, then she'd catch me and set me upright in the strong New England surf. I was thrilled by the wildness of the sea and my grandmother's fearless relationship to it. I loved that she didn't continually consult her mirror but looked as if she had been born to the shore, a kind of aquatic heiress.

None of the larger social issues had a chance of catching my attention in 1957. All that existed was my grandmother rising from the surf like a Dahomean queen, shaking her head free of the torturous, useless rubber cap, beaming down on me when I, at long last, took the first swim strokes on my own. She towered over me in the sun with a confidence that made simply dwelling in her presence a reward in itself. Under her gaze I felt like part of a long line of royalty. I was certain that everyone around us—Black and white—felt and respected her magnificence.

Although I intuited her power, I didn't know the real significance of our summer together as Black females in a white part of town. Unlike winter when we're protected by the concealment of coats, boots, and hats, the summer is a vulnerable time. I am left exposed, at odds with all the expectations handed down from the mainstream culture and its media: narrow hips, straight hair, flat stomach, small feet. But Lydia never seemed to notice. Her long, chorus-girl legs ended in size-nine shoes. She seemed unafraid to make herself even bigger, stretching the broad back of a woman with a purpose: teaching her granddaughter how to swim against the tide of prevailing opinion and propriety. It may have looked like a superfluous skill to those watching our lessons. After all, it was obvious I wouldn't be doing the backstroke on the Riviera or in the pool of a penthouse spa. Certainly nothing in the popular media had made the great outdoors seem a hospitable place for Blacks or women. It was a place in which, at best, we were meant to feel uncomfortable, and at worst—hunted. But the potential prospects for actually utilizing the skill were irrelevant to me; it was simply the skill itself that mattered. When I finally got it right I felt I held an invaluable life secret.

It wasn't until college that the specifics of slavery and the Middle Passage were made available to me. The magnitude of that "peculiar institution" was almost beyond my comprehension. It wasn't like anything else I'd learned in school about Black people in this country. It was impossibly contradictory trying to make my own connection to the descendants of slaves—myself, others I knew—and at the same time see slaves not exactly as Americans I might know but as Africans set adrift from their own, very different land. My initial reaction was, *Why didn't the slaves simply jump from the ships while still close to shore and swim home?* The child in me who'd been taught how to survive in water was crushed to learn my ancestors had not necessarily shared this skill. Years later, when I visited West Africa and found out about the poisonous, spiny fish inhabiting much of the inhospitable coastline, rocky and turbulent, I understood why swimming was not a local sport there as it is in New England. I often remember that innocent inquiry, and now every time I visit a beach I think of those ancestors and of Lydia.

The sea has been a fearful place for us. It swallowed us whole when there was no other escape from the holds of slave ships, and did so again more recently with the flimsy refugee flotillas from Haiti. To me, for whom the dark recesses of a tenement hallway were the most unknowable thing encountered in my first nine years, the ocean was a mystery of terrifying proportions. In teaching me to swim Lydia took away that fear. I understood something outside myself—the sea—and consequently something about myself as well. I was no longer simply a fat little girl. My body became a sea vessel—sturdy, enduring, graceful.

Before she died in the summer of 1988 I discovered that she herself didn't really swim that well. All that time I was splashing desperately, trying to learn the right rhythm—*face down, eyes closed, air out, face up, eyes open, air in, reach*—Lydia would be brushing the sandy bottom under the water to keep us both afloat. As she told me this it didn't seem such a big deal to her, but I was shocked. I reached back in my memory trying to put this new information together with the Olympic vision of her I'd always kept inside my head. At first I felt disappointed, tricked. Like I used to feel when I learned that my favorite movie stars were only five feet tall. But I later realized that it was an incredible act of bravery and intelligence for her to pass on to me a skill she herself had not quite mastered—a skill she knew would always bring me a sense of pride in accomplishment.

And it's not just the swimming, or the ability to stand on any beach anywhere and be proud of my large body, my African hair. It's being unafraid of the strong muscles in my own back, accepting control over my own life. Now when the weather turns cold and I don the layers of wool and down that protect me from the eastern winter, from those who think a Black woman can't do her job, from those who think I'm simply sexual prey, I remember the power of my grandmother's broad back and I imagine I'm wearing my swimsuit.

Face up, eyes open, air in, reach.

Polly Rose Gottlieb

from The Nine Lives of Billy Rose

*R*eader's Digest was kind enough not to mention the only one of Billy's nine careers at which he failed. Marriage. He was a five-time loser, and he often said, "Maybe I ain't cut out to be a husband, but I'm a sucker for the best two-dollar buy in town—a marriage license."

In 1928 he married one of Broadway's most brilliant stars, Fanny Brice, and during the next thirty-six years Billy chalked up a losing record of four more marriages and five divorces.

"According to the papers, I've lived nine lives," Billy commented once. "But they always leave out the key life of my crazy lives. The one I lived first— my life with Mama. She set the pattern for all my dreams and ambitions," Billy reminisced. "Looking back, my happiest years were the twelve great years with Eleanor."

It was early in the summer of 1937 when Billy, who was then still married to Fanny, called me and said, "Polly, I want you to go to Cleveland for six weeks."

"Cleveland?" I protested. "I don't know anyone in Cleveland."

"You will," said Billy. "I want you to meet and get to know a girl named Eleanor. Eleanor Holm."

When I walked into the Cleveland air terminal a week later, I saw the world's most beautiful athlete striding toward me. Eleanor was all smiles as she said, "So you're the kid sister Billy sent to look me over."

There was no stalling, no sparring. We both felt an immediate rapport. Eleanor hugged me tightly and said: "That brother of yours is really something. When he told me he was sending you here, I asked myself, 'Who needs it?'"

She laced her arm through mine as we started to walk. "I just met you," she said, "so how come I'm telling you this?" Her warm, hearty laugh rang out as she shook her head and added, "I know a place that makes a great chicken paprikash. Let's go there and talk about our favorite guy."

.

Billy, who was asked to stage a spectacular at the Cleveland Fair because of his success at the Fort Worth Centennial in 1936, had sweet-talked the tall Texans into paying him $1,000 a day for himself for 100 days.

"I spent a fortune of their money," related Billy, "and they couldn't have cared less, as long as I accomplished what they wanted. Amon Carter, Mr. Very Big in that neck of the woods, never forgot that I was the little guy who managed for the Fort Worth Centennial to take all the play away from the Dallas Fair only thirty-two miles away."

Billy chuckled when he said, "I was never much of a ballplayer, but I belted Dallas right out of the ball park with a seven-word slogan that I wrote and pasted up all over Texas: 'Dallas for Education, Fort Worth for Entertainment.'"

Eleanor and Johnny Weissmuller, Olympic champions and pretty fair country swimmers who held a couple of dozen world's records between them, were the stars of Billy's Aquacade in Cleveland. Billy not only coined the word "Aquacade" but, with his customary acumen, also registered it as a trademark. He never did forgive *Webster's Dictionary* for spelling it with a small "a." The dictionary people must have heard Billy's complaint. In the Third Edition, the word "Aquacade" has the big "A."

When Billy decided how he wanted to stage the first water show of his career, the experts told him it couldn't be done. So Billy went ahead and did it. As I watched his wondrous show, I recalled Billy's story of the way he convinced his skeptics.

"Gentlemen," Billy began, "you couldn't be more wrong! Your kind of thinking won't bring in a dime. If you want to make a barrel of money, we've got to charge the audience less than a buck for the greatest show they've ever seen. We've gotta use Canada for our backdrop, the moon and stars for our props, and Lake Erie for our swimming pool."

"But, Mr. Rose," protested one of the engineers, "where's your audience going to sit?"

"In a huge amphitheatre," Billy said. "Ten thousand seats right on the edge of the lake. And no top. The sky and the moon and the stars'll be our ceiling. Fancy enough props for the price?"

"Mr. Rose, you're forgetting something. Don't we need a stage?"

"What kind of a cockamamie question is that?" barked Billy. "Of course we need a stage. Build it three hundred and fifty feet wide and sixty feet deep from front to back. Then balance it on two big barges and float it in Lake Erie."

That's when the argument really began. How could an audience sitting on the shore see a stage floating in the lake?

"Gentlemen, gentlemen!" Bill interrupted. "Haven't you ever been on a ferry? I'm sure every one of you has stood in the front of a ferry and watched it buckle into its landing slip. That's what we'll do with our stage. Buckle it to the lumber in front of the first row of seats. Buckle it tight, tight as a snaredrum."

Another skeptic asked, "But if you attach the stage to the amphitheatre, where will the swimmers swim?"

Billy pulled himself up to his full five feet four and put his vision into words. "The audience is seated. Ten thousand ticket buyers, who paid from forty to ninety-nine cents! Now, strike up the band! Then, in precise alignment, start those barges inching the stage away. Not only will that audience begin to watch, it'll begin to feel! When the stage is seven feet from the audience, turn on the curtain."

A voice broke in to say, "What do you mean, 'turn on the curtain'?"

"I mean just what I said. This isn't any ordinary curtain. It's a curtain of water." The hubbub didn't stop Billy. "I want big spouts covering every inch of the first few feet of the apron and across the entire stage. I want that water to shoot up thirty feet. And it's gotta dance! It's gotta be bigger and more beautiful and better lit than any fountain in Versailles."

"Mr. Rose, I still don't understand where you plan to have the pool."

"When your stage is exactly forty feet away from the amphitheatre, stop those barges dead! There, gentlemen, between the stage and the audience, is your swimming pool, filled with the black and star-lit water of Lake Erie."

The next voice of protest was more patient. "Mr. Rose, how do we turn your fancy into fact? We've got limited money and even less time."

"That's *your* problem," Billy said softly. "You're the engineers and the bankers. I'm just a honky-tonk showman trying to make a fast buck."

Night after night audiences cheered and applauded as Billy's fancy became breathtaking fact. Hidden by the water curtain, the Aquacade swimmers formed a single line along the perimeter of the stage. Then the curtain went down and ten thousand spectators got their first look at a hundred and fifty aquaboys and aquabelles in shimmering white, skin-tight bathing suits.

The swimmers stood motionless for a long moment. Then they plunged into the water one at a time, a quarter of a second apart, rippling into Lake Erie like the snap of a long white leather whip. The show was on.

The dictionary defines "Aquacade" as "an elaborately staged water spectacle consisting of exhibitions of swimming and diving, acrobatics, and group evolutions, with musical accompaniment."

The dictionary doesn't say that all the featured swimmers and divers in every Billy Rose Aquacade were, with one beautiful exception, the world champions of their time. The exception was Esther Williams, who was in Billy's San Francisco Aquacade, and later became an exciting motion-picture star.

The dictionary also doesn't say that every Cleveland audience held its breath when Marshall Wayne, Olympic diving champion, did his two-and-a-half gainers and triple somersaults off the ten-meter-high board. Translated, ten meters is approximately forty feet, or the height of a four-story building, or an easy way to break your back when you're doing fancy high dives with a spotlight shining in your eyes. Nor does the dictionary tell that the laughter never stopped when the fabulous water clown Stubby Kreuger and his daredevil team of divers did their act. Nor does it describe the thrill of watching the greatest of American swimmers, Johnny Weissmuller.

Mr. Webster's book also doesn't note that exactly fifteen minutes after the show began, there was a blare of trumpets and then the announcement: "Ladies and gentlemen, the backstroke champion of the world, Miss Eleanor Holm!"

Eleanor, who is only five feet three, looked six feet tall when she marched to the center of the stage on her high-heeled silver slippers. She wore a leotard of silver sequins and a matching floor-length cape tied loosely around her shoulders. The audiences feasted their eyes and loved those moments when she took off her shoes and cape, and then with charming femininity tucked her dark thick hair inside her swim cap.

"Eleanor was darn near Nijinsky in a bathing cap when she backstroked the length of the pool," was Billy's comment.

Eleanor's performance featured her record-breaking backstroke at various speeds. She was electrifying as she sparkled and streaked through the black water. It was icy cold, but that never bothered Eleanor. What did bother her were the schools of minnows that would get wedged in her bathing suit. Watching her as she tried to outswim or dislodge the fish was a show in itself, but the audience never knew that the frantic minnows triggered her fantastic bursts of speed.

Eleanor had an open invitation to use Leonard Hanna's pool on his large farm in Willoughby, and she would take as many of us as she could squeeze into her car. The gourmet lunches were fabulous, and all of us put on weight except Eleanor, who claimed she swam it off every night, thanks to "those damned Lake Erie minnows!"

During our first week together, Eleanor kept asking, "How come your brother hasn't phoned me? Has he phoned you?" I told her he hadn't. Finally, on my eighth day in Cleveland, Billy called. He didn't even bother to say hello. He just said, "Well?"

"Billy, she's the greatest. I'm crazy about her."

"So am I," he said. "Think I ought to marry the girl if she'll have me?"

"You're crazy if you don't," was my answer.

As always in his life, Billy made headlines even when he wasn't trying. An eager-beaver reporter announced Billy's engagement to Eleanor while he was still married to Fanny Brice.

Fanny, with her deep understanding, took it in her stride when Billy flew out to Hollywood to tell her how he felt. Before Billy could deliver his well-rehearsed spiel, Fanny asked him, "Do you love her?"

Billy said, "Yes."

"That's all I want to know," said Fanny. "Good luck, kid."

Richard Halliburton

Letter, August 15, 1925

[*Athens—August 15, 1925.*] I'm the maddest man in Greece; I arrived yester-day to find the idiot American Express Co. had forwarded all my month's ac-cumulation of mail to *Naples*—though why Naples and not Liberia, only God knows.

Also the proudest! You have the honor to be the father of the *first and only American in history* to swim the Hellespont. Leander was the first Greek, Lord Byron the first Englishman, and Richard Halliburton the first American. Of course, I was headed straight for the Hellespont the moment I sailed from New York. As with the Matterhorn, I said nothing about it in advance for obvious rea-sons.

The morning after I wrote you from Constantinople, Rod and I caught a little Turkish steamer and sailed across the Sea of Marmora through the Dardanelles to the town of Dardanelles, sometimes called Chanak, on the Asi-atic shore. Straightway Rod and I complicated matters dreadfully by lugging our movie machine to a hill overlooking the Hellespont and taking a picture of the place I was going to swim. A few Turkish forts were in range. Between nag-ging police and a sailboat incapable of sailing upstream against a rousing wind, and a six-mile current, we lost three days in a row.

On the third day the wind became so violent we gave up temporarily and went to Troy, twenty miles away, in a wagon, and from sunup to sunset prowled over and about the most romantic and storied ruins on earth. Delaying too long to get home by light, we slept all night on the Scæan gate where Helen pointed out to Priam the armies of the Greeks, where Hector said goodbye to Andromache, and through which the Wooden Horse was dragged to Troy's destruction—truly a fine place to sleep.

Back to Dardanelles next day for more visés and fruitless requests to sail across to the European side—all a ruse, they said, to take forbidden pictures of their secret forts. But at last we got permission to cross over to the Gallipoli Grave Yard (30,000 British soldiers killed in the campaign). We were threatened with immediate execution if we went nearer Abydos, where the forts are. Once at Gallipoli, we spent the night with the British caretaker and next morning at dawn began to buck the six-miles-an-hour current with swirls around the peninsula of Abydos. We simply defied the police and felt we'd take our medicine if only we could swim first.

We reached a mile above Sestos after seven hours' rowing. I made Rod and the two sailboatmen pull for dear life while I steered and sailed, one mile an hour for seven hours, against wind and current. Leander swam directly across from Sestos to Abydos, but having a violent current and a wind that was whipping the water into a sea of whitecaps, I went on a mile and three-quarters higher up—a longer swim by that much, but longer time to get across before the current might sweep me past Abydos point. We lunched on sardines—no breakfast, and climbed a hill to take a sweeping panorama of *my* battlefield.

The exercise of climbing in the scorching sun had the usual physical effect on me. My knees shook when we got back, and my hands trembled so I could not have held a glass of water or lit a cigarette. I said to myself, "You're a physical wreck—can't climb a 150-foot hill without prostration and on top of it you presume to attempt a difficult and dangerous swim. You can't even *walk* five miles." That did me good.

So after a round of pictures—movie and still—we up-anchored and I paddled out into the racing current, the first swim in three years. I didn't know whether I had got more than two hundred feet, when I was the most surprised fish in the Hellespont to look around, after a *solid hour* of swimming, and find I was about a mile from shore—and a mile and a half below my starting point. My difficulty was with cold—the water was icy—and the waves beating and breaking over my head kept me swallowing salt water until I was thoroughly nauseated. But I was amazed at the ease with which I swam. I doubled, trebled my speed. As we approached Abydos point I had to fight to make any headway at all, going southwest about ten times as fast as I went south. But seeing the shore so close I stuck to it and presently my foot hit solid ground. Rod dragged me into the boat, gave me a swig of brandy and I was live as ever. He got pictures all the way across.

I can't explain it, and yet when I finished I could have done it again and faster than before. My physical state becomes an enigma to me more and more: completely exhausted by nine holes of golf, and yet capable of the endurance required for this hard swim.

Back at Dardanelles we found a Constantinople boat in the harbor and jumped aboard her before the Turks could find out what crimes we had committed. In 45 minutes we were steaming over the very water I'd swum in. That night on the boat my sunburn began to torment me, but except for this I had no other ill effects. We reached Constantinople in the morning, changed boats at once for an Athens-bound steamer, traversed the Hellespont for a third time, and arrived here yesterday afternoon—to learn that I had drowned in my attempt.*

Well, one more of my great aspirations is checked off. Only Olympus remains, and after writing here for five or six days we're off for the mountain. I've not dared open my eyes here in Athens. I want to clean up before plunging into Greece. I've no interest in modern Athens. It doesn't exist for me.

---

*The *New York Times* had so reported.

Jonathan Holden

The Swimming Pool

Long after he'd wearied of the work
I recall my father sloshing in hip boots,
ignoring the mosquitoes on his back
to lay by hand, around the stone
swimming pool he'd built, this tile
drain to divert the brook when it
turned brown in thunderstorms, how
he grunted as he pried up each sucking
shovelful of muck, his face
a shiny little mask of wrinkled sweat,
hating every minute of it.
And I remember how, later, in July,
when the wet heat would make you
claustrophobic and despair
he'd step up to that pool—
shy almost—gingerly dip in a toe,
exclaim wryly, then begin the ritual,
first rinse the arms,
then wash the chest,
his legs meanwhile feeling their way
on tiptoe as he waded forward, becoming
shorter and shorter, the cold lip
of the water crawling up his stomach
until, ready to receive the cold,
he'd lie back on his back and sigh,
then close his eyes as though
that pool could never give him back
enough or fast enough or long enough
all that he'd put into it.

A. E. Housman

Tarry, delight . . .

Tarry, delight, so seldom met,
  So sure to perish, tarry still;
Forbear to cease or languish yet,
  Though soon you must and will.

By Sestos town, in Hero's tower,
  On Hero's heart Leander lies;
The signal torch has burned its hour
  And sputters as it dies.

Beneath him, in the nighted firth,
  Between two continents complain
The seas he swam from earth to earth
  And he must swim again.

Barney Hutchinson

Cold Logic

This man likes to dive
In the cold seasons;
He dives, I suppose,
For divers reasons.

Annette Kellerman

from How to Swim

I first loved the ocean when I was a child because it made me curious. I wondered whether it really went down and down, if it would hold me up. I wanted to know what made it blue and to feel the white on a wave. My father told me that all animals swam except the monkey and the pig. And I didn't want to stay on their level. The pig, he said, always cut its throat in the water. That interested me greatly and I begged for the chance to throw one in the briny deep; but he firmly refused. And so I have never been sure about the tale. Some day I am going to buy a pig and try it.

I have been asked ten thousand times why I like to swim and I have given a different answer every time. You see the water always teaches me a new story. It is three times as large as the land and too big to be disturbed. Therefore it has not been crossed out by man and goes on and on, the most elemental thing in all the world. And why do I believe in swimming? To put it briefly, swimming is a pleasure and a benefit, a clean, cool, beautiful cheap thing we all from cats to kings can enjoy.

The man who has not given himself completely to the sun and wind and cold sting of the waves will never know all meanings of life. Swimming is more deeply woven into the fabric of man than any other form of motion. Athletics have scarcely begun to have a history; scientists tell us that walking is comparatively modern, but man swam before he was a man and he will swim till there is no more sea.

The way in which literature does not appreciate swimming surprises me. Poets have pushed the subject far away from them, even those who loved it. Lord Byron, who swam the Hellespont, barely mentions the fact. I only wish I could turn all this into poetry but I can only tell in a faulty way what a glorious human experience it is.

No where else in life can one find an experience bringing that wonderful sense of laziness and cares all blown away—at the same time rousing all forces of resistance. New confidence and power are born within you—for haven't you just overcome the depths of the sea?

But it works the other way, too. I have turned to the ocean when remembering only me and after I left the shore behind, I seemed to shrink and shrink till I was nothing but a flecky bubble and feared that the bubble would burst. And so I advise swimming as good to encourage the modesty of the soul.

There is nothing more democratic than swimming. Bathing is a society event but swimming out beyond the surf line is just plain social. Every one is happy and young and funny. No one argues. No one scolds. There is no time and no place where one may so companionably play the fool and not be called one.

I learn much from people in the way they meet the unknown of life, and water is a great test. If they come to it bravely they've gone far along the best way. I am sure no adventurer nor discoverer ever lived who could not swim. Swimming cultivates imagination; the man with the most is he who can swim his solitary course night or day and forget a black earth full of people that push.

This love of the unknown is the greatest of all the joys which swimming has for me. Though my swimming has earned me a goodly fortune I am still looking for my chest of gold in a cool dripping sea cave—though a professional mermaid for the movies I still wait to see my first real one sitting on a damp grey rock combing her long green hair.

A. M. Klein

Lone Bather

Upon the ecstatic diving board the diver,
poised for parabolas, lets go
lets go his manshape to become a bird.
Is bird, and topsy-turvy
the pool floats overhead, and the white tiles snow
their crazy hexagons. Is dolphin. Then
is plant with lilies bursting from his heels.

Himself, suddenly mysterious and marine,
bobs up a merman leaning on his hills.

Plashes and plays alone the deserted pool;
as those, is free, who think themselves unseen.
He rolls in his heap of fruit,
he slides his belly over
the melonrinds of water, curved and smooth and green.
Feels good: and trains, like little acrobats
his echoes dropping from the galleries;
circles himself over a rung of water;
swims fancy and gay; taking a notion, hides
under the satins of his great big bed, —
and then comes up to float until he thinks
the ceiling at his brow, and nowhere any sides.
His thighs are a shoal of fishes: scattered: he
turns with many gloves of greeting
towards the sunnier water and the tiles.

Upon the tiles he dangles from his toes
lazily the eight reins of his ponies.

An afternoon, far from the world
a street sound throws like a stone, with paper, through the glass.
Up, he is chipped enamel, grained with hair.

The gloss of his footsteps follows him to the showers,
the showers, and the male room, and the towel
which rubs the bird, the plant, the dolphin back again
personable plain.

Maxine Kumin

400-Meter Freestyle

The gun full swing the swimmer catapults and cracks
                                s
                                i
                                x
feet away onto that perfect glass he catches at
a
n
 d
throws behind him scoop after scoop cunningly moving
                                        t
                                        h
                                        e
water back to move him forward. Thrift is his wonderful
s
e
 c
ret; he has schooled out all extravagance. No muscle
                                r
                                 i
                                p
ples without compensation wrist cock to heel snap to
h
i
s
mobile mouth that siphons in the air that nurtures
                                  h
                                  i
                                  m
at half an inch above sea level so to speak.
 T
h
 e

astonishing whites of the soles of his feet rise
                              a
                                 n
                                 d
salute us on the turns. He flips, converts, and is gone
     a
l
     l
in one. We watch him for signs. His arms are steady at
                                        t
                                           h
                                           e
catch, his cadent feet tick in the stretch, they know
     t
h
     e
lesson well. Lungs know, too; he does not list for
                                   a
                                     i
                                     r
he drives along on little sips carefully expended
     b
u
     t
that plum red heart pumps hard cries hurt how soon
                                      i
                                        t
                                        s
near one more and makes its final surge
                         TIME: 4:25:9

Doris Lessing

Through the Tunnel

*G*oing to the shore on the first morning of the holiday, the young English boy stopped at a turning of the path and looked down at a wild and rocky bay, and then over to the crowded beach he knew so well from other years. His mother walked on in front of him, carrying a bright-striped bag in one hand. Her other arm, swinging loose, was very white in the sun. The boy watched that white, naked arm, and turned his eyes, which had a frown behind them, toward the bay and back again to his mother. When she felt he was not with her, she swung around. "Oh, there you are, Jerry!" she said. She looked impatient, then smiled. "Why, darling, would you rather not come with me? Would you rather—" She frowned, conscientiously worrying over what amusements he might secretly be longing for which she had been too busy or too careless to imagine. He was very familiar with that anxious, apologetic smile. Contrition sent him running after her. And yet, as he ran, he looked back over his shoulder at the wild bay; and all morning, as he played on the safe beach, he was thinking of it.

Next morning, when it was time for the routine of swimming and sunbathing, his mother said, "Are you tired of the usual beach, Jerry? Would you like to go somewhere else?"

"Oh, no!" he said quickly, smiling at her out of that unfailing impulse of contrition—a sort of chivalry. Yet, walking down the path with her, he blurted out, "I'd like to go and have a look at those rocks down there."

She gave the idea her attention. It was a wild-looking place, and there was no one there, but she said, "Of course, Jerry. When you've had enough, come to the big beach. Or just go straight back to the villa, if you like." She walked away, that bare arm, now slightly reddened from yesterday's sun, swinging. And he almost ran after her again, feeling it unbearable that she should go by herself, but he did not.

She was thinking, Of course he's old enough to be safe without me. Have I been keeping him too close? He mustn't feel he ought to be with me. I must be careful.

He was an only child, eleven years old. She was a widow. She was determined to be neither possessive nor lacking in devotion. She went worrying off to her beach.

As for Jerry, once he saw that his mother had gained her beach, he began the steep descent to the bay. From where he was, high up among red-brown rocks, it was a scoop of moving bluish green fringed with white. As he went lower, he saw that it spread among small promontories and inlets of rough, sharp rock, and the crisping, lapping surface showed stains of purple and darker blue. Finally, as he ran sliding and scraping down the last few yards, he saw an edge of white surf, and the shallow, luminous movement of water over white sand, and, beyond that, a solid, heavy blue.

He ran straight into the water and began swimming. He was a good swimmer. He went out fast over the gleaming sand, over a middle region where rocks lay like discolored monsters under the surface, and then he was in the real sea—a warm sea where irregular cold currents from the deep water shocked his limbs.

When he was so far out that he could look back not only on the little bay but past the promontory that was between it and the big beach, he floated on the buoyant surface and looked for his mother. There she was, a speck of yellow under an umbrella that looked like a slice of orange peel. He swam back to shore, relieved at being sure she was there, but all at once very lonely.

.

On the edge of a small cape that marked the side of the bay away from the promontory was a loose scatter of rocks. Above them, some boys were stripping off their clothes. They came running, naked, down to the rocks. The English boy swam toward them, and kept his distance at a stone's throw. They were of that coast, all of them burned smooth dark brown, and speaking a language he did not understand. To be with them, of them, was a craving that filled his whole body. He swam a little closer; they turned and watched him with narrowed, alert dark eyes. Then one smiled and waved. It was enough. In a minute, he had swum in and was on the rocks beside them, smiling with a desperate, nervous supplication. They shouted cheerful greetings at him, and then, as he preserved his nervous, uncomprehending smile, they understood that he was a foreigner strayed from his own beach, and they proceeded to forget him. But he was happy. He was with them.

They began diving again and again from a high point into a well of blue sea between rough, pointed rocks. After they had dived and come up, they swam around, hauled themselves up, and waited their turn to dive again. They were big boys—men to Jerry. He dived, and they watched him, and when he swam around to take his place, they made way for him. He felt he was accepted, and he dived again, carefully, proud of himself.

Soon the biggest of the boys poised himself, shot down into the water, and did not come up. The others stood about, watching. Jerry, after waiting for the sleek brown head to appear, let out a yell of warning; they looked at him idly and turned their eyes back toward the water. After a long time, the boy came up on the other side of a big dark rock, letting the air out of his lungs in a sputtering gasp and a shout of triumph. Immediately, the rest of them dived in. One moment, the morning seemed full of chattering boys; the next, the air and the surface of the water were empty. But through the heavy blue, dark shapes could be seen moving and groping.

Jerry dived, shot past the school of underwater swimmers, saw a black wall of rock looming at him, touched it, and bobbed up at once to the surface, where the wall was a low barrier he could see across. There was no one visible; under him, in the water, the dim shapes of the swimmers had disappeared. Then one, and then another of the boys came up on the far side of the barrier of rock, and he understood that they had swum through some gap or hole in it. He plunged down again. He could see nothing through the stinging salt water but the blank rock. When he came up, the boys were all on the diving rock, preparing to attempt the feat again. And now, in a panic of failure, he yelled up, in English, "Look at me! Look!," and he began splashing and kicking in the water like a foolish dog.

They looked down gravely, frowning. He knew the frown. At moments of failure, when he clowned to claim his mother's attention, it was with just this grave, embarrassed inspection that she rewarded him. Through his hot shame, feeling the pleading grin on his face like a scar that he could never remove, he looked up at the group of big brown boys on the rock and shouted, *"Bonjour! Merci! Au revoir! Monsieur, monsieur!,"* while he hooked his fingers round his ears and waggled them.

Water surged into his mouth; he choked, sank, came up. The rock, lately weighted with boys, seemed to rear up out of the water as their weight was removed. They were flying down past him, now, into the water; the air was full of falling bodies. Then the rock was empty in the hot sunlight. He counted one, two, three . . .

At fifty, he was terrified. They must all be drowning beneath him, in the watery caves of the rock! At a hundred, he stared around him at the empty hillside, wondering if he should yell for help. He counted faster, faster, to hurry them up, to bring them to the surface quickly, to drown them quickly—anything rather than the terror of counting on and on into the blue emptiness of the morning. And then, at a hundred and sixty, the water beyond the rock was full of boys blowing like brown whales. They swam back to the shore without a look at him.

He climbed back to the diving rock and sat down, feeling the hot roughness of it under his thighs. The boys were gathering up their bits of clothing and running off along the shore to another promontory. They were leaving to get away from him. He cried openly, fists in his eyes. There was no one to see him, and he cried himself out.

It seemed to him that a long time had passed, and he swam out to where he could see his mother. Yes, she was still there, a yellow spot under an orange umbrella. He swam back to the big rock, climbed up, and dived into the blue pool among the fanged and angry boulders. Down he went, until he touched the wall of rock again. But the salt was so painful in his eyes that he could not see.

He came to the surface, swam to shore and went back to the villa to wait for his mother. Soon she walked slowly up the path, swinging her striped bag, the flushed, naked arm dangling beside her. "I want some swimming goggles," he panted, defiant and beseeching.

She gave him a patient, inquisitive look as she said casually, "Well, of course, darling."

But now, now, now! He must have them this minute, and no other time. He nagged and pestered until she went with him to a shop. As soon as she had bought the goggles, he grabbed them from her hand as if she were going to claim them for herself, and was off, running down the steep path to the bay.

.

Jerry swam out to the big barrier rock, adjusted the goggles, and dived. The impact of the water broke the rubber-enclosed vacuum, and the goggles came loose. He understood that he must swim down to the base of the rock from the surface of the water. He fixed the goggles tight and firm, filled his lungs, and floated, face down, on the water. Now he could see. It was as if he had eyes of a different kind—fish-eyes that showed everything clear and delicate and wavering in the bright water.

Under him, six or seven feet down, was a floor of perfectly clean, shining white sand, rippled firm and hard by the tides. Two grayish shapes steered there, like long, rounded pieces of wood or slate. They were fish. He saw them nose toward each other, poise motionless, make a dart forward, swerve off, and come around again. It was like a water dance. A few inches above them, the water sparkled as if sequins were dropping through it. Fish again—myriads of minute fish, the length of his fingernail, were drifting through the water, and in a moment he could feel the innumerable tiny touches of them against his limbs. It was like swimming in flaked silver. The great rock the big boys had swum through rose sheer out of the white sand, black, tufted lightly with greenish weed. He could see no gap in it. He swam down to its base.

Again and again he rose, took a big chestful of air, and went down. Again and again he groped over the surface of the rock, feeling it, almost hugging it in the desperate need to find the entrance. And then, once, while he was clinging to the black wall, his knees came up and he shot his feet out forward and they met no obstacle. He had found the hole.

He gained the surface, clambered about the stones that littered the barrier rock until he found a big one, and, with this in his arms, let himself down over the side of the rock. He dropped, with the weight, straight to the sandy floor. Clinging tight to the anchor of stone, he lay on his side and looked in under the dark shelf at the place where his feet had gone. He could see the hole. It was an irregular, dark gap, but he could not see deep into it. He let go of his anchor, clung with his hands to the edges of the hole, and tried to push himself in.

He got his head in, found his shoulders jammed, moved them in sidewise, and was inside as far as his waist. He could see nothing ahead. Something soft and clammy touched his mouth, he saw a dark frond moving against the grayish rock, and panic filled him. He thought of octopuses, of clinging weed. He pushed himself out backward and caught a glimpse, as he retreated, of a harmless tentacle of seaweed drifting in the mouth of the tunnel. But it was enough. He reached the sunlight, swam to shore, and lay on the diving rock. He looked down into the blue well of water. He knew he must find his way through that cave, or hole, or tunnel, and out the other side.

First, he thought, he must learn to control his breathing. He let himself down into the water with another big stone in his arms, so that he could lie effortlessly on the bottom of the sea. He counted. One, two, three. He counted steadily. He could hear the movement of blood in his head. Fifty-one, fifty-two . . . His chest was hurting. He let go of the rock and went up into the air. He saw that the sun was low. He rushed to the villa and found his mother at her supper. She said only "Did you enjoy yourself?" and he said "Yes."

All night, the boy dreamed of the water-filled cave in the rock, and as soon as breakfast was over he went to the bay.

That night, his nose bled badly. For hours he had been underwater, learning to hold his breath, and now he felt weak and dizzy. His mother said, "I shouldn't overdo things, darling, if I were you."

That day and the next, Jerry exercised his lungs as if everything, the whole of his life, all that he would become, depended upon it. And again his nose bled at night, and his mother insisted on his coming with her the next day. It was a torment to him to waste a day of his careful self-training, but he stayed with her on that other beach, which now seemed a place for small children, a place where his mother might lie safe in the sun. It was not his beach.

He did not ask for permission, on the following day, to go to his beach. He went, before his mother could consider the complicated rights and wrongs of the matter. A day's rest, he discovered, had improved his count by ten. The big boys had made the passage while he counted a hundred and sixty. He had been counting fast, in his fright. Probably now, if he tried, he could get through that long tunnel, but he was not going to try yet. A curious, most unchildlike persistence, a controlled impatience, made him wait. In the meantime, he lay underwater on the white sand, littered now by stones he had brought down from the upper air, and studied the entrance to the tunnel. He knew every jut and corner of it, as far as it was possible to see. It was as if he already felt its sharpness about his shoulders.

He sat by the clock in the villa, when his mother was not near, and checked his time. He was incredulous and then proud to find he could hold his breath without strain for two minutes. The words "two minutes," authorized by the clock, brought the adventure that was so necessary to him close.

In another four days, his mother said casually one morning, they must go home. On the day before they left, he would do it. He would do it if it killed him, he said defiantly to himself. But two days before they were to leave—a day of triumph when he increased his count by fifteen—his nose bled so badly that he turned dizzy and had to lie limply over the big rock like a bit of seaweed, watching the thick red blood flow onto the rock and trickle slowly down to the sea. He was frightened. Supposing he turned dizzy in the tunnel? Supposing he died there, trapped? Supposing—His head went around, in the hot sun, and he almost gave up. He thought he would return to the house and lie down, and next summer, perhaps, when he had another year's growth in him—*then* he would go through the hole.

But even after he had made the decision, or thought he had, he found himself sitting up on the rock and looking down into the water, and he knew that now, this moment, when his nose had only just stopped bleeding, when his head was still sore and throbbing—this was the moment when he would try. If he did not do it now, he never would. He was trembling with fear that he would not go, and he was trembling with horror at that long, long tunnel under the rock, under the sea. Even in the open sunlight, the barrier rock seemed very wide and very heavy; tons of rock pressed down on where he would go. If he died there, he would lie until one day—perhaps not before next year—those big boys would swim into it and find it blocked.

He put on his goggles, fitted them tight, tested the vacuum. His hands were shaking. Then he chose the biggest stone he could carry and slipped over the edge of the rock until half of him was in the cool, enclosing water and half in the hot sun. He looked up once at the empty sky, filled his lungs once, twice, and then sank fast to the bottom with the stone. He let it go and began to count. He took the edges of the hole in his hands and drew himself into it, wriggling his shoulders in sidewise as he remembered he must, kicking himself along with his feet.

Soon he was clear inside. He was in a small rock-bound hole filled with yellowish-gray water. The water was pushing him up against the roof. The roof was sharp and pained his back. He pulled himself along with his hands—fast, fast—and used his legs as levers. His head knocked against something; a sharp pain dizzied him. Fifty, fifty-one, fifty-two . . . He was without light, and the water seemed to press upon him with the weight of rock. Seventy-one, seventy-two . . . There was no strain on his lungs. He felt like an inflated balloon, his lungs were so light and easy, but his head was pulsing.

He was being continually pressed against the sharp roof, which felt slimy as well as sharp. Again he thought of octopuses, and wondered if the tunnel might be filled with weed that could tangle him. He gave himself a panicky, convulsive kick forward, ducked his head, and swam. His feet and hands moved freely, as if in open water. The hole must have widened out. He thought he must be swimming fast, and he was frightened of banging his head if the tunnel narrowed.

A hundred, a hundred and one . . . The water paled. Victory filled him. His lungs were beginning to hurt. A few more strokes and he would be out. He was counting wildly; he said a hundred and fifteen, and then, a long time later, a hundred and fifteen again. The water was a clear jewel-green all around him. Then he saw, above his head, a crack running up through the rock. Sunlight was falling through it, showing the clean dark rock of the tunnel, a single mussel shell, and darkness ahead.

He was at the end of what he could do. He looked up at the crack as if it were filled with air and not water, as if he could put his mouth to it to draw in air. A hundred and fifteen, he heard himself say inside his head—but he had said that long ago. He must go on into the blackness ahead, or he would drown. His head was swelling, his lungs cracking. A hundred and fifteen, a hundred and fifteen pounded through his head, and he feebly clutched at rocks in the dark, pulling himself forward, leaving the brief space of sunlit water behind. He felt he was dying. He was no longer quite conscious. He struggled on in the darkness between lapses into unconsciousness. An immense, swelling pain filled his head, and then the darkness cracked with an explosion of green light. His hands, groping forward, met nothing, and his feet, kicking back, propelled him out into the open sea.

He drifted to the surface, his face turned up to the air. He was gasping like a fish. He felt he would sink now and drown; he could not swim the few feet back to the rock. Then he was clutching it and pulling himself up onto it. He lay face down, gasping. He could see nothing but a red-veined, clotted dark. His eyes must have burst, he thought: they were full of blood. He tore off his goggles and a gout of blood went into the sea. His nose was bleeding, and the blood had filled the goggles. He scooped up handfuls of water from the cool, salty sea, to splash on his face, and did not know whether it was blood or salt water he tasted. After a time, his heart quieted, his eyes cleared, and he sat up. He could see the local boys diving and playing half a mile away. He did not want them. He wanted nothing but to get back home and lie down.

．

In a short while, Jerry swam to shore and climbed slowly up the path to the villa. He flung himself on his bed and slept, waking at the sound of feet on the path outside. His mother was coming back. He rushed to the bathroom, thinking she must not see his face with bloodstains, or tearstains, on it. He came out of the bathroom and met her as she walked into the villa, smiling, her eyes lighting up.

"Have a nice morning?" she asked, laying her hand on his warm brown shoulder a moment.

"Oh, yes, thank you," he said.

"You look a bit pale." And then, sharp and anxious, "How did you bang your head?"

"Oh, just banged it," he told her.

She looked at him closely. He was strained. His eyes were glazed-looking. She was worried. And then she said to herself, "Oh, don't fuss! Nothing can happen. He can swim like a fish."

They sat down to lunch together.

"Mummy," he said, "I can stay under water for two minutes—three minutes, at least." It came bursting out of him.

"Can you, darling?" she said. "Well, I shouldn't overdo it. I don't think you ought to swim any more today."

She was ready for a battle of wills, but he gave in at once. It was no longer of the least importance to go to the bay.

Jenifer Levin

from Water Dancer

At 6:05 A.M. the sun had risen. Air temperature was seventy degrees and rising. Water temperature was fifty-three degrees Fahrenheit.

Dorey was greased and suited. She set her goggles for a good fit. Turning to Sarge, she suddenly pointed an accusing finger that, when she grinned, turned into a gun and her thumb the trigger. Bam, it went silently. Then she kissed its invisibly smoking barrel, aimed it again. Sarge dropped the plastic ointment container, hands up.

"Got me."

"Do I?"

"You've got me."

"The second time," she smiled calmly, "the second time things work." . . .

Sarge was careful not to touch her. "Breakfast feeling all right?"

Beneath the grease and goggles he could make out an apologetic expression. "I threw up."

He gave her a grin to stop any anxiety from showing. "Though you liked raw eggs." He checked his watch. Glancing up he noticed Ilana seated on the hood of the jeep, hair catching sunlight to sparkle silver. She'd strapped a bag of supplies over one shoulder and, when she saw them, smiled and waved.

He watched Dorey head towards the jeep. Her gray-greased back glistened. He couldn't hear what she said.

"It's all okay, Ilana. Everything."

Ilana just nodded.

Dorey's fingers fluttered. "I'll see you tomorrow."

Water sucked at land, at the rocks along it. It churned everything up and laid down a new surface, then crept back before the next surge. It made rocks smaller and smoother by microscopic measurements every minute of every day. It swept firm earth into soaked chaos. This was cold water that made you numb. This was water in which average human beings did not live for very long. It was rough water. Saltwater.

Dorey stepped into the water.

She took another step, slowly. Began to feel her toes again. Then she stopped just to look. It was that beautiful clear green-gray tint that made you remember warm things. Dorey stepped deeper, up to the knees. Shallow now, and receding. The tide would take her out past the breakers. This water made you think of coral reefs and sun and still it was so cold you almost couldn't believe it existed in the same world as the sun, on the same day, under the same sky. She stepped again. Ilana, she said. Then she wanted to jump out backward to warmth, seventy degrees and rising, and the land where Ilana was. The place she was going Ilana couldn't be in so with each step she lost her more and more.

Then something inside her clicked, the door to all that shut and was securely latched. Dorey breathed. Felt good. A little underweight, she'd have preferred to weigh another ten pounds and it was true she'd peaked for the fifth, not fourteenth, but this was a peak they'd worked on a year and she guessed she could ask it to stay through another day. She breathed deeply, went forward until water crept up her thighs. It was calm here near shore. The alphabet. She'd start out with the alphabet this time and run through that for the first two hours just to establish pace. She'd planned it all carefully. Alphabets for the first one hundred and twenty minutes and then she would do numbers up to three thousand. Then there was the tape Tycho'd sent up. She'd memorized it through those earphones. The tape was forty-seven minutes long. If she went through it song by song once, filled in the remaining thirteen minutes by calculating flip turns to every tenth stroke, that took her another hour and by then it was time for feeding. Then alphabets again. And later she'd be dreaming somewhere else anyway, no need for alphabets. Cold. She stepped waist-deep. She was ready. She had to walk out a way, feel it get shallower, then the suck of breakers on sandbars, then the pull tugging her towards them and she went along for the ride, sidestepped whitecaps, caught a swell and was no longer on her feet but kicking, lifting the right arm high, all of her in water. . . .

.

Of all the planets spinning that day through the planetary system, only one had on it the vast collections of liquid water called oceans. Descending to a certain depth, the human body would begin to compress. Eventually the external pressure of increasingly dense water would force the body to cave in. This was long, long before it hit bottom—the ocean floor—a longer distance than up Everest and longer than the 10 K. At bottom the floor was in a state of constant geological change. Shelves were crumbling, valleys deepening, plains and ridges shifting. The changes echoed up through pitch-dark cold, past levels where plants grew bleak white without sun, and sucking fish swallowed molecular configurations of plankton that glowed in perpetual night. The echoes bumped off ascending layers of shelf sloping into dry-topped continents. They spun up in zigzags, rumbled through decreasing blackness and density towards the first gray glimmerings of light. Bouncing, enmeshed in one another, the echoes of change sliced through to water surface. There they met air, sun, wind, and rain that fed water to the water. Meeting this, the echoes struggled along the surface as currents. Like the floor from which they'd ascended, they were in a state of constant change. So the current that ran parallel to the mainland shore of the San Antonio Strait could not be predicted long-range. It was subject to forces other than wind, or rain. All it did was writhe around itself, each of its multitudinous echoes struggling, snaking brutally along the ocean surface in a long, south-flowing stream.

At four minutes past ten in the morning on September 14, Dorey Thomas was swimming along the ocean surface at a rate of about two miles an hour—which, considering surface temperature and relative turbulence, was damned good time to be making. So she had swum nearly eight miles into the strait of San Antonio, heading east from Punta Provechosa. Another eight miles away, just about mid-channel, the current waited. It meandered. It would take her longer than just another four hours to reach there because, although she did not know it, the water temperature would soon drop by one degree and that would slow her down. Her change in pace would at first be unnoticeable, but by infinitesimal increments she would continue to slow until, at nightfall, her pace would appear drastically altered.

At five minutes past ten she stopped, backstroked methodically and was treading in water. It was time for her fourth feeding.

•

Well, Dorey told herself, see, you should have put on more weight. You're already cold.

She told herself she'd been colder before. Quebec. That year at Lac Louie. Or Ontario some days, sure. D breathe E F breathe G H breathe I J.

There was one sound in the world. It was flesh on water, each splash the same. It rang against the layers on her ears. S T breathe U V breathe. Each hand already numb. One of those hands would touch sand tomorrow and she wouldn't feel it at first it would be so numb but then a quick jolting sensation would quiver up the arm of the hand that was first to touch. K L breathe M N breathe O P.

Colder before and weighed less. How many fingers? Burns used to say as a joke. If you can count to ten you're okay in my book. Which direction you going? Know that and you're all right. Keep going that way that's all that counts, he said, I don't care if you freeze your butt off. Keep that pace and concentrate on where you're heading. Keep that pace and worry about yourself, forget the rest of those jokers in there. Let the water take care of them, you concentrate on where you're going and the water you're in.

U V breathe W X breathe Y Z breathe A B. That stroke of yours, Burns shook his head, distance stroke, distance, that's what you're doing there in this measly little pool. Maybe the 800 this year they'd said. Said that to Carol. The 800. Q R breathe S T breathe. No. She wouldn't slip back to then. Not to childhood or triumph. Not to despair either. This was it—now. Only now, the now was all that mattered. No backsliding. Not yet. Now was just the getting there, stroke, stroke, breath, numbers and the alphabets. No pools here no mothers here. No books here no lovers. Not now. Then was before. There was no past here, only water. Water always shifting, always in the present. Breathe. Don't slip back. Not now. Not yet. A B breathe C D. Burns. Remember. Old guy. Mean old guy. Said women were the tops at this stuff in his book, more endurance, less complaints.

Carol. It's cold.

No, she told herself, no you can't go back to then. Not now. Too early. Stay here. K L breathe M N breathe O P breathe Q R breathe and she caught herself, shivered smiles to herself, she could count to ten and go A to Z breathe A B breathe C D breathe and she knew, she was sure, of the direction. East. She was swimming the San Antonio Strait, she was going to cross it and touch land at the end. S T breathe U V. Pale lovely Pacific. It was frozen green-gray and not a fish in sight.

D breathe E F breathe G H breathe I J. Time for her feeding now. She stopped to tread and then the whistle shrilled once twice three times, up to five so she backstroked and was treading again. Cold but it was all right. You're okay, she said. You know where you're going, where you're crossing to.

It was five after one in the afternoon. She grabbed for the cup. . . .

You're hungry and you ought to eat. Here, eat this. She did. Couldn't see her hand reach for the liquid but knew it was out there somewhere, heading in the right direction and shuddering uncontrollably like her teeth. What went down hurt her lips and tongue. They were puffy with salt and raw.

Remember where you're going. East. Remember stay here for a while because you haven't hit that current yet. Important. Stay.

Carol.

Not yet.

It was cold.

When the moon goes high in the—

Stay.

She did. Lifted the right arm, stroked, stroked, breathed to her right. She swallowed saltwater. Then something forced its way up from her stomach, all the heat vomiting out of her. She had to stop. Rolled over on her back, shaking. Couldn't keep it down. I'm sick, she said. Sarge I'm sick. Oh come on, it said. It was a voice she'd heard before. Come on, don't be a cry baby. You're just fine. You know the story. You're strong so stop sniveling.

She rolled back over quickly, lifted the right arm, the left, breathed, again. Swimming. There now, see, that's better, that's the way it is meant to be. You're doing well, see how well.

Who are you? she asked.

Dorey Thomas.

Well it's good to meet you. Thank you. Thanks a lot. Dorey Thomas the swimmer?

The swimmer. Listen. Let me tell you a secret. All these terrible things, they aren't happening to you. The cold. The sick feeling. These things are not happening. Not to you. They are happening to me. So relax.

I'm sick.

Stop complaining. Come on. Faster. Don't you want to make good time? Well then. Let's get moving.

Here, all here. Hands arms neck head, bench press, lats.

What about your legs?

Leg press. Hamstrings quadriceps. Not much good at it.

That's okay. Keep kicking, you know you're strong.

Yes. Well I do. Thanks. When the moon goes high in the sky I also rise and my eyes are tired from so much looking at the sea. No. That's not the way it goes. Before dawn I also rise and my eyes. Breathe. Are tired. Breathe. Okay now. Sure I'm still crossing the San Antonio Strait, I am in water. They said try the 800, Carol, just try—

Not yet. Stay here. You have to.

—the 800, the Regionals. See how she does at—

Get back here.

—and they were surprised weren't they.

Dorey! Dorey Thomas! Stay a while.

She did. One two three four up to ten. Alphabet once more, one more time just to make sure. Hands arms shoulders neck all right. Breathe. Torso yes. Breathe. Thighs calves breathe. Toes count them. How many, Burns? Count to ten and where are you heading? East in the strait of San Antonio. To touch sand tomorrow. Uh-huh.

She was okay. She knew where she was and where she was going to and there was someone out in the fog now, telling her try this, this is broth. Broth and a vanilla cookie, try it champ. She did. It was three o'clock. . . .

.

Ilana . . . was feeling unsettled—not seasick, but a little fragmented and nowhere near hungry. . . .

"Hello." When she touched Sarge's shoulder he turned. "Tired?"

He shook his head. "Thinking."

"It's almost four."

"Right."

"I can feed her this time, Sarge, if you're tired. I'd like to."

Minutes later, she'd changed clothes. Ilana imagined herself sliding along aluminum, feeling for a grip. Would it be like climbing cliffs. She'd balance the feeding stick and hot cup in one hand. If there were cookies or any other solid food it would be wrapped in plastic. She focused on the image of herself doing this. Once she had a clear picture of how she would appear, she knew she could do it easily. It was a matter if visual cognizance—for her, all movement was.

She stepped down rope rungs.

That's when she felt the cold. Spraying against the bared top of her chest it was salty and numbing. Gasping, she'd forgotten what it was like. She took her time before crouching to sit, slide along those few feet out to the pontoon's end with careful balance while her legs hung, feelingless, in water. The waves had diminished during the last hour. None washed over her. Still, it was cold. . . .

Braced against the drum, she looked up. The face staring blindly in her direction, bobbing between waves, could have been anyone's. Could have been but was not. Somewhere, in the blank line of the nose, the opened mouth, Ilana searched out a lover. Thought maybe she'd found her. Then she was leaning over to reach, extending the cup-tipped feeding stick across water. She spoke clearly. Had to repeat everything until the words stopped making sense, but finally she was heard.

"Ilana?"

She was relieved. Yes, she said, yes it's me. What Dorey said next was unrecognizable. The sound came out all swollen. I don't understand, Ilana said, again please, tell me again. Dorey did. Finally Ilana thought she understood.

"You're okay?"

"Okay."

"Drink this, Dorey. Here. To your right. Your right. To the right. Drink this. All of it. To the right."

"I'm a little crazy now Ilana."

What, Ilana said, tell me again, I'm listening. Listening. I am. Tell me. Again. I'm sorry, one more time. Once more. Crazy? You are? Crazy but okay?

"Uh-huh."

"Good. That's good. It's the best way to be."

Ilana I'm a little crazy now, it happens like this a lot but I'm okay. Still here. There was something I wanted to tell you. Can't talk. Feel sick. Well a little. Still here. Something I'd like to tell you now while I'm still here in the water.

"Later."

Ilana understood. She began the slow slide back to ship. Around the midriff of the feeding stick, her fingers shook with cold.

Tycho calculated carefully, then shifted course to the north. It was a subtle change at first, east to northeast, but by the time the eastern sky'd begun to darken they were heading nearly due north. In the west the sun was dark orange and just starting its fade. Air temperature was sixty-eight degrees and falling. Water temperature was fifty-two point three degrees Fahrenheit and winds were with them this time, blowing from the southwest. Waves were erratic. Some five-footers. Still they were, like the winds, slamming along in the right direction.

Just before twilight was the time when ghosts rode echoes right up to the surface of the San Antonio Strait. They were the strait's lost spirits, and most had left their bodies behind in its water over a century ago. Along the perimeters of the current they hovered silently, huddled close together without touching in the deepening gray.

There's another, one said in Spanish. Pointed soundlessly. Dorey looked up. They were conferring about something, it seemed. Her. She didn't understand the Spanish, it was being spoken too quickly. Still she caught a couple of words.

Another what?

Otro nadador. Another swimmer.

But this one's a woman.

Nadadora. Estará lo mismo.

No. Perhaps it won't be the same.

Perhaps.

They were silent again. Looking up, she thought she'd caught a hint of her name being spoken but no. Only gray tranquility that clamped over her now like a snow-cold glove. What was there in the world but the sound of water, those relentless splashes ringing against both her ears until she almost did not hear them because everything had become them. Her arms stroking water. Her arms causing splashes. Arms rendering her ears deaf. Watching, the spirits stepped from their perch atop waves. One sat on her shoulders.

Knock knock.

Go away.

Knock knock.

Who's there, she sobbed.

Guess.

Go away.

No I won't. Guess.

I don't know.

Do you want me to tell you? Do you?

Please, she said, you don't understand. I have to concentrate now.

Knock knock.

Who's there?

Matt.

Who?

You know. Matt Olssen, me. Remember me? I beat you in Quebec.

Not by much.

Hah. Want to shake hands?

The hand crawled over her shoulder. It caressed the raw line of her neck. Fingers found her lips and pried them apart to poke into her mouth. The fingers were salt-tasting. They were bone. She screamed and kept swimming. Then the weight on her shoulders lifted, mouth emptied, she'd thrown up again and was swimming north, chattering teeth biting once in a while into her tongue. Her toes were gone.

She concentrated.

Now came a noticeable tug from the east, water just slightly more turbulent and its direction confused. Closer. Getting closer. The skin along her spine burned. Its burning was a bright line of flame in ice, a tingle of expectation. That current. She swallowed more water, threw up the rest of last hour's feeding.

Fog on her goggles darkened with evening. North. She concentrated. Counted each splash up to ten and then started over. In front of her yawned an enormous mouth. Its lips were full, slime-smeared, its insides black and cavernous and it had no teeth. Whoosh, it went. Sucking. It sucked her to the east now, lips glistening. She fought to keep heading north and it laughed. So little, it mocked. You're so little.

Who are you?

Water.

Oh, she said. She was afraid.

Someone else was talking, that swimmer. Better concentrate. Just concentrate now, that's right. Keep the pace.

But the water.

Keep that pace. Cut out all this whining, huh? Remember this isn't happening to you, it is happening to me. Remember.

Dorey Thomas. She wanted to cry with relief.

Right. Let's get going. We can do it.

Too small.

No you're not.

She paused, confused. Small. But you're bigger than me, are you a giant.

No, said Dorey, I'm something better now, don't you remember?

I'm sorry, she cried, I forgot.

Think a minute. Let's swim now. Uh-huh. Just think.

Something better? No. Well I don't know. Tell me.

You haven't really forgotten. Do you want me to tell you anyway?

What? she stroked. Stroked. Breathed. What are you?

Dorey smiled. I—she glowed proudly—am a water dancer.

She breathed. Then wanted to throw open her arms with a burst of recognition. Ah, she said. A water dancer. Well so am I.

Well then *concentrate*.

She did.

It was five o'clock. . . .

.

Sometimes what she imagined was a beam of light attached to the topmost cap emanating from her forehead. It was similar to the kind worn by coal-miners, spotlighting the dismal route ahead.

Sometimes she worried about sharks, then remembered that none had ever been spotted here. This was the San Antonio Strait. She guessed they preferred less difficult water.

Sometimes what happened was the cold went completely through her, pierced her chest, and rode out somewhere in the vicinity of her spine. It came in waves like gusts of wind. Each wave of ice was electric shock.

She'd slowed again to less than a mile an hour. South-flowing, the current pushed them. Tycho tilted them slightly northeast again, readjusting until she'd snapped back on course. If it was going to take this long, he decided, they ought to be consistently on the right trail.

"Here, dear. Here's some food."

The voice's faint sound filled her with longing, and a sense of expectation for which she could not account.

"Who's there?"

"Ilana. This is Ilana."

She stopped. Tried to think. Then she had it and gave a grin that split her lips but they were too numb to feel it. "Ah. Are you my lover?"

"Yes."

"Still?"

"Yes," Ilana lied.

Dorey swallowed some liquid and spat out the rest. Blindly, she back-stroked a little. Water swirled into her mouth, she felt it creep down her throat and mix unsettled with what she'd just consumed. Most of it water anyway. *Lover.* Why not. Bugs had them. Sharks had them. Animals had them men had them and so would she. A lover. For a second she felt part of what she floated in, inside of it as it was inside her, integral aspect of the water-covered world. For a second, there was peace. She felt her eyelids sink down and she turned suddenly, listened carefully, heard the whistles signaling which direction. Bear left, the signals said. Arm raised, muscles felt torn. Arm raised. Breathe. She went on ahead. . . .

.

"Ilana!"

At one in the morning she was treading, trying bleakly to yell.

"Ilana!"

Ilana stepped down the rope. On metal she balanced. Something rang dully in her head and at first she thought it was the incessant rhythm of exhaustion but after a while she knew that, no, it was something else altogether, some realization she was wavering at the edge of. When water washed over her thighs she shuddered. Fifty-three degrees and steady was cold enough. Personally she liked it in the eighties.

Out along the pontoon she'd left a boat behind. Whatever she was heading for was different, she knew, than anything she had done in the past. And perhaps it was weariness that brought these tears to her eyes now, here, in the middle of an ocean at an hour past midnight but she didn't think so.

"I'm here."

"Ilana."

"Yes."

Features blanched, swollen, unfamiliar, the swimmer faced her by instinct and reached, hand dropped weakly, splashed the water.

"Ilana what time is it."

Ilana thought before answering. When she spoke it was with care. "Oh, don't worry about the time. You're doing fine."

"One o'clock? It's only one o'clock?"

"No. I don't know."

"Then," the voice slurred, "how do you know it's not."

Ilana took deep breaths. "Because," she said, "you are almost there."

"What?"

"You're almost there. Get going now, don't you feel good about that?"

"*Liar.*"

In the head-splitting light, Ilana rubbed her cheek with those long fingers of hers. The fingers came away wet, whether with sea or tears she didn't know and didn't care.

"Liar. You're lying to me."

"Dorey. I've never lied to you. Not ever, remember?"

Dorey paused silently, treading. Well it was true. Then it could not be one o'clock and still the middle of the strait if she were almost there, could it. Maybe the stars had already faded. And it was nearly dawn. Well maybe. Ilana was there. She reached. No, they hadn't lied to each other. She remembered. No betrayal.

Almost there, Ilana coaxed. Almost there so don't you worry about the time now, not now, you just concentrate on swimming. Just swim now, all right? You're fine, you're doing very well, believe me.

Dorey believed her. It was Ilana saying these things, after all, Ilana who didn't lie. She ate part of a cookie they'd crumbled in liquid but threw it up. She guessed if she were almost there she had just better swim. Ilana was right. Sure.

So somewhere after one o'clock in the morning Dorey Thomas, more than halfway across the strait of San Antonio, gave up on time. She let it leave her. Realized, once she felt it slough off, how much energy she'd been expending keeping track of alphabets and Spanish words of songs, keeping track of feedings and what they meant in relation to distance. Now that she was no longer spending precious calories on thoughts of time, she could concentrate on one thing alone: stroking through water, maintaining the specific rhythm of a pace she'd worked towards all her life. There was no further purpose in this—no goal of time towards which the strokes could be counted because she'd lost track of time and, losing time, lost sight of all specificity. The space between where she was each instant and the shoreline she struggled to approach was now immeasurable. The only goal left her—if it could indeed be called a goal—was the rhythmic continuation of strokes through water.

She concentrated.

Each stroke an end in itself. There was no other purpose in the world than this, she knew, to stroke through water and that way keep going. Every stroke the same so every stroke was an infinity of strokes, in the dead of night each infinity measured by the sound of a splash. . . .

.

Carol, remember that day. I was little. Walking into the kitchen. He put an arm around your neck and kissed. He winked at me. It was raining. I had a jelly sandwich.

Remember at the beach. I climbed on your shoulders. That way I was over the waves. You bounced. You played horse.

Dorey reached for sun. Just as it was about to envelop her it faded. Something sat on her shoulders. It seemed a weight from outside, like a leaden shoe. She wondered who was stepping against her back. Wasn't fair.

Carol?

Think we're there yet?

The weight got heavier. Much more of that and her shoulders would cave in, she knew. No more giant. Back when she was a giant maybe she could have carried it. Maybe. No. Because she'd been a giant, and even then all it took was one wave. One wave and poof. Giant broke in two. Humpty Dumpty.

Well I tried, Carol. For you. To be that strong. See. You needed it. But it wasn't possible. I was barely strong enough for one. See when you stop being a giant it's so lonely. Lonely. Still lonely. All right. But I can touch now. Getting there. Stronger now. I guess. I know. And no giant. No. Just going for it. Going for broke. Free, you said, it is possible to be free. That's the part I liked. Believed. Still do.

That frozen feeling in the center of her chest seemed to waver then, massive glacier teetering on the edge of some vast cavern before it tipped, crumbled, dissolved and she reached, reached, breathed easier now from the center of her chest where the sun glowed hot, bright, unsmothered by ice. Still the weight crouched, gripped with monkey hands on her shoulders. She breathed out sun and heard the hiss of melting ice down in the cavern there. It was a sound almost of lament, far-off wails heard in some jungle, a dark female cry. Dorey listened carefully. Her right, she knew, to stop for just this second and understand something. The glacier had been water after all. Frozen water. Not permanent. Not indestructible. At least she was less destructible than ice. Hot blood inside stronger than the cold. For now. Strong. She could breathe easier. And it was her right to listen, to hear the dark sounds of dying. Or, pounding against it, her own pulse-beat. Dancing. And know she was alive.

The lie. It was a lie Carol. That I was doing it for you. Sure. It was for that glow. What's left under everything. Get rid of everything else and you feel it. The glow. Not giving up. Making it through. That's all. Alive. Cold but feel that, that glow. Alive.

The weight pressed down. Everything hurt.

How much longer?

Remember? What you told me once. What I believed?

By the beach. I was twelve. You told me that day. You can be free darling, it is possible if only you're willing to pay the price and the price is very high. Simply a choice. You must need it more than anything. You must want it more than love.

It was too cold to feel anymore. She'd dropped down below the earth into water and was starving, filthy, no chance to clean right now and no strength left to stop. Just keep going. She'd dropped down below where people didn't go unless they had to, where nothing changed but the wind and time didn't exist. But something sat right there on her shoulders, crying, insistent. Sounded like an infant. Dorey pulled out the scissors. Sorry, she said, I am sorry. She'd have cried but nothing left. Sorry. I would carry you now Carol if I had the strength. Except I'm not a giant anymore. Just enough left for me. Forgive me. Forgive me. I have to make it. Carol it's what you wanted.

She cut.

The scissors dropped, sank out of sight. From below rose blade-shaped traces of blood, and between Dorey's shoulders the cord flapped, spliced, oozing, with nothing at its other end. She picked up the pace slightly. With each stroke the cord shriveled and dried until it was nothing but dessicated, unneeded skin, and the skin washed away from her by saltwater.

.

"How much longer?"

"Not much. You're almost there."

Perched on the pontoon, she said it mechanically. It was four o'clock and stars had died, moon vanished in an ash-colored sky.

"But how much? How long?"

"Keep going," she said, "you're almost there."

In clammy predawn, Ilana felt her shoulders droop. The lines on her face she could just about feel through her skin. How deeply they'd etched themselves. Winds had calmed to nothing so what shrouded the water now was a vast stillness. Even their voices seemed muted by it, echoes nonexistent. Parallel to them the *Lazarilla* had slowed. If you squinted from deck you could make out figures standing still, watching. They hung there over the rails. They froze like shadows in the dark.

"Almost," Ilana whispered. "Almost there."

It was true. When the sun rose they'd see the mainland shore and see it was close. Now, though, it was hard to believe things were on the verge of dawn. They seemed, instead, to be on the edge of some black well, a sewer of ink into which the world would slide.

"Go away," she sobbed. Her tongue filled her mouth. "I don't believe you anymore."

Ilana leaned far over. She shoved the half-finished cup back towards the face. "Please believe me. Keep going. You're almost there."

Dorey rolled over. Hands reached for goggles. Then she slid into a backstroke before rolling over again, faced the voice that hounded her right back into the cold, goggles intact, hands clenched below the surface.

"Ilana, what are you doing to me."

She started to swim again. . . .

.

Sarge reached up over the side. Ilana gripped his hand. He realized they were shaking hands firmly, solemnly, like friends sealing a contract. When her hand had left his, Sarge thought of other things. First he focused on water. He focused on the water and then on the oven inside him. It was less an oven than a volcano of sorts, hot incubating bed of lava which he'd feed himself at will. Gripping rope, his hands shook. He wondered why and then knew it was because he was afraid. He was afraid of water. He was afraid of jumping into it. Was this water special water. Different from any other water. Was it separate from all other water on earth because it had his son's heart thumping faintly through it and a piece of him along with it.

Sarge focused on her. His son was dead and he'd never have him again. Dorey Thomas was alive and swimming across the San Antonio Strait and he was her trainer. She was three miles from touching the mainland sand. That was all. She was a swimmer swimming. Water changed with the rain. He couldn't know that this very same water had taken his son. That had been years ago. Maybe it was not the same water. Even though all water was the same still it was not the same, and so he could be afraid of water and realize he'd been all his life without knowing it, realize that the San Antonio Strait in his head would always be there, death-giving, terrifying, and forever apart from the reality of the water before him now. There was no San Antonio Strait in the absolute. It changed by the day, by the hour. And the swimmer in there was not his son nor daughter and would never be his lover. Still she was a swimmer—and in that, the most essential sense of that, she was his. He'd nurtured the part of her that would survive.

Sarge let go. He dropped cleanly into water. Poured lava out of him, out and out, ice penetrated but not to the core. There was at his core something red, bubbling and alive, that the ice skirted around and couldn't cut through. Gasping, he waited. Then the boundaries were established. Cold crawled around but past a certain layer wouldn't enter. Through the density his arms cut slowly. He swam out to where she waited. He stopped to tread a few feet away.

"Hello."

The skin of her face was raw and swollen. She was blind, deaf too, effectively muted for all he could understand of what she said. Something inside him ached just to touch her. That was forbidden here. She was the swimmer and must cross unaided, touching was a violation. Sarge stayed where he was. Facing her, more than an arm's length away, this was the closest they would ever be. She was effectively isolated by cold and pain and her own desire, and the world she occupied now could not be touched, it was surrounded by water.

He saw her head wobble slightly, begin to fall forward. Sarge splashed at her. "Stay awake!"

She did. She started a listless breaststroke. He slid alongside between her and the pontoons, passed Tycho without looking his way. Sarge was all concentration now. He focused on her and willed her awake for the rest of this crossing however long it took.

Dorey stopped, legs began a leaden sink. He flailed arms again. He beat up quite a fuss.

"Stay awake!"

The swollen head shook stiffly. She rolled onto her back.

"Awake!" he ordered. "Let's go!" He splashed some more at her, caused her to swallow it and sputter and then he heard a sob. She'd turned face to the water and lifted the right arm, breath, stroke, and another. Slowly he moved alongside her. Ice crept against his bones, dulled sensation. Sarge stabbed it back with the life inside him. He jerked it out and poured it out on ice and the ice screamed while it melted and then some more ice formed, hovered at the oven gates, waiting. Stay awake! he told her. Around them was ice water, sleep-inducing, that would coat you like snow and deep-freeze the pump that was your heart. What they had against it was the liquid inside them, blood bouncing strongly back to help the heart generate heat, bouncing from all muscles and capillaries, running through veins keeping the engine alive. Outside was cold water, life inside them hot water, both bodies of water held apart by the thinnest partition of flesh and bone. Wear down the partition enough, Sarge knew, and the inside water dissolved into the outside surrounding it. He swam. Stay awake, he warned her. Stay awake lady, stay awake baby, stay awake now champ come on kid stay awake come on. It would be so easy sometimes to allow the dissolution of boundaries to take place. And he wasn't going to let that happen. Not now. Not to his swimmer.

After a while, if you stood on deck you'd see both bodies swimming at the same pace. Sometimes they'd stop, one yell and splash at the other and then they'd continue.

In the east, you could see the mainland shore. You could see hills rising black into sky. The sky was yellowing there, then light gray, then blue-gray as it crept west. Soon the first flame-orange mound of sun would appear between hills.

One by one, lights on both ships in the San Antonio Strait went off. On the *Lazarilla* shadow bodies belonging to voices heard by radio all night straightened, stood tall and male, and silently waved. Off the escort's starboard side the swimmers moved, capped heads turning gently towards one another in unison. Arms lifted, shoulders rolled. Once in a while red skin flashed against the dawn-lit water. . . .

"You're almost there."

She inched her head forward. The cup waited, she could smell it. Lips tried to find the rim and they swelled around it.

"Almost there," said Ilana.

Sweet liquid burned down her throat, hurt her tongue, and she tried to scream. Another sip. Another. Had to. Then it hurt too much and brought back the nausea. She shook her head. No. No more. Too sick. Almost there, that's what Ilana said and Ilana wouldn't have lied. Well she'd better not waste time then. Couldn't afford to throw up. Precious energy spent.

"Going," she said. Ilana understood. She looked to Sarge for reassurance and he nodded. Let her go. Believe it or not she's all right.

Dorey stroked sideways in the water, then she'd stopped and was treading again, facing the pontoon. Ilana leaned forward. The repetition was patient, methodical. Ilana listened harder. She could feel her ears straining as if both were hands reaching for something just beyond reasonable grasp. In the patience, the repetitious care with which the words were repeated for her, she got a glimpse of something familiar and of something enduring and realized that, apparent or not, this enduring center was alive in the body speaking before her. It was what had pushed so far, so hard, for more than a day now, had done so without sleep or the relief of being warmed by touch. Dorey, she said. Ilana smiled, relieved, finally recognizing her. She listened. Then she had it.

"Ilana. Do you know me now?"

"Yes," said Ilana, "I am proud."

"See you," Dorey blurted.

When she began to swim again, Ilana let her head sink tiredly to her hand. She was older physically and irrevocably. Hair all gray. Too old to bear children. Too much of that water inside had dried up by now. Still, what she'd recognized in Dorey—or what she'd finally recognized as Dorey—was there in her, too, she knew. What was it but a capacity for some incessant kind of behavior. An incessance that made you put one foot before the other when you no longer wanted to, or made you send one arm stroking when nothing was left to propel it. As if the instinct to survive lived deeper in them than desire itself, deeper than consciousness. That was what she'd recognized, this instinct as base as blood, and like blood it ran through both of them.

Sarge climbed out of the water. He hung for a minute on the ladder's bottom rung, pulled off goggles and blinked. Watched her swim. Unbelievably slow, each stroke still had to it a certain elegance. Or maybe it was simply that the strokes continued after so long which made him proud, and held for him a certain fascination. Sarge watched, then shut his eyes. Shivering fingers tightened on rope while he hung there in the morning. That was to him beauty, and strength in the ideal. He knew it. That reaching for something. It was his way of moving through the world. For an instant he experienced a strange, removed sense of peace.

Sarge pulled himself up and over, sat on deck in the first streaks of sunlight. No grease remained on his body and his skin shone raw, quivering with cold. . . .

·

In the last mile, the water calmed to a lovely stillness. It reflected a cloudless sky, tinted the sky's reflected image slightly green. Flame-gold sun crawled above the horizon. It was a perfect day.

The closer they got to shore, the more the air changed. It was heavier, less pure. It was sweeter. Gulls swooped against the sky, struck water for fish. They'd rise, small catch flapping in beaks, their wings fluffed to shake off water. Sometimes they'd circle. One would break away, torpedo the water with a scream of triumph.

Dorey heard one thing now, one series of sounds. It was the breathe, stroke, stroke that coincided with the boom, thump, thump of her heart. That heart constituted a powerful sort of engine. Fifty beats, normally, was what it took to propel her through a minute. Sometimes less. And now it seemed to her to have slowed considerably, immeasurable time stretching between each pulsation, each pause delineated by the suck of a breath. There was nothing else in the world but this. Each stroke took her farther away from what she'd been before. One stroke a lover. One stroke a giant. The strokes disappeared with the water they propelled through. She left them all behind. So what she headed towards was unknown, the land she touched would be a strange one. She'd arrive bereft of all the elements by which she could quantify the shape of a day, or qualify her place within it. Arrive stripped, therefore different. . . .

At 7:38 A.M. Dorey picked up pace a little. Water on the outside of her goggles had gotten lighter. She guessed sand. Then something inside her cracked open, bled out. Silently, breath spilling back into saltwater, she felt sounds coming from her totally muted by water. She was crying. She didn't know why. Just for the pain, maybe, that had turned to ice long ago, or for all those things that were now lost. Every stroke stripping more and more of it away. She was changing. That meant leaving skin behind. Her head wanted to bust open. Well she'd sleep soon, once she got there, sleep and it would be okay then.

Okay and maybe she'd never do this again, not ever, not unless she had to. Right. Only if she had to. She promised herself. Muffled, Dorey was sobbing. It hurt. She needed to drink water. To bathe. She was hungry.

The water grew even lighter, goggles clouds in front of her that brightened the closer they got to the sun. She wasn't hungry anymore. Not dirty. Just trembling, she was just trembling all over with a happiness that seemed absolute, it was hot like fever, kept her moving in the foreign light of a strange kind of ecstasy. The 800, something whispered. Come on. You can do an 800.

She started to.

Come on. You are almost there, you know. Dorey. Keep going. Come on lady. Come on baby come on kid come on champ keep that pace come on. Too much for you? No. No, well, I'm glad to hear that. Glad, understand. Come on. You can do an 800.

She did.

What flew by her now were visions of sand. Her fingers clutched at sand and each time it was a mirage. She cried and kept going. Then her left hand hit a mirage and stuck. Fingers moved against the mirage. They burrowed in deep. Her fingers clawed at the grainy texture and squirmed with the unfamiliarity of it, this sense of touch. Other hand groped sightlessly forward. She reached and the right set of fingers touched too. She was on hands and knees in sand, head above water, and what washed over her back was sunlight.

"Did it," she said. The words squeezed out around her tongue.

There was noise. Voices. Splashing. She looked up, pinpointed one voice among many. "You've made it and it's a few feet to the beach. Would you like a hand?"

Uh-uh. She shook her head. Started to crawl. The water splashed with her. It swept up towards shore. She inched along and didn't stop until her hands touched sand that was dry and then she kept going, a little more she told herself, just a little more, get those legs out of the water too. Her feet. Well she thought she'd lost them long ago. But now they were touching sand too, and the sand was dry. She'd kept goggles on so was effectively blind, but knew it by that touch. It was the sense of touch that distinguished her from fish, that set her apart from the water she'd been in. Had to be separate from something in order to touch it.

"May I?" Hands hovered at her goggle straps. She nodded.

Ilana removed them carefully. The eyes were almost shut. Light shot into them, blinding. Dorey reached to cover her eyes.

"Can you walk?"

She didn't know. She reached for Ilana's hand anyway and then she was standing. She looked awful. She was alternately bleached by salt and rubbed raw by it, swollen with water and nothing but skin and bones. The worn suits hung from her. She looked like some monster baby, crazed eyes half shut. Her tongue swelled out between her lips. She was shaking all over.

Record books would state that Dorey Thomas emerged on the mainland shore just before 8:15 A.M. The crossing had taken 26 hours, 9 minutes, 33 seconds.

A couple of journalists were there taking pictures. There'd be a big story in the local paper. There'd be a one-line mention in the *Times,* and a blurb in *Sports-Year.*

Her feet left a couple of uncertain imprints in sand. Then she stopped, everything spinning. She let go of Ilana's hand. Took two steps on her own, then was falling forward. The bodies around her seemed far away, and out of them all she recognized the one she was falling towards.

"Sarge."

"You're one tired baby."

"Am I?" she said, but he didn't understand.

She was overexposed, close to shock, sputtering breath. She looked just about dead. She was dripping water, and alive. Sarge caught her when she crumpled. Sick and proud, her eyes blinked up at his. He held her tight as if it would keep her with him forever, then let go of that impossibility and his touch became gentle. Did it, she said. He lifted her in his arms.

Jack London

The Kanaka Surf

*T*he tourist women, under the hau-tree arbor that lines the Moana Hotel beach, gasped when Lee Barton and his wife Ida emerged from the bathhouse. And as the pair walked past them and down to the sand, they continued to gasp. Not that there was anything about Lee Barton provocative of gasps. The tourist women were not of the sort to gasp at sight of a mere man's swimming-suited body, no matter with what swelling splendor of line and muscle such body was invested. Nevertheless, trainers and conditioners of men would have drawn deep breaths of satisfaction at contemplation of the physical spectacle of him. But they would not have gasped in the way the women did, whose gasps were indicative of moral shock.

Ida Barton was the cause of their perturbation and disapproval. They disapproved, seriously so, at the first instant's glimpse of her. They thought—such ardent self-deceivers were they—that they were shocked by her swimming suit. But Freud has pointed out how persons, where sex is involved, are prone sincerely to substitute one thing for another thing, and to agonize over the substituted thing as strenuously as it if were the real thing.

Ida Barton's swimming suit was a very nice one, as women's suits go. Of thinnest of firm-woven black wool, with white trimmings and a white belt line, it was high-throated, short-sleeved, and brief-skirted. Brief as was the skirt, the leg tights were no less brief. Yet on the beach in front of the adjacent Outrigger Club, and entering and leaving the water, a score of women, not provoking gasping notice, were more daringly garbed. Their men's suits, as brief of leg tights and skirts, fitted them as snugly, but were sleeveless after the way of men's suits, the armholes deeply low cut and in cut, and, by the exposed armpits, advertiseful that the wearers were accustomed to 1916 décolleté.

So it was not Ida Barton's suit, although the women deceived themselves into thinking it was. It was, first of all, say, her legs; or, first of all, say, the totality of her, the sweet and brilliant jewel of her femininity bursting upon them. Dowager, matron, and maid, conserving their soft-fat muscles or protecting their hothouse complexions in the shade of the hau-tree arbor, felt the immediate challenge of her. She was menace as well, an affront of superiority in their own chosen and variously successful game of life.

But they did not say it. They did not permit themselves to think it. They thought it was the suit, and said so to one another, ignoring the twenty women more daringly clad but less perilously beautiful. Could one have winnowed out of the souls of these disapproving ones what lay at bottom of their condemnation of her suit, it would have been found to be the sex-jealous thought: *that no woman, so beautiful as this one, should be permitted to show her beauty.* It was not fair to them. What chance had they in the conquering of males with so dangerous a rival in the foreground?

They were justified. As Stanley Patterson said to his wife, where the two of them lolled wet in the sand by the tiny fresh-water stream that the Bartons waded in order to gain the Outrigger Club beach:

"Lord god of models and marvels, behold them! My dear, did you ever see two such legs on one small woman? Look at the roundness and taperingness. They're boy's legs. I've seen featherweights go into the ring with legs like those. And they're all woman's legs, too. Never mistake them in the world. The arc of the front line of that upper leg! And the balanced adequate fullness at the back! And the way the opposing curves slender into the knee that *is* a knee! Makes my fingers itch. Wish I had some clay right now."

"It's a true human knee," his wife concurred, no less breathlessly; for, like her husband, she was a sculptor. "Look at the joint of it working under the skin. It's got form, and blessedly is not covered by a bag of fat." She paused to sigh, thinking of her own knees. "It's correct and beautiful and dainty. Charm! If ever I beheld the charm of flesh it is now. I wonder who she is."

Stanley Patterson, gazing ardently, took up his half of the chorus.

"Notice that the round muscle pads on the inner sides which make most women appear knock-kneed are missing? They're boy's legs, firm and sure—"

"And sweet woman's legs, soft and round," his wife hastened to balance. "And look, Stanley! See how she walks on the balls of her feet. It makes her seem light as swan's-down. Each step seems just a little above the earth, and each other step seems just a little higher above until you get the impression she is flying, or just about to rise and begin flying . . . "

So Stanley and Mrs. Patterson. But they were artists, with eyes therefore unlike the next batteries of human eyes Ida Barton was compelled to run, and that laired on the Outrigger lanais (verandas) and in the hau-tree shade of the closely adjoining Seaside. The majority of the Outrigger audience was composed, not of tourist guests, but of club members and old-timers in Hawaii. And even the old-time women gasped.

"It's positively indecent," said Mrs. Hanley Black to her husband, herself a too-stout-in-the-middle matron of forty-five, who had been born in the Hawaiian Islands and who had never heard of Ostend.

Hanley Black surveyed his wife's criminal shapelessness and voluminousness of antediluvian, New England swimming dress with a withering, contemplative eye. They had been married a sufficient number of years for him frankly to utter his judgment:

"That strange woman's suit makes your own look indecent. You appear as a creature shameful, under a grotesqueness of apparel striving to hide some secret awfulness."

"She carries her body like a Spanish dancer," Mrs. Patterson said to her husband, for the pair of them had waded the little stream in pursuit of the vision.

"By George, she does," Stanley Patterson concurred. "Reminds me of Estrellita. Torso just well enough forward, slender waist, not too lean in the stomach, and with muscles like some lad boxer's armoring that stomach to fearlessness. She has to have them to carry herself that way and to balance the back muscles. See that muscled curve of the back! It's Estrellita's."

"How tall would you say?" his wife queried.

"There she deceives," was the appraised answer. "She might be five feet one, or five feet three or four. It's that way she has of walking that you described as almost about to fly."

"Yes, that's it," Mrs. Patterson concurred. "It's her energy, her seemingness of being on tiptoe with rising vitality."

Stanley Patterson considered for a space.

"That's it," he enounced. "She *is* a little thing. I'll give her five two in her stockings. And I'll weigh her a mere one hundred and ten, or eight, or fifteen at the outside."

"She won't weigh a hundred and ten," his wife declared with conviction.

"And with her clothes on, plus her carriage (which is builded of her vitality and will), I'll wager she'd never impress anyone with her smallness."

"I know her type," his wife nodded. "You meet her out and you have the sense that, while not exactly a fine, large woman, she's a whole lot larger than the average. And now, age?"

"I'll give you best, there," he parried.

"She might be twenty-five, she might be thirty-eight . . ."

But Stanley Patterson had impolitely forgotten to listen.

"It's not her legs alone," he cried on enthusiastically. "It's the all of her. Look at the delicacy of that forearm. And the swell of line to the shoulder. And that biceps! It's alive. Dollars to drowned kittens she can flex a respectable knot of it. . . ."

No woman, much less an Ida Barton, could have been unconscious of the effect she was producing along Waikiki Beach. Instead of making her happy in the small vanity way, it irritated her.

"The cats," she laughed to her husband. "And to think I was born here an almost even third of a century ago! But they weren't nasty then. Maybe because there weren't any tourists. Why, Lee, I learned to swim right here on this beach in front of the Outrigger. We used to come out with daddy for vacations and for week-ends and sort of camp out in a grass house that stood right where the Outrigger ladies serve tea now. And centipedes fell out of the thatch on us while we slept, and we all ate poi and opihis and raw *aku*, and nobody wore much of anything for the swimming, and squidding, and there was no real road to town. I remember times of big rain when it was so flooded we had to go in by canoe, out through the reef and in by Honolulu Harbor."

"Remember," Lee Barton added, "it was just about that time that the youngster that became me arrived here for a few weeks' stay on our way around. I must have seen you on the beach at that very time—one of the kiddies that swam like fishes. Why, merciful me, the women here were all riding cross saddle, and that was long before the rest of the social female world outgrew its immodesty and came around to sitting simultaneously on both sides of a horse. I learned to swim on the beach here at that time myself. You and I may even have tried body surfing on the same waves, or I may have splashed a handful of water into your mouth and been rewarded by your sticking out your tongue at me—"

Interrupted by an audible gasp of shock from a spinster-appearing female sunning herself hard by and angularly in the sand in a swimming suit monstrously unbeautiful, Lee Barton was aware of an involuntary and almost perceptible stiffening on the part of his wife.

"I smile with pleasure," he told her. "It serves only to make your valiant little shoulders the more valiant. It may make you self-conscious, but it likewise makes you absurdly self-confident."

For, be it known in advance, Lee Barton was a superman and Ida Barton a superwoman—or at least they were personalities so designated by the cub book reviewers, flat-floor men and women, and scholastically emasculated critics, who, from across the dreary levels of their living, can descry no glorious humans overtopping their horizons. These dreary folk, echoes of the dead past and importunate and self-elected pallbearers for the present and future, proxy livers of life and vicarious sensualists that they are in a eunuch sort of way, insist, since their own selves, environments, and narrow agitations of the quick are mediocre and commonplace, that no man or woman can rise above the mediocre and commonplace.

Lacking gloriousness in themselves, they deny gloriousness to all mankind; too cowardly for whimsy and derring-do, they assert whimsy and derring-do ceased at the very latest no later than the Middle Ages; flickering little tapers themselves, their feeble eyes are dazzled to unseeingness of the flaming conflagrations of other souls that illumine their skies. Possessing power in no greater quantity than is the just due of pygmies, they cannot conceive of power greater in others than in themselves. In those days there were giants; but, as their moldy books tell them, the giants are long since passed and only the bones of them remain. Never having seen the mountains, there are no mountains.

In the mud of their complacently perpetuated barnyard pond, they assert that no bright-browed, bright-appareled, shining figures can be outside of fairy books, old histories, and ancient superstitions. Never having seen the stars, they deny the stars. Never having glimpsed the shining ways nor the mortals that tread them, they deny the existence of the shining ways as well as the existence of the high-bright mortals who adventure along the shining ways. The narrow pupils of their eyes in the center of the universe, they image the universe in terms of themselves, of their meager personalities make pitiful yardsticks with which to measure the high-bright souls, saying: "Thus long are all souls, and no longer; it is impossible that there should exist greater-statured souls than we are, and our gods know that we are great of stature."

·

But all, or nearly all on the beach, forgave Ida Barton her suit and form when she took the water. A touch of her hand on her husband's arm, indication and challenge in her laughing face, and the two ran as one for half a dozen paces and leaped as one from the hard-wet sand of the beach, their bodies describing flat arches of flight ere the water was entered.

There are two surfs at Waikiki: the big, bearded-man surf that roars far out beyond the diving stage; the smaller, gentler, wahine, or woman, surf that breaks upon the shore itself. Here is a great shallowness, where one may wade a hundred or several hundred feet to get beyond depth. Yet, with a good surf on outside, the wahine surf can break three or four feet, so that, close in against the shore, the hard-sand bottom may be three feet or three inches under the welter of surface foam. To dive from the beach into this, to fly into the air off racing feet, turn in mid-flight so that heels are up and head is down, and so to enter the water headfirst, requires wisdom of waves, timing of waves, and a trained deftness in entering such unstable depths of water with pretty, unapprehensive, headfirst cleavage while at the same time making the shallowest possible of dives.

It is a sweet and pretty and daring trick, not learned in a day nor learned at all without many a mild bump on the bottom or close shave of fractured skull or broken neck. Here, on the spot where the Bartons so beautifully dived, two days earlier a Stanford track athlete had broken his neck. His had been an error in timing the rise and subsidence of a wahine wave.

"A professional," Mrs. Hanley Black sneered to her husband at Ida Barton's feat.

"Some vaudeville tank girl," was one of the similar remarks with which the women in the shade complacently reassured one another; finding, by way of the weird mental processes of self-illusion, a great satisfaction in the money caste distinction between one who worked for what she ate and themselves who did not work for what they ate.

It was a day of heavy surf on Waikiki. In the wahine surf it was boisterous enough for good swimmers. But out beyond, in the *Kanaka*, or man, surf, no one ventured. Not that the score or more of young surf-riders, loafing on the beach, could not venture there, or were afraid to venture there; but because their biggest outrigger canoes would have been swamped, and their surfboards would have been overwhelmed in the too-immense overtopple and downfall of the thundering monsters. They themselves, most of them, could have swum, for man can swim through breakers which canoes and surfboards cannot surmount; but to ride the backs of the waves, rise out of the foam to stand full length in the air above and with heels winged with the swiftness of horses to fly shoreward, was what made sport for them and brought them out from Honolulu to Waikiki.

The captain of Number Nine canoe, himself a charter member of the Outrigger and a many-times medalist in long-distance swimming, had missed seeing the Bartons take the water and first glimpsed them beyond the last festoon of bathers who clung to the life lines. From then on, from his vantage of the upstairs lanai, he kept his eyes on them. When they continued out past the steel diving stage where a few of the hardiest divers disported, he muttered vexedly under his breath, "damned malihinis!"

Now malihini means newcomer, tenderfoot; and, despite the prettiness of their stroke, he knew that none except malihinis would venture into the racing channel beyond the diving stage. Hence, the vexation of the captain of Number Nine. He descended to the beach, with a low word here and there picked a crew of the strongest surfers, and returned to the lanai with a pair of binoculars. Quite casually, the crew, six of them, carried Number Nine to the water's edge, saw paddles and everything in order for a quick launching, and lolled about carelessly on the sand. They were guilty of not advertising that anything untoward was afoot, although they did steal glances up to their captain straining through the binoculars.

What made the channel was the fresh-water stream. Coral cannot abide fresh water. What made the channel race was the immense shoreward surf-fling of the sea. Unable to remain flung up on the beach, pounded ever back toward the beach by the perpetual shoreward rush of the Kanaka surf, the up-piled water escaped to the sea by way of the channel and in the form of undertow along the bottom under the breakers. Even in the channel the waves broke big, but not with the magnificent bigness of terror as to right and left. So it was that a canoe or a comparatively strong swimmer could dare the channel. But the swimmer must be a strong swimmer indeed who could successfully buck the current in. Wherefore the captain of Number Nine continued his vigil and his muttered damnation of malihinis, disgustedly sure that these two malihinis would compel him to launch Number Nine and go after them when they found the current too strong to swim in against. As for himself, caught in their predicament, he would have veered to the left toward Diamond Head and come in on the shoreward fling of the Kanaka surf. But then, he was no one other than himself, a bronze Hercules of twenty-two, the whitest blood man ever burned to mahogany brown by a subtropic sun, with body and lines and muscles very much resembling the wonderful ones of Duke Kahanamoku. In a hundred yards the world champion could invariably beat him a second flat; but over a distance of miles he could swim circles around the champion.

No one of the many hundreds on the beach, with the exception of the captain and his crew, knew that the Bartons had passed beyond the diving stage. All who had watched them start to swim out had taken for granted that they had joined the others on the stage.

The captain suddenly sprang upon the railing of the lanai, held on to a pillar with one hand, and again picked up the two specks of heads through the glasses. His surmise was verified. The two fools had veered out of the channel toward Diamond Head and were directly seaward of the Kanaka surf. Worse, as he looked, they were starting to come in through the Kanaka surf.

He glanced down quickly to the canoe, and even as he glanced, and as the apparently loafing members quietly arose and took their places by the canoe for the launching, he achieved judgment. Before the canoe could get abreast in the channel, all would be over with the man and woman. And, granted that it could get abreast of them, the moment it ventured into the Kanaka surf it would be swamped, and a sorry chance would the strongest swimmer of them have of rescuing a person pounding to pulp on the bottom under the smashes of the great bearded ones.

The captain saw the first Kanaka wave, large of itself but small among its fellows, lift seaward behind the two speck swimmers. Then he saw them strike a crawl stroke, side by side, faces downward, full lengths outstretched on surface, their feet sculling like propellers and their arms flailing in rapid overhand strokes as they spurted speed to approximate the speed of the overtaking wave, so that, when overtaken, they would become part of the wave and travel with it instead of being left behind it. Thus, if they were coolly skilled enough to ride outstretched on the surface and the forward face of the crest instead of being flung and crumpled or driven headfirst to bottom, they would dash shoreward, not propelled by their own energy but by the energy of the wave into which they had become incorporated.

And they did it! "*Some* swimmers," the captain of Number Nine made announcement to himself under his breath. He continued to gaze eagerly. The best of swimmers could hold such a wave for several hundred feet. But could they? If they did, they would be a third of the way through the perils they had challenged. But, not unexpected by him, the woman failed first, her body not presenting the larger surfaces that her husband's did. At the end of seventy feet she was overwhelmed, being driven downward and out of sight by the tons of water in the overtopple. Her husband followed, and both appeared swimming beyond the wave they had lost.

The captain saw the next wave first. "If they try to body-surf on that, *good night*," he muttered; for he knew the swimmer did not live who would tackle it. Beardless itself, it was father of all bearded ones, a mile long, rising up far out beyond where the others rose, towering its solid bulk higher and higher till it blotted out the horizon and was a giant among its fellows ere its beard began to grow as it thinned its crest to the overcurl.

But it was evident that the man and woman knew big water. No racing stroke did they make in advance of the wave. The captain inwardly applauded as he saw them turn and face the wave and wait for it. It was a picture that of all on the beach he alone saw, wonderfully distinct and vivid in the magnification of the binoculars. The wall of the wave was truly a wall, mounting, ever mounting, and thinning, far up, to a transparency of the colors of the setting sun shooting athwart all the green and blue of it. The green thinned to lighter green that merged blue even as he looked. But it was a blue gem brilliant with innumerable sparkle points of rose and gold flashed through it by the sun. On and up, to the sprouting beard of growing crest, the color orgy increased until it was a kaleidoscopic effervescence of transfusing rainbows.

Against the face of the wave showed the heads of the man and woman like two sheer specks. Specks they were, of the quick, adventuring among the blind elemental forces, daring the Titanic buffets of the sea. The weight of the down-fall of that father of waves, even then imminent above their heads, could stun a man or break the fragile bones of a woman. The captain of Number Nine was unconscious that he was holding his breath. He was oblivious of the man. It was the woman. Did she lose her head or courage, or misplay her muscular part for a moment, she could be hurled a hundred feet by that giant buffet and left wrenched, helpless, and breathless to be pulped on the coral bottom and sucked out by the undertow to be battened on by the fish sharks too cowardly to take their human meat alive.

Why didn't they dive deep, and with plenty of time, the captain wanted to know, instead of waiting till the last tick of safety and the first tick of peril were one? He saw the woman turn her head and laugh to the man, and his head turn in response. Above them, overhanging them, as they mounted the body of the wave, the beard, creaming white, then frothing into rose and gold, tossed upward into a spray of jewels. The crisp offshore trade wind caught the beard's fringes and blew them backward and upward yards and yards into the air. It was then, side by side, and six feet apart, that they dived straight under the overcurl even then disintegrating to chaos and falling. Like insects disappearing into the convolutions of some gorgeous, gigantic orchid, so they disappeared, as beard and crest and spray and jewels, in many tons, crashed and thundered down just where they had disappeared the moment before but where they were no longer.

Beyond the wave they had gone through they finally showed, side by side, still six feet apart, swimming shoreward with a steady stroke until the next wave should make them body-surf it or face and pierce it. The captain of Number Nine waved his hand to his crew in dismissal and sat down on the lanai railing, feeling vaguely tired, and still watching the swimmers through his glasses.

"Whoever and whatever they are," he murmured, "they aren't malihinis. They simply can't be malihinis."

·

Not all days, and only on rare days, is the surf heavy at Waikiki; and, in the days that followed, Ida and Lee Barton, much in evidence on the beach and in the water, continued to arouse disparaging interest in the breasts of the tourist ladies, although the Outrigger captains ceased from worrying about them in the water. They would watch the pair swim out and disappear in the blue distance, and they might, or might not, chance to see them return hours afterward. The point was that the captains did not bother about their returning because they *knew* they would return.

The reason for this was that they were not malihinis. They belonged. In other words, or, rather, in the potent Islands word, they were *kamaaina*.

Kamaaina men and women of forty remembered Lee Barton from their child-hood days, when, in truth, he had been a malihini, though a very young speci-men. Since that time, in the course of various long stays, he had earned the ka-maaina distinction.

As for Ida Barton, young matrons of her own age (privily wondering how she managed to keep her figure) met her with arms around and hearty Hawaiian kisses. Grandmothers must have her to tea and reminiscence in old gardens of forgotten houses which the tourist never sees. Less than a week after her arrival, the aged Queen Liliuokalani must send for her and chide her for neglect. And old men, on cool and balmy lanais, toothlessly maundered to her about Grandpa Captain Wilton, of before their time but whose wild and lusty deeds and pranks, told them by their fathers, they remembered with gusto—Grandpa Captain Wilton, or David Wilton, or "All Hands," as the Hawaiians of that re-mote day had affectionately renamed him—All Hands, ex-Northwest trader, the godless, beachcombing, clipper-shipless, and shipwrecked skipper who had stood on the beach at Kailua and welcomed the very first of the missionaries, off the brig *Thaddeus*, in the year 1820, and who, not many years later, made a scan-dalous runaway marriage with one of their daughters, quieted down and served the Kamehamehas long and conservatively as Minister of the Treasury and Chief of the Customs, and acted as intercessor and mediator between the mis-sionaries on one side and the beachcombing crowd, the trading crowd, and the Hawaiian chiefs on the variously shifting other side.

Nor was Lee Barton neglected. In the midst of the dinners and lunches, the luaus and poi suppers, and swims and dances in aloha to both of them, his time and inclination were claimed by the crowd of lively youngsters of old Kohala days who had come to know that they possessed digestions and various other internal functions and who had settled down to somewhat of sedateness, who roistered less, and who played bridge much and went to baseball often. Also, similarly oriented, was the old poker crowd of Lee Barton's younger days, which crowd played for more consistent stakes and limits, while it drank min-eral water and orange juice and timed the final round of "Jacks" never later than midnight.

Appeared, through all the rout of entertainment, Sonny Grandison, Hawaiian-born, Hawaiian-prominent, who, despite his youthful forty-one years, had declined the proffered governorship of the Territory. Also, he had ducked Ida Barton in the surf at Waikiki a quarter of a century before, and, still earlier, vacationing on his father's great Lakanaii cattle ranch, had hair-raisingly initi-ated her, and various other tender tots of from five to seven years of age, into his boys' band, "The Cannibal Head-Hunters" or "The Terrors of Lakanaii." Still further, his Grandpa Grandison and her Grandpa Wilton had been business and political comrades in the old days.

Educated at Harvard, he had become for a time a world-wandering scientist and social favorite. After serving in the Philippines, he had accompanied various expeditions through Malaysia, South America, and Africa in the post of official entomologist. At forty-one he still retained his traveling commission from the Smithsonian Institution, while his friends insisted that he knew more about sugar "bugs" than the expert entomologists employed by him and his fellow sugar planters in the Experiment Station. Bulking large at home, he was the best-known representative of Hawaii abroad. It was the axiom among traveled Hawaiian folk that wherever over the world they might mention they were from Hawaii, the invariable first question asked of them was: "And do you know Sonny Grandison?"

In brief, he was a wealthy man's son who had made good. His father's million he inherited he had increased to ten millions, at the same time keeping up his father's benefactions and endowments and overshadowing them with his own.

But there was still more to him. A ten years' widower, without issue, he was the most eligible and most pathetically sought-after marriageable man in all Hawaii. A clean-and-strong-featured brunet, tall, slenderly graceful, with the lean runners' stomach, always fit as a fiddle, a distinguished figure in any group, the graying of hair over his temples (in juxtaposition to his young-textured skin and bright, vital eyes) made him appear even more distinguished. Despite the social demands upon his time, and despite his many committee meetings and meetings of boards of directors and political conferences, he yet found time and space to captain the Lakanaii polo team to more than occasional victory, and on his own island of Lakanaii vied with the Baldwins of Maui in the breeding and importing of polo ponies.

.

Given a markedly strong and vital man and woman, when a second equally markedly strong and vital man enters the scene, the peril of a markedly strong and vital triangle of tragedy becomes imminent. Indeed, such a triangle of tragedy may be described, in the terminology of the flat-floor folk, as "super" and "impossible." Perhaps, since within himself originated the desire and the daring, it was Sonny Grandison who first was conscious of the situation, although he had to be quick to anticipate the sensing intuition of a woman like Ida Barton. At any rate, and undebatable, the last of the three to attain awareness was Lee Barton, who promptly laughed away what was impossible to laugh away.

His first awareness, he quickly saw, was so belated that half his hosts and hostesses were already aware. Casting back, he realized that for some time any affair to which he and his wife were invited found Sonny Grandison likewise invited. Wherever the two had been, the three had been. To Kahuku or to Haleiwa, to Ahuimanu, or to Kaneohe for the coral gardens, or to Koko Head for a picnicking and a swimming, somehow it invariably happened that Ida rode in Sonny's car or that both rode in somebody's car. Dances, luaus, dinners, and outings were all one; the three of them were there.

Having become aware, Lee Barton could not fail to register Ida's note of happiness ever rising when in the same company with Sonny Grandison, and her willingness to ride in the same cars with him, to dance with him, or to sit out dances with him. Most convincing of all was Sonny Grandison himself. Forty-one, strong, experienced, his face could no more conceal what he felt than could be concealed a lad of twenty's ordinary lad's love. Despite the control and restraint of forty years he could no more mask his soul with his face than could Lee Barton, of equal years, fail to read that soul through so transparent a face. And often, to other women, talking, when the topic of Sonny came up, Lee Barton heard Ida express her fondness for Sonny, or her almost too-eloquent appreciation of his polo playing, his work in the world, and his general all-rightness of achievement.

About Sonny's state of mind and heart, Lee had no doubts. It was patent enough for the world to read. But how about Ida, his own dozen years' wife of a glorious love match? He knew that woman, ever the mysterious sex, was capable any time of unguessed mystery. Did her frank comradeliness with Grandison token merely frank comradeliness and childhood contacts continued and recrudesced into adult years? Or did it hide, in woman's subtler and more secretive ways, a heat of heart and return of feeling that might even outbalance what Sonny's face advertised?

Lee Barton was not happy. A dozen years of utmost and postnuptial possession of his wife had proved to him, so far as he was concerned, that she was his one woman in the world, and that the woman was unborn, much less unglimpsed, who could for a moment compete with her in his heart, his soul, and his brain. Impossible of existence was the woman who could lure him away from her, much less overbid her in the myriad, continual satisfactions she rendered him.

Was this, then, he asked himself, the dreaded contingency of all fond Benedicts, to be her first "affair"? He tormented himself with the ever iterant query, and, to the astonishment of the reformed Kahala poker crowd of wise and middle-aged youngsters as well as to the reward of the keen scrutiny of the dinner-giving and dinner-attending women, he began to drink King William instead of orange juice, to bully up the poker limit, to drive of nights his own car more than rather recklessly over the Pali and Diamond Head roads, and, ere dinner or lunch or after, to take more than an average man's due of Old Fashioned cocktails and Scotch highs.

All the years of their marriage, she had been ever complaisant toward him in his card playing. This complaisance, to him, had become habitual. But now that doubt had arisen, it seemed to him that he noted an eagerness in her countenancing of his poker parties. Another point he could not avoid noting was that Sonny Grandison was missed by the poker and bridge crowds. He seemed to be too busy. Now where was Sonny, while he, Lee Barton, was playing? Surely not always at committee and boards of directors' meetings. Lee Barton made sure of this. He easily learned that at such times Sonny was more than usually wherever Ida chanced to be—at dances, or dinners, or moonlight swimming parties, or, the very afternoon he had flatly pleaded rush of affairs as an excuse not to join Lee and Langhorne Jones and Jack Holstein in a bridge battle at the Pacific Club—that afternoon he had played bridge at Dora Niles' home with three women, one of whom was Ida.

Returning, once, from an afternoon's inspection of the great dry-dock building at Pearl Harbor, Lee Barton, driving his machine against time in order to have time to dress for dinner, passed Sonny's car; and Sonny's one passenger, whom he was taking home, was Ida. One night, a week later, during which interval he had played no cards, he came home at eleven from a stag dinner at the University Club, just preceding Ida's return from the Alstone poi supper and dance. And Sonny had driven her home. Major Franklin and his wife had first been dropped off by them, they mentioned, at Fort Shafter, on the other side of town and miles away from the beach.

Lee Barton, after all, mere human man, as a human man unfailingly meeting Sonny in all friendliness, suffered poignantly in secret. Not even Ida dreamed that he suffered; and she went her merry, careless, laughing way, secure in her own heart, although a trifle perplexed at her husband's increase in number of pre-dinner cocktails.

Apparently, as always, she had access to almost all of him; but now she did not have access to his unguessable torment nor to the long parallel columns of mental bookkeeping running their total balances from moment to moment, day and night, in his brain. In one column were her undoubtable spontaneous expressions of her usual love and care for him, her many acts of comfort-serving and of advice-asking and advice-obeying. In another column, in which the items increasingly were entered, were her expressions and acts which he could not but classify as dubious. Were they what they seemed? Or were they of duplicity compounded, whether deliberately or unconsciously? The third column, longest of all, totaling most in human heart appraisements, was filled with items relating directly or indirectly to her and Sonny Grandison. Lee Barton did not deliberately do this bookkeeping. He could not help it. He would have liked to avoid it. But in his fairly ordered mind the items of entry, of themselves and quite beyond will on his part, took their places automatically in their respective columns.

In his distortion of vision, magnifying apparently trivial detail which half the time he felt he magnified, he had recourse to MacIlwaine, to whom he had once rendered a very considerable service. MacIlwaine was chief of detectives. "Is Sonny Grandison a womaning man?" Barton had demanded. MacIlwaine had said nothing. "Then he is a womaning man," had been Barton's declaration. And still the chief of detectives had said nothing.

Briefly afterward, ere he destroyed it as so much dynamite, Lee Barton went over the written report. Not bad, not really bad, was the summarization; but not too good after the death of his wife ten years before. That had been a love match almost notorious in Honolulu society because of the completeness of infatuation, not only before, but after marriage, and up to her tragic death when her horse fell with her a thousand feet off Nahiku Trail. And not for a long time afterward, MacIlwaine stated, had Grandison been guilty of interest in any woman. And whatever it was, it had been unvaryingly decent. Never a hint of gossip or scandal; and the entire community had come to accept that he was a one-woman man and would never marry again. What small affairs MacIlwaine had jotted down he insisted that Sonny Grandison did not dream were known by another person outside the principals themselves.

Barton glanced hurriedly, almost shamedly, at the several names and incidents, and knew surprise ere he committed the document to the flames. At any rate, Sonny had been most discreet. As he stared at the ashes, Barton pondered how much of his own younger life, from his bachelor days, resided in old MacIlwaine's keeping. Next, Barton found himself flushing, to himself, at himself. If MacIlwaine knew so much of the private lives of community figures, then had not he, her husband and protector and shielder, planted in MacIlwaine's brain a suspicion of Ida?

.

"Anything on your mind?" Lee asked his wife that evening, as he stood holding her wrap while she put the last touches to her dressing.

This was in line with their old and successful compact of frankness, and he wondered, while he waited her answer, why he had refrained so long from asking her.

"No," she smiled. "Nothing particular. . . . Afterward . . . perhaps. . . . "

She became absorbed in gazing at herself in the mirror while she dabbed some powder on her nose and dabbed it off again.

"You know my way, Lee," she added after the pause. "It takes me time to gather things together in my own way—when there are things to gather; but when I do, you always get them. And often there's nothing in them, after all, I find, and so you are saved the nuisance of them."

She held out her arms for him to place the wrap about her—her valiant little arms that were so wise and steellike in battling with the breakers, and that yet were such just mere woman's arms, round and warm and white, delicious as a woman's arms should be, with the canny muscles, masking under soft round-ness of contour and fine, smooth skin, capable of being flexed at will by the will of her.

He pondered her, with a grievous hurt and yearning of appreciation—so delicate she seemed, so porcelain fragile that a strong man could snap her in the crook of his arm.

"We must hurry!" she cried, as he lingered in the adjustment of the flimsy wrap over her flimsy prettiness of gown. "We'll be late. And if it showers up Nuuanu, putting the curtains up will make us miss the second dance."

He made a note to observe with whom she danced that second dance, as she preceded him across the room to the door; while at the same time he plea-sured his eye in what he had so often named to himself as the spirit-proud, flesh-proud walk of her.

"You don't feel I'm neglecting you in my too-much poker?" he tried again, by indirection.

"Mercy, no! You know I just love you to have your card orgies. They're tonic for you. And you're so much nicer about them, so much more middle-aged. Why, it's almost years since you sat up later than one."

It did not shower up Nuuanu, and every overhead star was out in a clear trade-wind sky. In time at the Inchkeeps for the second dance, Lee Barton ob-served that his wife danced it with Grandison—which, of itself, was nothing un-usual, but which became immediately a registered item in Barton's mental books.

An hour later, depressed and restless, declining to make one of a bridge foursome in the library and escaping from a few young matrons, he strolled out into the generous grounds. Across the lawn, at the far edge, he came upon the hedge of night-blooming cereus. To each flower, opening after dark and fading, wilting, perishing with the dawn, this was its one night of life. The great, cream-white blooms, a foot in diameter and more, lilylike and waxlike, white beacons of attraction in the dark, penetrating and seducing the night with their per-fume, were busy and beautiful with their brief glory of living.

But the way along the hedge was populous with humans, two by two, male and female, stealing out between the dances or strolling the dances out while they talked in low, soft voices and gazed upon the wonder of flower love. From the lanai drifted the love-caressing strains of "Hanalei" sung by the singing boys. Vaguely Lee Barton remembered—perhaps it was from some Maupassant story—the abbé, obsessed by the theory that behind all things were the pur-poses of God and perplexed so to interpret the night, who discovered at the last that the night was ordained for love.

The unanimity of the night, as betrayed by flowers and humans, was a hurt to Barton. He circled back toward the house along a winding path that skirted within the edge of shadow of the monkeypods and algaroba trees. In the obscurity, where his path curved away into the open again, he looked across a space of a few feet where, on another path in the shadow, stood a pair in each other's arms. The impassioned, low tones of the man had caught his ear and drawn his eyes, and at the moment of his glance, aware of his presence, the voice ceased and the two remained immobile, furtive, in each other's arms.

He continued to walk, sombered by the thought that in the gloom of the trees was the next progression from the openness of the sky over those who strolled the night-flower hedge. Oh, he knew the game when of old no shadow was too deep, no ruse of concealment too furtive, to veil a love moment. After all, humans were like flowers, he meditated. Under the radiance from the lighted lanai, ere entering the irritating movement of life again to which he belonged, he paused to stare, scarcely seeing, at a flaunt of display of scarlet double-hibiscus blooms. And abruptly all that he was suffering, all that he had just observed, from the night-blooming hedge and the two-by-two love-murmuring humans to the pair like thieves in each other's arms, crystallized into a parable of life enunciated by the day-blooming hibiscus upon which he gazed, now at the end of its day. Bursting into its bloom after the dawn, snow-white, warming to pink under the hours of sun and quickening to scarlet with the dark from which its beauty and its being would never emerge, it seemed to him that it epitomized man's life and passion.

What further connotations he might have drawn he was never to know; for from behind, in the direction of the algarobas and monkeypods, came Ida's unmistakably serene and merry laugh. He did not look, being too afraid of what he knew he would see, but retreated hastily, almost stumbling, up the steps to the lanai. Despite that he knew what he was to see, when he did turn his head and beheld his wife and Sonny, the pair he had seen thieving in the dark, he went suddenly dizzy and paused, supporting himself with a hand against a pillar and smiling vacuously at the grouped singing boys who were pulsing the sensuous night into richer sensuousness with their *"honi ka ua wikiwiki"* refrain.

The next moment he had wet his lips with his tongue, controlled his face and flesh, and was bantering with Mrs. Inchkeep. But he could not waste time, or he would have to encounter the pair he could hear coming up the steps behind him.

"I feel as if I had just crossed the Great Thirst," he told his hostess, "and that nothing less than a highball will preserve me."

She smiled permission and nodded toward the smoking lanai, where they found him talking sugar politics with the oldsters when the dance began to break up.

Quite a party of half a dozen machines were starting for Waikiki, and he found himself billeted to drive the Leslies and Burnstons home, though he did not fail to note that Ida sat in the driver's seat with Sonny in Sonny's car. Thus, she was home ahead of him and brushing her hair when he arrived. The parting of bed-going was usual, on the face of it, although he was most rigid in his successful effort for casualness as he remembered whose lips had pressed hers last before his.

Was, then, woman the utterly unmoral creature as depicted by the German pessimists? he asked himself, as he tossed under his reading lamp unable to sleep or read. At the end of an hour he was out of bed and into his medicine case, and took a heavy sleeping-powder. An hour later, afraid of his thoughts and the prospect of a sleepless night, he took another powder. At one-hour intervals he twice repeated the dosage. But so slow was the action of the drug that dawn had broken ere his eyes closed.

At seven he was awake again, dry-mouthed, feeling stupid and drowsy, yet incapable of dozing off for more than several minutes at a time. He abandoned the idea of sleep, ate breakfast in bed, and devoted himself to the morning papers and the magazines. But the drug effect held, and he continued briefly to doze through his eating and reading. It was the same when he showered and dressed, and, though the drug had brought him little forgetfulness during the night, he felt grateful for the dreaming lethargy with which it possessed him through the morning.

It was when his wife arose, her serene and usual self, and came into him smiling and roguish, delectable in her kimono, that the whim madness of the opium in his system seized upon him. When she had clearly and simply shown that she had nothing to tell him under their ancient compact of frankness, he began building his opium lie. Asked how he had slept, he replied:

"Miserably. Twice I was routed wide awake with cramps in my feet. I was almost too afraid to sleep again. But they didn't come back, though my feet are sorer than blazes."

"Last year you had them," she reminded him.

"Maybe it's going to become a seasonal affliction," he smiled. "They're not serious, but they're horrible to wake up to. They won't come again till tonight, if they come at all, but in the meantime I feel as if I had been bastinadoed."

.

In the afternoon of the same day, Lee and Ida Barton made their shallow dive from the Outrigger beach, and went on, at a steady stroke, past the diving stage to the big water beyond the Kanaka surf. So quiet was the sea that when, after a couple of hours, they turned and lazily started shoreward through the

Kanaka surf they had it all to themselves. The breakers were not large enough to be exciting, and the last languid surfboarders and canoeists had gone into shore. Suddenly, Lee turned over on his back.

"What is it?" Ida called from twenty feet away.

"My foot—cramp," he answered calmly, though the words were twisted out through clenched jaws of control.

The opium still had its dreamy way with him, and he was without excitement. He watched her swimming toward him with so steady and unperturbed a stroke that he admired her own self-control, although at the same time doubt stabbed him with the thought that it was because she cared so little for him, or, rather, so much immediately more for Grandison.

"Which foot?" she asked, as she dropped her legs down and began treading water beside him.

"The left one—ouch! Now it's both of them."

He doubled his knees, as if involuntarily, raised his head and chest forward out of the water, and sank out of sight in the down wash of a scarcely cresting breaker. Under no more than a brief several seconds, he emerged spluttering and stretched out on his back again.

Almost he grinned, although he managed to turn the grin into a pain grimace, for his simulated cramp had become real. At least in one foot it had, and the muscles convulsed painfully.

"The right is the worst," he muttered, as she evinced her intention of laying hands on his cramp and rubbing it out. "But you'd better keep away. I've had cramps before, and I know I'm liable to grab you if these get any worse."

Instead, she laid her hands on the hard-knotted muscles and began to rub and press and bend.

"Please," he gritted through his teeth. "You must keep away. Just let me lie out here—I'll bend the ankle and toe joints in the opposite ways and make it pass. I've done it before and know how to work it."

She released him, remaining close beside him and easily treading water, her eyes upon his face to judge the progress of his own attempt at remedy. But Lee Barton deliberately bent joints and tensed muscles in the directions that would increase the cramp. In his bout the preceding year with the affliction, he had learned, lying in bed and reading when seized, to relax and bend the cramps away without even disturbing his reading. But now he did the thing in reverse, intensifying the cramp, and, to his startled delight, causing it to leap into his right calf. He cried out with anguish, apparently lost control of himself, attempted to sit up, and was washed under by the next wave.

He came up, spluttered, spread-eagle on the surface, and had his knotted calf gripped by the strong fingers of both Ida's small hands.

"It's all right," she said, while she worked. "No cramp like this lasts very long."

"I didn't know they could be so savage," he groaned. "If only it doesn't go higher! They make one feel so helpless."

He gripped the biceps of both her arms in a sudden spasm, attempting to climb out upon her as a drowning man might try to climb out on an oar and sinking her down under him. In the struggle under water, before he permitted her to wrench clear, her rubber cap was torn off and her hairpins pulled out, so that she came up gasping for air and half blinded by her wet-clinging hair. Also, he was certain he had surprised her into taking in a quantity of water.

"Keep away!" he warned, as he spread-eagled with acted desperateness.

But her fingers were deep into the honest pain wrack of his calf, and in her he could observe no reluctance of fear.

"It's creeping up," he grunted through tight teeth, the grunt itself a half-controlled groan.

He stiffened his whole right leg, as with another spasm, hurting his real minor cramps but flexing the muscles of his upper leg into the seeming hardness of cramp.

The drug still worked in his brain, so that he could playact cruelly while at the same time he appraised and appreciated her stress of control and will that showed in her drawn face, and the terror of death in her eyes, with beyond it and behind it, in her eyes and through her eyes, the something more of the spirit of courage and higher thought and resolution.

Still further, she did not enunciate so cheap a surrender as, "I'll die with you." Instead, provoking his admiration, she did say quietly: "Relax. Sink until only your lips are out. I'll support your head. There must be a limit to cramp. No man ever died of cramp on land. Then in the water no strong swimmer should die of cramp. It's bound to reach its worst and pass. We're both strong swimmers and coolheaded—"

He distorted his face and deliberately dragged her under. But when they emerged, still beside him, supporting his head as she continued to tread water, she was saying:

"Relax. Take it easy. I'll hold your head up. Endure it. Live through it. Don't fight it. Make yourself slack—slack in your mind; and your body will slack. Yield. Remember how you taught me to yield to the undertow."

An unusually large breaker for so mild a surf curled overhead, and he climbed out on her again sinking both of them under as the wave crest overfell and smashed down.

"Forgive me," he mumbled through pain-clenched teeth, as they drew in their first air again. "And leave me." He spoke jerkily, with pain-filled pauses between his sentences. "There is no need for both of us to drown. I've got to go. It will be in my stomach at any moment, and then I'll drag you under and be unable to let go of you. Please, please, dear, keep away. One of us is enough. You've plenty to live for."

She looked at him in reproach so deep that the last vestige of the terror of death was gone from her eyes. It was as if she had said, and more than if she had said: "I have only you to live for."

Then Sonny did not count with her as much as he did!—was Barton's exultant conclusion. But he remembered her in Sonny's arms under the monkeypods and determined on further cruelty. Besides, it was the lingering potion in him that suggested this cruelty. Since he had undertaken this acid test, urged the poppy juice, then let it be a real acid test.

He doubled up and went down, emerged, and apparently strove frantically to stretch out in the floating position. And she did not keep away from him.

"It's too much!" he groaned, almost screamed. "I'm losing my grip. I've got to go. You can't save me. Keep away and save yourself."

But she was to him, striving to float his mouth clear of the salt, saying: "It's all right. It's all right. The worst is right now. Just endure it a minute more and it will begin to ease."

He screamed out, doubled, seized her, and took her down with him. And he nearly did drown her, so well did he playact his own drowning. But never did she lose her head nor succumb to the fear of death so dreadfully imminent. Always, when she got her head out, she strove to support him while she panted and gasped encouragement in terms of: "Relax . . . Relax . . . Slack . . . Slack out . . . At any time . . . now . . . you'll pass . . . the worst . . . No matter how much it hurts . . . it will pass . . . You're easier now . . . aren't you?"

And then he would put her down again, going from bad to worse in his illtreatment of her; making her swallow pints of salt water, secure in the knowledge that it would not definitely hurt her. Sometimes they came up for brief emergencies, for gasping seconds in the sunshine on the surface, and then were under again, dragged under by him, rolled and tumbled under by the curling breakers.

Although she struggled and tore herself from his grips, in the times he permitted her freedom she did not attempt to swim away from him, but, with fading strength and reeling consciousness, invariably came to him to try to save him. When it was enough, in his judgment, and more than enough, he grew quieter, left her released, and stretched out on the surface.

"A-a-h," he sighed long, almost luxuriously, and spoke with pauses for breath. "It is passing. It seems like heaven. My dear, I'm water-logged, yet the mere absence of that frightful agony makes my present state sheerest bliss."

She tried to gasp a reply but could not.

"I'm all right," he assured her. "Let us float and rest up. Stretch out, your-self, and get your wind back."

And for half an hour, side by side, on their backs, they floated in the fairly placid Kanaka surf. Ida Barton was the first to announce recovery by speaking first.

"And how do you feel now, man of mine?" she asked.

"I feel as if I'd been run over by a steam-roller," he replied. "And you, poor darling?"

"I feel I'm the happiest woman in the world. I'm so happy I could almost cry, but I'm too happy even for that. You had me horribly frightened for a time. I thought I was going to lose you."

Lee Barton's heart pounded up. Never a mention of losing herself. This, then, was love, and all real love, proved true—the great love that forgot self in the loved one.

"And I'm the proudest man in the world," he told her; "because my wife is the bravest woman in the world."

"Brave!" she repudiated "I love you. I never knew how much, how really much, I loved you as when I was losing you. And now let's work for shore. I want you all alone with me, your arms around me, while I tell you all you are to me and shall always be to me."

In another half hour, swimming strong and steadily, they landed on the beach and walked up the hard, wet sand among the sand loafers and sun baskers.

"What were the two of you doing out there?" queried one of the Outrigger captains. "Cutting up?"

"Cutting up," Ida Barton answered with a smile.

"We're the village cut-ups, you know," was Lee Barton's assurance.

.

That evening, the evening's engagement canceled, found the two, in a big chair, in each other's arms.

"Sonny sails tomorrow noon," she announced casually and irrelevant to anything in the conversation. "He's going out to the Malay Coast to inspect what's been done with that lumber and rubber company of his."

"First I've heard of his leaving us," Lee managed to say, despite his surprise.

"I was the first to hear of it," she added. "He told me only last night."

"At the dance?"

She nodded.

"Rather sudden, wasn't it?"

"Very sudden." Ida withdrew herself from her husband's arms and sat up. "And I want to talk to you about Sonny. I've never had a real secret from you before. I didn't intend ever to tell you. But it came to me today, out in the Kanaka surf, that if we passed out it would be something left behind us unsaid."

She paused, and Lee, half anticipating what was coming, did nothing to help her, save to girdle and press her hand in his.

"Sonny rather lost his—his head over me," she faltered. "Of course, you must have noticed it. And—and last night he wanted me to run away with him. Which isn't my confession at all—"

Still Lee Barton waited.

"My confession," she resumed, "is that I wasn't the least bit angry with him—only sorrowful and regretful. My confession is that I rather slightly, only rather more than slightly, lost my own head. That was why I was kind and gentle to him last night. I am no fool. I knew it was due. And—oh, I know, I'm just a feeble female of vanity compounded—I was proud to have such a man swept off his feet by me, by little me. I encouraged him. I have no excuse. Last night would not have happened had I not encouraged him. And I, and not he, was the sinner last night when he asked me. And I told him no, impossible, as you should know why without my repeating it to you. And I was maternal to him, very much maternal. I let him take me in his arms, let myself rest against him, and, for the first time because it was to be the forever last time, let him kiss me and let myself kiss him. You—I know you understand—it was his renunciation. And I didn't love Sonny. I don't love him. I have loved you, and you only, all the time."

She waited, and felt her husband's arm pass around her shoulder and under her own arm, and yielded to his drawing down of her to him.

"You did have me worried more than a bit," he admitted, "until I was afraid I was going to lose you. And—" He broke off in patent embarrassment, then gripped the idea courageously. "Oh, well, you know you're my one woman. Enough said."

She fumbled the match box from his pocket and struck a match to enable him to light his long-extinct cigar.

"Well," he said, as the smoke curled about them, "knowing you as *I* know you, the *all* of you, all I can say is that I'm sorry for Sonny for what he's missed—awfully sorry for him, but equally glad for me. And—one other thing: five years hence I've something to tell you, something rich, something ridiculously rich and all about me and the foolishness of me over you. Five years. Is it a date?

"I shall keep it if it is fifty years," she sighed, as she nestled closer to him.

Thomas Lux

Tarantulas on the Lifebuoy

For some semitropical reason
when the rains fall
relentlessly they fall

into swimming pools, these otherwise
bright and scary
arachnids. They can swim
a little, but not for long

and they can't climb the ladder out.
They usually drown—but
if you want their favor,
if you believe there is justice,
a reward for not loving

the death of ugly
and even dangerous (the eel, hog snake,
rats) creatures, if

you believe these things, then
you would leave a lifebuoy
or two in your swimming pool at night.

And in the morning
you would haul ashore
the huddled, hairy survivors

and escort them
back to the bush, and know,
be assured that at least these saved,
as individuals, would not turn up

again someday
in your hat, drawer,
or the tangled underworld

of your socks, and that even—
when your belief in justice
merges with your belief in dreams—
they may tell the others

in a sign language
four times as subtle
and complicated as man's

that you are good,
that you love them,
that you would save them again.

Colleen J. McElroy

Learning to Swim at Forty-Five

I could not whistle and walk in storms
along Lake Michigan's shore . . .
I could not swallow the lake.
—CLARENCE MAJOR

Having given up hope for a high-wire act
I've taken to water and the quicksilver
Danger of working words hand over hand.
At the edge of the pool I am locked in gravity
And remember the jeers at girl scout camp
Where *catfish* meant anyone who lived in a ghetto
With no pools and no need to tan and everyone
Spent more time learning how to keep their hair
From *going bad* than they did learning breaststrokes.

And yes, Clarence, I learned to swallow the lake
Including all that it held and what I was told
By Mrs. Fitzsimmons of Harris Stowe Teachers
Who later said I couldn't hold the elements
Of tone or the way words break and run like rain,
The *Hecates* and *Africs* filling the page
Until it grows buoyant under the weight of sonnets,
A feat she believed so unconsciously automatic
It arrived full blown at birth.

For forty years I've lived under the pull of air,
All the while knowing survival meant learning
To swim in strange waters. *Just jump in and do it*
They yelled at camp, then tossed me heels over head
Their humor an anchor dragging me down.
There I defied training films and descended just once,
My body stone weight and full of the first primal fear
Of uncurling from the water belly of a mother country.
There I could not whistle in the face of the storm
And even my legs were foreign.

Poetry like swimming cannot be learned
Fitzsimmons insisted as I rubbed the smooth skin
Behind my ears where gill flaps had failed to appear.
Now years later, I voluntarily step below the surface
And there beneath the chlorine blue, I am finally reptilian
And so close to the Middle Passage, I will pay any price
For air. If silence has a smell, it is here
Where my breath fizzles in a champagne of its own making,
Where I must learn to sing to the rhythms of water
The strange currents and patterns of moons and tides.

Fitzsimmons, it doesn't happen all at once. To swim
You must learn to labor under the threat of air lost
Forever and hold fear close to you like a safety net.
You must imagine the body, the way it floats and extends
First like an anchor, then a lizard or a dead leaf.
Direction is some point where the sun is inverted and sweet
Air hammers the brain with signals that must be ignored.
You learn to take risks, to spread yourself thin,
You learn to look *through a glass darkly*
And in your darkness, build elegies of your own rhythms,
And yes Fitzsimmons, you learn when to swallow
The lake and when to hold to the swell of it.

Walter Russell Mead

Bold Strokes

*T*he colors were intense, surreal, as in a dream. My mother, wrapped in silks and seated on a throne of Turkish carpets, seemed halfway to the sky. She peered down at me from an infinite distance and waved. I had rarely felt this alone; on swift, clean strokes my father sped by me. She can't help me, I thought, and *he* won't.

I took a deep breath, but a wave swept up and filled my mouth with salt water. I choked and coughed; the blue-green water closed over my head.

This was no dream, to be dutifully remembered and repeated on the analyst's couch; it was real. It was September 1991, and my father was swimming, and I was trying to swim, from Asia to Europe across the Hellespont.

The Hellespont is a narrow—not narrow enough—strait through which the waters of the Black Sea pour into the Mediterranean. It separates Europe and Asia and has been one of the main crossroads for the world's armies and traders from the time of the Trojan War.

It is named for someone who drowned there. Helle and Phrixus, we are told, fled their abusive stepmother on the back of a flying ram with a fleece of pure gold. Helle slid off and fell into the waterway that still bears her name.

Later, the ram died and the Golden Fleece was hung in a temple in what is now the Republic of Georgia. Jason and the Argonauts sailed through the

Hellespont on their quest for the Fleece; at the time, the waters were chiefly known for the Clashing Rocks, which smashed any ship trying to sail through, and for the Harpies, giant birds with a woman's face and a poor disposition.

People have been swimming the Hellespont—now officially called the Dardanelles—for years. In ancient times, the improbably named Hero, a temple virgin on the European side, was in love with Leander, a young man from Asia. On nights when she felt like it, she put a lantern in the tower of the temple and Leander would swim the four miles to reach her. Early in the morning, he would swim back, and everybody was happy. Hero had her lover, the townspeople in Sestos thought they had a temple virgin.

These situations rarely last. One night, a storm came up after Leander had taken the plunge. The light in the tower went out, and in the morning, Hero found Leander's body on the shore.

Thus began, inauspiciously enough, a tradition that persists to our times. The poet Byron, a crack swimmer at Harrow, swam the Hellespont at 22. His first effort ended in failure, but on the second try, he made it across.

Byron's poetry may have been romantic, but his impressions of the Hellespont were not. "The current," he wrote in a letter to a friend, "renders it hazardous, so much so, that I doubt whether Leander's conjugal powers must not have been exhausted in his passage to paradise."

Given Byron's theory, swimming the Hellespont may not be the most natural way to mark a fortieth wedding anniversary, but my father didn't care. An athlete from a family of athletes, he took to swimming ten years ago, and he took to it bad.

As he neared 60 and his fortieth anniversary, he began to look for "trophy events." It wasn't enough to be the fastest piranha in the pool where he swam every morning in Washington, D.C.; he wanted long-distance swims. A residual sense of reality has, so far, kept him out of the English Channel, but every year he swims four miles in open ocean at the mouth of the Chesapeake Bay, and when he learned I was going to Turkey, he had only one request.

"Find out what you can about swimming the Hellespont," he said.

I did; it's possible. In fact, I met Hüseyin Uluaslan, a local historian and journalist who guided his first American across thirty-two years ago. "See," said Hüseyin, "I'll show you." And he pulled out an issue of *Life* from 1960 that showed him next to a dripping teenager. I glanced through the article; the boy didn't finish the swim, but Hüseyin got him out of the water alive.

"I don't know," I said to Hüseyin. "My father just turned 60. Do you think he can make it?"

He thought for a moment. "I've had people in their fifties swim," he said, "but never anyone over 60."

When the Indomitable One heard this, he was ready to pack. Visions of the *Guinness Book of World Records* danced in his head.

That is how Dad got into the water. My story is more complicated. While my dad comes from a long line of athletes, my mother does not. I take after her, and five years of muscular Christianity in a New England prep school did nothing to cure me of my dislike of and incapacity for physical endeavor of any kind. My brothers, sad to say, take after Dad. Chris plays polo with crowned heads; Philip was varsity crew at Princeton, has rowed for the United States in international competition and, alarmed that he was getting out of shape, recently ran the New York City Marathon to keep himself from going stale.

In theory, the bookish, klutzy brother is supposed to be compensated. The athletic brothers are supposed to be as strong as oxen, but no smarter. This is not the way it works in my family. The polo player is fluent in Japanese and French, and his opinions on Japanese investment trends are constantly being quoted by major news organizations here and abroad.

"Oh, look," as my mother often says to me on the phone, "they've quoted Chris again in *The Wall Street Journal!*" As for the oarsman, he is currently a straight-A student adding an M.D. to his Wharton M.B.A. It's a difficult family.

I can't seem to win. I had a book published several years ago, and although nobody much bought it, the reviews were complimentary. I brought a copy to my parents. "What do you think, Mom?" I asked.

"It's very nice," she said, cradling in her arms my sister's first son, the second grandchild. "But there's one thing I want you to remember."

"What's that?" I asked.

"One grandchild is worth five books."

From time to time, I've tried to keep up. My polo-playing brother and a friend once talked me into hiking up Mount Whitney, the highest peak in California. I don't remember much about it now, besides sitting and wheezing desperately on a rock by the trail while a group of Brownies marched by—singing. I was 18 then and in my prime. I'm pushing 40 now, and I'm thicker and slower than I used to be. The most exercise I usually get in the water is washing my hair—but none of this kept me out of the Hellespont.

The tongue, warn the Scriptures, is a tiny rudder that steers the big ship. "What are you doing this summer?" friends would ask from time to time.

"Oh," I would say casually, "I'm thinking of swimming the Hellespont with my father."

Their jaws would drop in the most satisfactory way and I would go on, offhandedly describing the swim. "It's not too far," said the man who'd rarely swum across a pool. "Just a couple of miles. Of course, with the currents, the route is a little longer—maybe four."

They would stand around silently while I rattled on. "The currents can be treacherous," I would say learnedly. "But I've found a local guide who will hire fishermen to go with us on a boat and point out the way."

As my audience grew, I would go on to tell them about Hero and Leander and to note that the best place to swim is in a military zone. The Hellespont remains a strategic waterway; most Soviet shipping, as it was still being called, passes through it. Would-be swimmers have to get permission from Turkish authorities—or they'll be shot. My listeners gasped; I basked.

A few weeks of this, and I was trapped. Having boasted about the swim to everyone I knew, I would have to do something about it. Leander swam for love, Byron for art; I was going to swim the Hellespont for shame—and with my dad.

The best time to swim the strait is late summer. Spring and early summer are bad: The Central and Eastern European snowpacks run off into the Black Sea and then down through the Hellespont into the Mediterranean. By Labor Day, though, the currents are relatively calm, and the water stays warm through October. My parents' fortieth wedding anniversary fell late in August 1991. We picked Labor Day for the swim.

For most of the summer, my thoughts were fixed on the swim. I ground out lap after weary lap in the pool at my gym, cursing my stupidity and trying vainly to adjust those annoying little goggles to keep the water out of my eyes. A quarter-mile, a half-mile; by late June, I was up to a mile or more a day and supplementing that with long bike rides.

About the time I began to feel that, physically, I had a reasonable shot at the swim, the emotional side of the trip hit me: twenty days in a car—with my parents. We hadn't spent twenty days alone together since December 1953, when Chris was born.

Like a lot of American families, ours is part bright and modern, part twisted ancestral roots. My parents come from small towns in South Carolina, and we came north together, when I went to prep school and my parents started new jobs in Washington.

On one level, we've adjusted. We're modern people now. No more chickens on the front steps, no more stills out back. We get our liquor at the store like everybody else. And, at least on the surface, we've managed a convincing imitation of the civilized family life—cool and bland—that upper-middle-class Yankees seem to lead.

But put us together for long, and we start to revert. After three or four days, we're back to sitting on the porch, drinking brown liquor, eating boiled peanuts and embellishing stories about one another until they turn into legends: the time Aunt Laura drove her Toyota into the Atlantic, the night we stored the pigs in Grandma's tub for the big barbecue, and so on through the years.

Like most professional people in the U.S. today, I have a working, day-to-day adult identity that is different, purposefully different, from the identity I had as a member of my parents' nuclear family. I live hundreds of miles from them, see them only occasionally, and I am comfortable in this new identity—in which friends and colleagues see a more controlled, carefully groomed version of whom I am. The apple likes to think it has fallen a long way from the tree.

Coming back to family undermines all that. All the old raw nerves are exposed once again. You are with people who know what you're like under your skin. You are with people who watched your personality come together over the years, who saw you dissolve helplessly into tears of frustration at 2; who saw, and pitied, the awkward struggles of adolescence.

And you are not only with the people who saw you come into the world, you are with the people among whom you can't forget that you will one day be leaving. My father was 30 once and he's 60 now; to be with him is to face facts I prefer to ignore.

Despite all this baggage, we had a wonderful trip. I didn't need, much, to assert my independence; my parents didn't need, much, to assert their control. Somehow, in the past fifteen years, we've disarmed and miraculously, ended up falling in like with one another.

Some moments were tense. My father and I are both used to navigating and planning; the buck deer locked antlers now and then, but we learned to ease up. We managed. We compromised. My parents proved to be game and adventurous travelers, ready to pick up and go on impulse and without reservations—and ready, too, to put up with the snarls and inconvenience this occasionally produces. We had unforgettable moments together: standing on a mountainside on the Black Sea coast, breathing in the wild mint; sunset on a hilltop in Cappadocia as one by one the muezzins in the surrounding villages sent up their echoing calls to prayer; gin-and-cherry juice cocktails on the roof terrace of our Istanbul hotel, with views of the Blue Mosque, the Hagia Sophia and the ships on the Bosphorus.

The Hellespont, though, was the high point of our trip, and not just because of the swim. There may be no spot on earth where the currents of history flow so strongly. The oldest walls at Troy were built almost 5,000 years ago; from that time to this, the strait has been a source of riches and a battleground of civilizations. Eight hundred and sixty-six years after the Trojan War, Alexander the Great sailed across from Macedon to conquer Asia; he plunged naked from his boat, swam ashore and ran three times around the tomb of Achilles.

During the Persian Wars, King Xerxes I had a pontoon bridge built across the strait so that his vast army could cross over to Greece. A huge storm swept up the channel and smashed the bridge to bits; the royal executioner solemnly lashed the water for its insubordination, and Xerxes built a new bridge.

Rome was supposed to have been founded from here. Aeneas, the son of Aphrodite, carried his father out of the burning ruins of Troy and sailed to Italy.

Instructed by the gods, he built a new city, and from it, eventually, came Rome. Julius Caesar, who passed by here en route to the battle where he said *"Veni, vidi, vici,"* was descended from Aeneas, and from Caesar's time on, the Roman emperors came to the Hellespont to pay tribute to their Trojan ancestors.

Saint Paul stopped here, too, and went from the Troad (the region surrounding Troy) to bring Christianity to Europe. Twelve hundred years later, the bearers of a new faith came here as well. The Ottomans crossed the Hellespont into Europe and built a castle that still survives—and is part of NATO's defense system. Thanks to their crossing, the Ottomans went on to surround and ultimately conquer Constantinople, and, except for a few islanders, Christianity is now as dead in the Troad as the paganism that it replaced.

The Hellespont has played a role in modern times, too. During World War I, Winston Churchill tried and failed to send the British Navy through to occupy Istanbul, knock the Ottoman Empire out of the war and break the blockade that was strangling czarist Russia. The Gallipoli campaign that followed was one of the bloodiest of the war. Turks date their modern history from this victory; Kemal Atatürk, the Turkish general who defeated Churchill, went on to establish the Turkish Republic and is now venerated by the Turks as the Washington, Jefferson, Lincoln and Roosevelt of their country.

We toured the tragic and magnificent battlefields of Gallipoli and walked the walls of Troy. I found a pear tree growing among the ruins of the palace of Priam (king of Troy at the time of the Trojan War) and brought a pear to my mother. But my father and I were unable to concentrate fully; he was anticipating, and I was dreading, the swim.

Hüseyin had set everything up. We had permits and signal flags from the Turkish military—useful to avoid having one's boat fired on by the sentries. We had a boat, and fishermen who knew the best route across the choppy and treacherous waters. We had Vaseline to rub on ourselves to help keep us warm during the two-hour swim. We had, in short, everything we needed, except a good excuse to drop the whole project.

The morning of the swim, we got up early and drove to the docks. Hüseyin and the boat were waiting. The wind was cold, the waves were ominously high. "Four feet," I estimated.

"Six," said Dad. We compromised on eight.

"The sooner you start," said Hüseyin, "the better. The wind picks up in the morning—and so does the shipping traffic in the channel."

The boat took us a couple miles up the waterway from the city of Çanakkale to the site of ancient Abydos, where Leander had lived. We covered ourselves in Vaseline as my mother wrapped herself securely in her shawls and arranged the pillows and carpets that Hüseyin had thoughtfully set around the deck. Dad was chipper; I was resigned. We jumped in. It was much worse than I had expected.

All the time I'd spent in pools that summer wasn't much help in the ocean. There are no lanes painted on the floor of the ocean, and pools don't have waves.

I turned my head to breathe and a wave slapped salt water down my throat. I raised my hand to stroke and the water slipped away, leaving my arm uselessly plowing the air. Five minutes of this and I was convinced that I would never make it across.

Dad had no such doubts. This water was warmer and no rougher than that at the mouth of the Chesapeake; he soon pulled ahead of me with strong, sure strokes. Hüseyin and the crew tried to position the boat between us, to keep us both in view. As the distance widened, they zigzagged across the channel to make sure we were both heading in the right direction—and that we were both above water.

I never really wanted to do this, I was thinking as I floundered. I'll never make it. I should quit. Except for the occasional jellyfish, there was nothing to see in the water; above it there was only the depressing vista of two shores. One of them never seemed to drop back, and the other one wasn't getting any closer. I started to panic. I was sure I would fail. What a pointless and stupid thing to do, I kept thinking. I don't need to swim this. It was neurotic and idiotic; I was perfectly safe and, physically, perfectly capable of staying afloat long enough to struggle to the opposite shore, but after ten minutes in the water I was a total psychological wreck.

I kept going; I'm still not quite sure why. I think even in the panic and muddle, I realized that one way or another, I was going to have to deal with these feelings and with what they made me do. It would be cheaper and easier to swim the damn Hellespont than to agonize about not doing it in therapy later. I remembered something Chesterton once said—"If a thing is worth doing, it's worth doing badly"—and that's how I swam the Hellespont. I began to count strokes—bad strokes, good strokes, it didn't matter. Two thousand five hundred, I figured, and I should be making some progress.

Sixteen hundred strokes later, I had made it across the strongest part of the current when the boat cut in front of me. After much shouting and confusion in English and Turkish, I understood. A couple of large ships were headed down the shipping lane, and our boat would have to pull me out of the way. The crew tossed me a life preserver attached to a line. I grabbed it, and the boat roared off.

This was much worse than the swimming. I was blinded by a cascade of white water, and my arms were nearly pulled out of their sockets. I couldn't shout to get the boat to slow down—nobody could hear me over the noise of the engine, and, anyway, I couldn't open my mouth without drowning in spray. The boat towed me around in a huge circle away from the ships. My bathing suit was slipping down my thighs, my arms at last were too weak to hold on any longer, and I dropped the life preserver to hitch up my shorts and start swimming again.

I was back in the middle of the current, and started slogging once more: 1,601, 1,602, 1,603.

Five hundred strokes later, Europe started to look a little closer. By this time, I was past the current again and able to enjoy myself a little. The weather, though rough, was beautiful. The hills above the water were gloriously green, the sky almost cloudless. Even the whitecaps, so annoying close-up, had their charm when considered as part of the view rather than as obstacles to swimming.

Two and a half hours after starting out, I dragged myself up the wild, rocky shore of Europe. I picked up a couple of rocks as souvenirs and put them in the pocket of my bathing suit; they dissolved into sand as I swam the hundred yards out to the boat.

Hüseyin and the crew pulled me over the side, wrapped me in towels and poured me some brandy. There were plums from Mount Ida and Turkish pastries. My father, who'd finished an hour ahead of me, was dry and well-rested, although, I was slightly gratified to note, he had cracked a rib coming up into the boat and was in more pain than I was.

I'm not sure what the point of all this was—except maybe the pointlessness. It's impossible to feel anything but dwarfed by the Hellespont. Five thousand years of history laugh as you swim. My father and I will pass on, leaving no more mark of our presence than do the waves that lap at the shores. Priam's walls, Paul's religion, Xerxes's bridge, Churchill's flotilla—much bigger plans than ours have come to nothing in these waters.

But then, our plans, though small, hadn't come to nothing. We had mounted a successful amphibious operation where Leander and Churchill had failed. Though I'd almost lost my shorts, I managed to keep them, thus making the swim with more dignity than had Alexander the Great. And it was a sunny day, a fine swim, and something special to do with some of the people I love.

There are now three grandchildren in the family, and my father is already counting the years until they are old enough to swim with him. Fifteen or so, he thinks. He'll be well into his seventies, but he has no plans to slow down. *Inshallah*, as they say in Turkey—God willing—we'll come back, with the polo player, the supermom and the oarsman, and try it again. If I can, I'll be standing in the prow of the boat with the rest of them, rubbing Vaseline all over myself and asking why I'm doing it.

Meanwhile, I recently read about two islands that are only three miles apart in the Bering Strait. One is in Russia and one is in America; they straddle the international date line as well as the line between Asia and North America. Of course, we'd need to get wet suits. . . .

Rohinton Mistry

Swimming Lessons

*T*he old man's wheelchair is audible today as he creaks by in the hallway: on some days it's just a smooth whirr. Maybe the way he slumps in it, or the way his weight rests has something to do with it. Down to the lobby he goes, and sits there most of the time, talking to people on their way out or in. That's where he first spoke to me a few days ago. I was waiting for the elevator, back from Eaton's with my new pair of swimming-trunks.

"Hullo," he said. I nodded, smiled.

"Beautiful summer day we've got."

"Yes," I said, "it's lovely outside."

He shifted the wheelchair to face me squarely. "How old do you think I am?"

I looked at him blankly, and he said, "Go on, take a guess."

I understood the game; he seemed about seventy-five although the hair was still black, so I said, "Sixty-five?" He made a sound between a chuckle and a wheeze: "I'll be seventy-seven next month." Close enough.

I've heard him ask that question several times since, and everyone plays by the rules. Their faked guesses range from sixty to seventy. They pick a lower number when he's more depressed than usual. He reminds me of Grandpa as he sits on the sofa in the lobby, staring out vacantly at the parking lot. Only difference is, he sits with the stillness of stroke victims, while Grandpa's Parkinson's disease would bounce his thighs and legs and arms all over the place. When he could no longer hold the *Bombay Samachar* steady enough to read, Grandpa took to sitting on the veranda and staring emptily at the traffic passing outside Firozsha Baag. Or waving to anyone who went by in the compound: Rustomji, Nariman Hansotia in his 1932 Mercedes-Benz, the fat ayah Jaakaylee with her shopping-bag, the *kuchrawalli* with her basket and long bamboo broom.

The Portuguese woman across the hall has told me a little about the old man. She is the communicator for the apartment building. To gather and disseminate information, she takes the liberty of unabashedly throwing open her door when newsworthy events transpire. Not for Portuguese Woman the furtive peerings from thin cracks or spyholes. She reminds me of a character in a movie, *Barefoot In The Park* I think it was, who left empty beer cans by the landing for anyone passing to stumble and give her the signal. But PW does not need beer cans. The gutang-khutang of the elevator opening and closing is enough.

The old man's daughter looks after him. He was living alone till his stroke, which coincided with his youngest daughter's divorce in Vancouver. She returned to him and they moved into this low-rise in Don Mills. PW says the daughter talks to no one in the building but takes good care of her father.

Mummy used to take good care of Grandpa, too, till things became complicated and he was moved to the Parsi General Hospital. Parkinsonism and osteoporosis laid him low. The doctor explained that Grandpa's hip did not break because he fell, but he fell because the hip, gradually growing brittle, snapped on that fatal day. That's what osteoporosis does, hollows out the bones and turns effect into cause. It has an unusually high incidence in the Parsi community, he said, but did not say why. Just one of those mysterious things. We are the chosen people where osteoporosis is concerned. And divorce. The Parsi community has the highest divorce rate in India. It also claims to be the most westernized community in India. Which is the result of the other? Confusion again, of cause and effect.

The hip was put in traction. Single-handed, Mummy struggled valiantly with bedpans and dressings for bedsores which soon appeared like grim spectres on his back. *Mamaiji,* bent double with her weak back, could give no assistance. My help would be enlisted to roll him over on his side while Mummy changed the dressing. But after three months, the doctor pronounced a patch upon Grandpa's lungs, and the male ward of Parsi General swallowed him up. There was no money for a private nursing home. I went to see him once, at Mummy's insistence. She used to say that the blessings of an old person were the most valuable and potent of all, they would last my whole life long. The ward had rows and rows of beds; the din was enormous, the smells nauseating, and it was just as well that Grandpa passed most of his time in a less than conscious state.

But I should have gone to see him more often. Whenever Grandpa went out, while he still could in the days before parkinsonism, he would bring back pink and white sugar-coated almonds for Percy and me. Every time I remember Grandpa, I remember that; and then I think: I should have gone to see him more often. That's what I also thought when our telephone-owning neighbour, esteemed by all for that reason, sent his son to tell us the hospital had phoned that Grandpa died an hour ago.

The postman rang the doorbell the way he always did, long and continuous; Mother went to open it, wanting to give him a piece of her mind but thought better of it, she did not want to risk the vengeance of postmen, it was so easy for them to destroy letters; workers nowadays thought no end of themselves, strutting around like peacocks, ever since all this Shiv Sena agitation about Maharashtra for Maharashtrians, threatening strikes and Bombay bundh all the time, with no respect for the public; bus drivers and conductors were the worst, behaving as if they owned the buses and were doing favours to commuters, pulling the bell before you were in the bus, the driver purposely braking and moving with big jerks to make the standees lose their balance, the conductor so rude if you did not have the right change.

But when she saw the airmail envelope with a Canadian stamp her face lit up, she said wait to the postman, and went in for a fifty paisa piece, a little baksheesh for you, she told him, then shut the door and kissed the envelope, went in running, saying my son has written, my son has sent a letter, and Father looked up from the newspaper and said, don't get too excited, first read it, you know what kind of letters he writes, a few lines of empty words, I'm fine, hope you are all right, your loving son—that kind of writing I don't call letter-writing.

Then Mother opened the envelope and took out one small page and began to read silently, and the joy brought to her face by the letter's arrival began to ebb; Father saw it happening and knew he was right, he said read aloud, let me also hear what our son is writing this time, so Mother read: My dear Mummy and Daddy, Last winter was terrible, we had record-breaking low temperatures all through February and March, and the first official day of spring was colder than the first official day of winter had been, but it's getting warmer now. Looks like it will be a nice warm summer. You asked about my new apartment. It's small, but not bad at all. This is just a quick note to

*let you know I'm fine, so you won't worry about me. Hope everything is okay
at home.*

*After Mother put it back in the envelope, Father said everything about
his life is locked in silence and secrecy, I still don't understand why he bothered to visit us last year if he had nothing to say; every letter of his has been a
quick note so we won't worry—what does he think we worry about, his health,
in that country everyone eats well whether they work or not, he should be worrying about us with all the black market and rationing, has he forgotten already how he used to go to the ration-shop and wait in line every week; and
what kind of apartment description is that, not bad at all; and if it is a Canadian weather report I need from him, I can go with Nariman Hansotia
from A Block to the Cawasji Framji Memorial Library and read all about it,
there they get newspapers from all over the world.*

The sun is hot today. Two women are sunbathing on the stretch of patchy lawn
at the periphery of the parking lot. I can see them clearly from my kitchen.
They're wearing bikinis and I'd love to take a closer look. But I have no binoculars. Nor do I have a car to saunter out to and pretend to look under the
hood. They're both luscious and gleaming. From time to time they smear lotion over their skin, on the bellies, on the inside of the thighs, on the shoulders. Then one of them gets the other to undo the string of her top and spread
some there. She lies on her stomach with the straps undone. I wait. I pray that
the heat and haze make her forget, when it's time to turn over, that the straps
are undone.

But the sun is not hot enough to work this magic for me. When it's time to
come in, she flips over, deftly holding up the cups, and reties the top. They
arise, pick up towels, lotions and magazines, and return to the building.

This is my chance to see them closer. I race down the stairs to the lobby.
The old man says hullo. "Down again?"

"My mailbox," I mumble.

"It's Saturday," he chortles. For some reason he finds it extremely funny.
My eye is on the door leading in from the parking lot.

Through the glass panel I see them approaching. I hurry to the elevator
and wait. In the dimly lit lobby I can see their eyes are having trouble adjusting
after the bright sun. They don't seem as attractive as they did from the kitchen
window. The elevator arrives and I hold it open, inviting them in with what I
think is a gallant flourish. Under the fluorescent glare in the elevator I see their
wrinkled skin, aging hands, sagging bottoms, varicose veins. The lustrous trick
of sun and lotion and distance has ended.

I step out and they continue to the third floor. I have Monday night to look
forward to, my first swimming lesson. The high school behind the apartment

building is offering, among its usual assortment of macramé and ceramics and pottery classes, a class for non-swimming adults.

The woman at the registration desk is quite friendly. She even gives me the opening to satisfy the compulsion I have about explaining my non-swimming status.

"Are you from India?" she asks. I nod. "I hope you don't mind my asking, but I was curious because an Indian couple, husband and wife, also registered a few minutes ago. Is swimming not encouraged in India?"

"On the contrary," I say. "Most Indians swim like fish. I'm an exception to the rule. My house was five minutes walking distance from Chaupatty beach in Bombay. It's one of the most beautiful beaches in Bombay, or was, before the filth took over. Anyway, even though we lived so close to it, I never learned to swim. It's just one of those things."

"Well," says the woman, "that happens sometimes. Take me, for instance. I never learned to ride a bicycle. It was the mounting that used to scare me, I was afraid of falling." People have lined up behind me. "It's been very nice talking to you," she says, "hope you enjoy the course."

The art of swimming had been trapped between the devil and the deep blue sea. The devil was money, always scarce, and kept the private swimming clubs out of reach; the deep blue sea of Chaupatty beach was grey and murky with garbage, too filthy to swim in. Every so often we would muster our courage and Mummy would take me there to try and teach me. But a few minutes of paddling was all we could endure. Sooner or later something would float up against our legs or thighs or waists, depending on how deep we'd gone in, and we'd be revulsed and stride out to the sand.

Water imagery in my life is recurring. Chaupatty beach, now the high-school swimming pool. The universal symbol of life and regeneration did nothing but frustrate me. Perhaps the swimming pool will overturn that failure.

When images and symbols abound in this manner, sprawling or rolling across the page without guile or artifice, one is prone to say, how obvious, how skilless; symbols, after all, should be still and gentle as dewdrops, tiny, yet shining with a world of meaning. But what happens when, on the page of life itself, one encounters the ever-moving, all-engirdling sprawl of the filthy sea? Dewdrops and oceans both have their rightful places; Nariman Hansotia certainly knew that when he told his stories to the boys of Firozsha Baag.

The sea of Chaupatty was fated to endure the finales of life's everyday functions. It seemed that the dirtier it became, the more crowds it attracted: street urchins and beggars and beachcombers, looking through the junk that washed up. (Or was it the crowds that made it dirtier?—another instance of cause and effect blurring and evading identification.)

Too many religious festivals also used the sea as repository for their finales.

Its use should have been rationed, like rice and kerosene. On Ganesh Chaturthi, clay idols of the god Ganesh, adorned with garlands and all manner of finery, were carried in processions to the accompaniment of drums and a variety of wind instruments. The music got more frenzied the closer the procession got to Chaupatty and to the moment of immersion.

Then there was Coconut Day, which was never as popular as Ganesh Chaturthi. From a bystander's viewpoint, coconuts chucked into the sea do not provide as much of a spectacle. We used the sea, too, to deposit the leftovers from Parsi religious ceremonies, things such as flowers, or the ashes of the sacred sandalwood fire, which just could not be dumped with the regular garbage but had to be entrusted to the care of Avan Yazad, the guardian of the sea. And things which were of no use but which no one had the heart to destroy were also given to Avan Yazad. Such as old photographs.

After Grandpa died, some of his things were flung out to sea. It was high tide; we always checked the newspaper when going to perform these disposals; an ebb would mean a long walk in squelchy sand before finding water. Most of the things were probably washed up on shore. But we tried to throw them as far out as possible, then waited a few minutes; if they did not float back right away we would pretend they were in the permanent safekeeping of Avan Yazad, which was a comforting thought. I can't remember everything we sent out to sea, but his brush and comb were in the parcel, his *kusti,* and some Kemadrin pills, which he used to take to keep the parkinsonism under control.

Our paddling sessions stopped for lack of enthusiasm on my part. Mummy wasn't too keen either, because of the filth. But my main concern was the little guttersnipes, like naked fish with little buoyant penises, taunting me with their skills, swimming underwater and emerging unexpectedly all around me, or pretending to masturbate—I think they were too young to achieve ejaculation. It was embarrassing. When I look back, I'm surprised that Mummy and I kept going as long as we did.

I examine the swimming-trunks I bought last week. Surf King, says the label, Made in Canada–Fabriqué Au Canada. I've been learning bits and pieces of French from bilingual labels at the supermarket too. These trunks are extremely sleek and streamlined hipsters, the distance from waistband to pouch tip the barest minimum. I wonder how everything will stay in place, not that I'm boastful about my endowments. I try them on, and feel that the tip of my member lingers perilously close to the exit. Too close, in fact, to conceal the exigencies of my swimming lesson fantasy: a gorgeous woman in the class for non-swimmers, at whose sight I will be instantly aroused, and she, spying the shape of my desire, will look me straight in the eye with her intentions; she will come home with me, to taste the pleasures of my delectable Asian brown body whose strangeness has intrigued her and unleashed uncontrollable surges of passion inside her throughout the duration of the swimming lesson.

I drop the Eaton's bag and wrapper in the garbage can. The swimming-trunks cost fifteen dollars, same as the fee for the ten weekly lessons. The garbage bag is almost full. I tie it up and take it outside. There is a medicinal smell in the hallway; the old man must have just returned to his apartment.

PW opens her door and says, "Two ladies from the third floor were lying in the sun this morning. In bikinis."

"That's nice," I say, and walk to the incinerator chute. She reminds me of Najamai in Firozsha Baag, except that Najamai employed a bit more subtlety while going about her life's chosen work.

PW withdraws and shuts her door.

Mother had to reply because Father said he did not want to write to his son till his son had something sensible to write to him, his questions had been ignored long enough, and if he wanted to keep his life a secret, fine, he would get no letters from his father.

But after Mother started the letter he went and looked over her shoulder, telling her what to ask him, because if they kept on writing the same questions, maybe he would understand how interested they were in knowing about things over there; Father said go on, ask him what his work is at the insurance company, tell him to take some courses at night school, that's how everyone moves ahead over there, tell him not to be discouraged if his job is just clerical right now, hard work will get him ahead, remind him he is a Zoroastrian: manashni, gavashni, kunashni, better write the translation also: good thoughts, good words, good deeds—he must have forgotten what it means, and tell him to say prayers and do kusti at least twice a day.

Writing it all down sadly, Mother did not believe he wore his sudra and kusti anymore, she would be very surprised if he remembered any of the prayers; when she had asked him if he needed new sudras he said not to take any trouble because the Zoroastrian Society of Ontario imported them from Bombay for their members, and this sounded like a story he was making up, but she was leaving it in the hands of God, ten thousand miles away there was nothing she could do but write a letter and hope for the best.

Then she sealed it, and Father wrote the address on it as usual because his writing was much neater than hers, handwriting was important in the address and she did not want the postman in Canada to make any mistake; she took it to the post office herself, it was impossible to trust anyone to mail it ever since the postage rates went up because people just tore off the stamps for their own use and threw away the letter, the only safe way was to hand it over the counter and make the clerk cancel the stamps before your own eyes.

Berthe, the building superintendent, is yelling at her son in the parking lot. He tinkers away with his van. This happens every fine-weathered Sunday. It must be the van that Berthe dislikes because I've seen mother and son together in other quite amicable situations.

Berthe is a big Yugoslavian with high cheekbones. Her nationality was disclosed to me by PW. Berthe speaks a very rough-hewn English, I've overheard her in the lobby scolding tenants for late rents and leaving dirty lint screens in the dryers. It's exciting to listen to her, her words fall like rocks and boulders, and one can never tell where or how the next few will drop. But her Slavic yells at her son are a different matter, the words fly swift and true, well-aimed missiles that never miss. Finally, the son slams down the hood in disgust, wipes his hands on a rag, accompanies mother Berthe inside.

Berthe's husband has a job in a factory. But he loses several days of work every month when he succumbs to the booze, a word Berthe uses often in her Slavic tirades on those days, the only one I can understand, as it clunks down heavily out of the tight-flying formation of Yugoslavian sentences. He lolls around in the lobby, submitting passively to his wife's tongue-lashings. The bags under his bloodshot eyes, his stringy moustache, stubbled chin, dirty hair are so vulnerable to the poison-laden barbs (poison works the same way in any language) emanating from deep within the powerful watermelon bosom. No one's presence can embarrass or dignify her into silence.

No one except the old man who arrives now. "Good morning," he says, and Berthe turns, stops yelling, and smiles. Her husband rises, positions the wheelchair at the favourite angle. The lobby will be peaceful as long as the old man is there.

.

It was hopeless. My first swimming lesson. The water terrified me. When did that happen, I wonder, I used to love splashing at Chaupatty, carried about by the waves. And this was only a swimming pool. Where did all that terror come from? I'm trying to remember.

Armed with my Surf King I enter the high school and go to the pool area. A sheet with instructions for the new class is pinned to the bulletin board. All students must shower and then assemble at eight by the shallow end. As I enter the showers three young boys, probably from a previous class, emerge. One of them holds his nose. The second begins to hum, under his breath: Paki Paki, smell like curry. The third says to the first two: pretty soon all the water's going to taste of curry. They leave.

It's a mixed class, but the gorgeous woman of my fantasy is missing. I have to settle for another, in a pink one-piece suit, with brown hair and a bit of a stomach. She must be about thirty-five. Plain-looking.

The instructor is called Ron. He gives us a pep talk, sensing some nervousness in the group. We're finally all in the water, in the shallow end. He demonstrates floating on the back, then asks for a volunteer. The pink one-piece suit wades forward. He supports her, tells her to lean back and let her head drop in the water.

She does very well. And as we all regard her floating body, I see what was not visible outside the pool: her bush, curly bits of it, straying out at the pink Spandex V. Tongues of water lapping against her delta, as if caressing it teasingly, make the brown hair come alive in a most tantalizing manner. The crests and troughs of little waves, set off by the movement of our bodies in a circle around her, dutifully irrigate her; the curls alternately wave free inside the crest, then adhere to her wet thighs, beached by the inevitable trough. I could watch this forever, and I wish the floating demonstration would never end.

Next we are shown how to grasp the rail and paddle, face down in the water. Between practising floating and paddling, the hour is almost gone. I have been trying to observe the pink one-piece suit, getting glimpses of her straying pubic hair from various angles. Finally, Ron wants a volunteer for the last demonstration, and I go forward. To my horror he leads the class to the deep end. Fifteen feet of water. It is so blue, and I can see the bottom. He picks up a metal hoop attached to a long wooden stick. He wants me to grasp the hoop, jump in the water, and paddle, while he guides me by the stick. Perfectly safe, he tells me. A demonstration of how paddling propels the body.

It's too late to back out; besides, I'm so terrified I couldn't find the words to do so even if I wanted to. Everything he says I do as if in a trance. I don't remember the moment of jumping. The next thing I know is, I'm swallowing water and floundering, hanging on to the hoop for dear life. Ron draws me to the rails and helps me out. The class applauds.

We disperse and one thought is on my mind: what if I'd lost my grip? Fifteen feet of water under me. I shudder and take deep breaths. This is it. I'm not coming next week. This instructor is an irresponsible person. Or he does not value the lives of non-white immigrants. I remember the three teenagers. Maybe the swimming pool is the hangout of some racist group, bent on eliminating all non-white swimmers, to keep their waters pure and their white sisters unogled.

The elevator takes me upstairs. Then gutang-khutang. PW opens her door as I turn the corridor of medicinal smells. "Berthe was screaming loudly at her husband tonight," she tells me.

"Good for her," I say, and she frowns indignantly at me.

.

The old man is in the lobby. He's wearing thick wool gloves. He wants to know how the swimming was, must have seen me leaving with my towel yesterday. Not bad, I say.

"I used to swim a lot. Very good for the circulation." He wheezes. "My feet are cold all the time. Cold as ice. Hands too."

Summer is winding down, so I say stupidly, "Yes, it's not so warm any more."

The thought of the next swimming lesson sickens me. But as I comb through the memories of that terrifying Monday, I come upon the straying curls of brown pubic hair. Inexorably drawn by them, I decide to go.

It's a mistake, of course. This time I'm scared even to venture in the shallow end. When everyone has entered the water and I'm the only one outside, I feel a little foolish and slide in.

Instructor Ron says we should start by reviewing the floating technique. I'm in no hurry. I watch the pink one-piece pull the swim-suit down around her cheeks and flip back to achieve perfect flotation. And then reap disappointment. The pink Spandex triangle is perfectly streamlined today, nothing strays, not a trace of fuzz, not one filament, not even a sign of post-depilation irritation. Like the airbrushed parts of glamour magazine models. The barrenness of her impeccably packaged apex is a betrayal. Now she is shorn like the other women in the class. Why did she have to do it?

The weight of this disappointment makes the water less manageable, more lung-penetrating. With trepidation, I float and paddle my way through the remainder of the hour, jerking my head out every two seconds and breathing deeply, to continually shore up a supply of precious, precious air without, at the same time, seeming too anxious and losing my dignity.

I don't attend the remaining classes. After I've missed three, Ron the instructor telephones. I tell him I've had the flu and am still feeling poorly, but I'll try to be there the following week.

He does not call again. My Surf King is relegated to an unused drawer. Total losses: one fantasy plus thirty dollars. And no watery rebirth. The swimming pool, like Chaupatty beach, has produced a stillbirth. But there is a difference. Water means regeneration only if it is pure and cleansing. Chaupatty was filthy, the pool was not. Failure to swim through filth must mean something other than failure of rebirth—failure of symbolic death? Does that equal success of symbolic life? death of a symbolic failure? death of a symbol? What is the equation?

The postman did not bring a letter but a parcel, he was smiling because he knew that every time something came from Canada his baksheesh was guaranteed, and this time because it was a parcel Mother gave him a whole rupee, she was quite excited, there were so many stickers on it besides the stamps, one for Small Parcel, another Printed Papers, a red sticker saying In-

sured; she showed it to Father, and opened it, then put both hands on her cheeks, not able to speak because the surprise and happiness was so great, tears came to her eyes and she could not stop smiling, till Father became impatient to know and finally got up and came to the table.

When he saw it he was surprised and happy too, he began to grin, then hugged Mother saying our son is a writer, and we didn't even know it, he never told us a thing, here we are thinking he is still clerking away at the insurance company, and he has written a book of stories, all these years in school and college he kept his talent hidden, making us think he was just like one of the boys in the Baag, shouting and playing the fool in the compound, and now what a surprise; then Father opened the book and began reading it, heading back to the easy chair, and Mother so excited, still holding his arm, walked with him, saying it was not fair him reading it first, she wanted to read it too, and they agreed that he would read the first story, then give it to her so she could also read it, and they would take turns in that manner.

Mother removed the staples from the padded envelope in which he had mailed the book, and threw them away, then straightened the folded edges of the envelope and put it away safely with the other envelopes and letters she had collected since he left.

The leaves are beginning to fall. The only ones I can identify are maple. The days are dwindling like the leaves. I've started a habit of taking long walks every evening. The old man is in the lobby when I leave, he waves as I go by. By the time I'm back, the lobby is usually empty.

Today I was woken up by a grating sound outside that made my flesh crawl. I went to the window and saw Berthe raking the leaves in the parking lot. Not in the expanse of patchy lawn on the periphery, but in the parking lot proper. She was raking the black tarred surface. I went back to bed and dragged a pillow over my head, not releasing it till noon.

When I return from my walk in the evening, PW, summoned by the elevator's gutang-khutang, says, "Berthe filled six big black garbage bags with leaves today."

"Six bags!" I say. "Wow!"

.

Since the weather turned cold, Berthe's son does not tinker with his van on Sundays under my window. I'm able to sleep late.

Around eleven, there's a commotion outside. I reach out and switch on the clock radio. It's a sunny day, the window curtains are bright. I get up, curious, and see a black Olds Ninety-Eight in the parking lot, by the entrance to the building. The old man is in his wheelchair, bundled up, with a scarf wound several times round his neck as though to immobilize it, like a surgical collar. His daughter and another man, the car-owner, are helping him from the wheelchair into the front seat, encouraging him with words like: that's it, easy does it, attaboy. From the open door of the lobby, Berthe is shouting encouragement too, but hers is confined to one word: yah, repeated at different levels of pitch and volume, with variations on vowel-length. The stranger could be the old man's son, he has the same jet black hair and piercing eyes.

Maybe the old man is not well, it's an emergency. But I quickly scrap that thought—this isn't Bombay, an ambulance would have arrived. They're probably taking him out for a ride. If he is his son, where has he been all this time, I wonder.

The old man finally settles in the front seat, the wheelchair goes in the trunk, and they're off. The one I think is the son looks up and catches me at the window before I can move away, so I wave, and he waves back.

In the afternoon I take down a load of clothes to the laundry room. Both machines have completed their cycles, the clothes inside are waiting to be transferred to dryers. Should I remove them and place them on top of a dryer, or wait? I decide to wait. After a few minutes, two women arrive, they are in bathrobes, and smoking. It takes me a while to realize that these are the two disappointments who were sunbathing in bikinis last summer.

"You didn't have to wait, you could have removed the clothes and carried on, dear," says one. She has a Scottish accent. It's one of the few I've learned to identify. Like maple leaves.

"Well," I say, "some people might not like strangers touching their clothes."

"You're not a stranger, dear," she says, "you live in this building, we've seen you before."

"Besides, your hands are clean," the other one pipes in. "You can touch my things any time you like."

Horny old cow. I wonder what they've got on under their bathrobes. Not much, I find, as they bend over to place their clothes in the dryers.

"See you soon," they say, and exit, leaving me behind in an erotic wake of smoke and perfume and deep images of cleavages. I start the washers and depart, and when I come back later, the dryers are empty.

PW tells me, "The old man's son took him out for a drive today. He has a big beautiful black car."

I see my chance, and shoot back: "Olds Ninety-Eight."

"What?"

"The car," I explain, "it's an Oldsmobile Ninety-Eight."

She does not like this at all, my giving her information. She is visibly nettled, and retreats with a sour face.

Mother and Father read the first five stories, and she was very sad after read-ing some of them, she said he must be so unhappy there, all his stories are about Bombay, he remembers every little thing about his childhood, he is thinking about it all the time even though he is ten thousand miles away, my poor son, I think he misses his home and us and everything he left behind, because if he likes it over there why would he not write stories about that, there must be so many new ideas that his new life could give him.

But Father did not agree with this, he said it did not mean that he was unhappy, all writers worked in the same way, they used their memories and experiences and made stories out of them, changing some things, adding some, imagining some, all writers were very good at remembering details of their lives.

Mother said, how can you be sure that he is remembering because he is a writer, or whether he started to write because he is unhappy and thinks of his past, and wants to save it all by making stories of it; and Father said that is not a sensible question, anyway, it is now my turn to read the next story.

The first snow has fallen, and the air is crisp. It's not very deep, about two inches, just right to go for a walk in. I've been told that immigrants from hot countries always enjoy the snow the first year, maybe for a couple of years more, then inevitably the dread sets in, and the approach of winter gets them fretting and moping. On the other hand, if it hadn't been for my conversation with the woman at the swimming registration desk, they might now be saying that India is a nation of non-swimmers.

Berthe is outside, shovelling the snow off the walkway in the parking lot. She has a heavy, wide pusher which she wields expertly.

The old radiators in the apartment alarm me incessantly. They continue to broadcast a series of variations on death throes, and go from hot to cold and cold to hot at will, there's no controlling their temperature. I speak to Berthe about it in the lobby. The old man is there too, his chin seems to have sunk deeper into his chest, and his face is a yellowish grey.

"Nothing, not to worry about anything," says Berthe, dropping rough-hewn chunks of language around me. "Radiator no work, you tell me. You feel cold, you come to me, I keep you warm," and she opens her arms wide, laughing. I step back, and she advances, her breasts preceding her like the gallant prows of two ice-breakers. She looks at the old man to see if he is appreciating the act: "You no feel scared, I keep you safe and warm."

But the old man is staring outside, at the flakes of falling snow. What thoughts is he thinking as he watches them? Of childhood days, perhaps, and snowmen with hats and pipes, and snowball fights, and white Christmases, and

Christmas trees? What will I think of, old in this country, when I sit and watch the snow come down? For me, it is already too late for snowmen and snowball fights, and all I will have is thoughts about childhood thoughts and dreams, built around snowscapes and winter-wonderlands on the Christmas cards so popular in Bombay; my snowmen and snowball fights and Christmas trees are in the pages of Enid Blyton's books, dispersed amidst the adventures of the Famous Five, and the Five Find-Outers, and the Secret Seven. My snowflakes are even less forgettable than the old man's, for they never melt.

·

It finally happened. The heat went. Not the usual intermittent coming and going, but out completely. Stone cold. The radiators are like ice. And so is everything else. There's no hot water. Naturally. It's the hot water that goes through the rads and heats them. Or is it the other way around? Is there no hot water because the rads have stopped circulating it? I don't care, I'm too cold to sort out the cause and effect relationship. Maybe there is no connection at all.

I dress quickly, put on my winter jacket, and go down to the lobby. The elevator is not working because the power is out, so I take the stairs. Several people are gathered, and Berthe has announced that she has telephoned the office, they are sending a man. I go back up the stairs. It's only one floor, the elevator is just a bad habit. Back in Firozsha Baag they were broken most of the time. The stairway enters the corridor outside the old man's apartment, and I think of his cold feet and hands. Poor man, it must be horrible for him without heat.

As I walk down the long hallway, I feel there's something different but can't pin it down. I look at the carpet, the ceiling, the wallpaper: it all seems the same. Maybe it's the freezing cold that imparts a feeling of difference.

PW opens her door: "The old man had another stroke yesterday. They took him to the hospital."

The medicinal smell. That's it. It's not in the hallway any more.

In the stories that he'd read so far Father said that all the Parsi families were poor or middle-class, but that was okay; nor did he mind that the seeds for the stories were picked from the sufferings of their own lives; but there should also have been something positive about Parsis, there was so much to be proud of: the great Tatas and their contribution to the steel industry, or Sir Dinshaw Petit in the textile industry who made Bombay the Manchester of the East, or Dadabhai Naoroji in the freedom movement, where he was the first to use the word swaraj, *and the first to be elected to the British Parliament where he carried on his campaign; he should have found some way to bring some of these wonderful facts into his stories, what would people reading these stories think, those who did not know about Parsis—that the whole community was full of* cranky, bigoted people; and in reality it was the richest, most advanced and philanthropic community in India, and he did not need to tell his own son that Parsis had a reputation for being generous and family-oriented. And he could have written something also about the historic background, how Parsis came to India from Persia because of Islamic persecution in the seventh century, and were the descendants of Cyrus the Great and the magnificent Persian Empire. He could have made a story of all this, couldn't he?

Mother said what she liked best was his remembering everything so well, how beautifully he wrote about it all, even the sad things, and though he changed some of it, and used his imagination, there was truth in it.

My hope is, Father said, that there will be some story based on his Canadian experience, that way we will know something about our son's life there, if not through his letters then in his stories; so far they are all about Parsis and Bombay, and the one with a little bit about Toronto, where a man perches on top of the toilet, is shameful and disgusting, although it is funny at times and did make me laugh, I have to admit, but where does he get such an imagination from, what is the point of such a fantasy; and Mother said that she would also enjoy some stories about Toronto and the people there; it puzzles me, she said, why he writes nothing about it, especially since you say that writers use their own experience to make stories out of.

Then Father said this is true, but he is probably not using his Toronto experience because it is too early; what do you mean, too early, asked Mother and Father explained it takes a writer about ten years time after an experience before he is able to use it in his writing, it takes that long to be absorbed internally and understood, thought out and thought about, over and over again, he haunts it and it haunts him if it is valuable enough, till the writer is comfortable with it to be able to use it as he wants; but this is only one theory I read somewhere, it may or may not be true.

That means, said Mother, that his childhood in Bombay and our home here is the most valuable thing in his life just now, because he is able to remember it all to write about it, and you were so bitterly saying he is forgetting where he came from; and that may be true, said Father, but that is not what the theory means, according to the theory he is writing of these things because they are far enough in the past for him to deal with objectively, he is able to achieve what critics call artistic distance, without emotions interfering; and what do you mean emotions, said Mother, you are saying he does not feel anything for his characters, how can he write so beautifully about so many sad things without any feelings in his heart?

But before Father could explain more, about beauty and emotion and inspiration and imagination, Mother took the book and said it was her turn now and too much theory she did not want to listen to, it was confusing and

did not make as much sense as reading the stories, she would read them her
way and Father could read them his.

My books on the windowsill have been damaged. Ice has been forming on the
inside ledge, which I did not notice, and melting when the sun shines in. I
spread them in a corner of the living-room to dry out.

The winter drags on. Berthe wields her snow pusher as expertly as ever, but
there are signs of weariness in her performance. Neither husband nor son is ever seen outside with a shovel. Or anywhere else, for that matter. It occurs to me
that the son's van is missing, too.

The medicinal smell is in the hall again, I sniff happily and look forward to
seeing the old man in the lobby. I go downstairs and peer into the mailbox, see
the blue and magenta of an Indian aerogramme with Don Mills, Ontario, Canada in Father's flawless hand through the slot.

I pocket the letter and enter the main lobby. The old man is there, but not
in his usual place. He is not looking out through the glass door. His wheelchair
is facing a bare wall where the wallpaper is torn in places. As though he is not
interested in the outside world any more, having finished with all that, and now
it's time to see inside. What does he see inside, I wonder? I go up to him and say
hullo. He says hullo without raising his sunken chin. After a few seconds his
grey countenance faces me. "How old do you think I am?" His eyes are dull
and glazed; he is looking even further inside than I first presumed.

"Well, let's see, you're probably close to sixty-four."

"I'll be seventy-eight next August." But he does not chuckle or wheeze. Instead, he continues softly, "I wish my feet did not feel so cold all the time. And
my hands." He lets his chin fall again.

In the elevator I start opening the aerogramme, a tricky business because a
crooked tear means lost words. Absorbed in this while emerging, I don't notice
PW occupying the centre of the hallway, arms folded across her chest: "They
had a big fight. Both of them have left."

I don't immediately understand her agitation. "What . . . who?"

"Berthe. Husband and son both left her. Now she is all alone."

Her tone and stance suggest that we should not be standing here talking but
do something to bring Berthe's family back. "That's very sad," I say, and go in. I
picture father and son in the van, driving away, driving across the snow-covered
country, in the dead of winter, away from wife and mother; away to where? how
far will they go? Not son's van nor father's booze can take them far enough. And
the further they go, the more they'll remember, they can take it from me.

All the stories were read by Father and Mother, and they were sorry when the
book was finished, they felt they had come to know their son better now, yet

there was much more to know, they wished there were many more stories; and this is what they mean, said Father, when they say that the whole story can never be told, the whole truth can never be known; what do you mean, they say, asked Mother, who they, and Father said writers, poets, philosophers. I don't care what they say, said Mother, my son will write as much or as little as he wants to, and if I can read it I will be happy.

The last story they liked the best of all because it had the most in it about Canada, and now they felt they knew at least a little bit, even if it was a very little bit, about his day-to-day life in his apartment; and Father said if he continues to write about such things he will become popular because I am sure they are interested there in reading about life through the eyes of an immigrant, it provides a different viewpoint; the only danger is if he changes and becomes so much like them that he will write like one of them and lose the important difference.

The bathroom needs cleaning. I open a new can of Ajax and scour the tub. Sloshing with mug from bucket was standard bathing procedure in the bathrooms of Firozsha Baag, so my preference now is always for a shower. I've never used the tub as yet; besides, it would be too much like Chaupatty or the swimming pool, wallowing in my own dirt. Still, it must be cleaned.

When I've finished, I prepare for a shower. But the clean gleaming tub and the nearness of the vernal equinox give me the urge to do something different today. I find the drain plug in the bathroom cabinet, and run the bath.

I've spoken so often to the old man, but I don't know his name. I should have asked him the last time I saw him, when his wheelchair was facing the bare wall because he had seen all there was to see outside and it was time to see what was inside. Well, tomorrow. Or better yet, I can look it up in the directory in the lobby. Why didn't I think of that before? It will only have an initial and a last name, but then I can surprise him with: hullo Mr. Wilson, or whatever it is.

The bath is full. Water imagery is recurring in my life: Chaupatty beach, swimming pool, bathtub. I step in and immerse myself up to the neck. It feels good. The hot water loses its opacity when the chlorine, or whatever it is, has cleared. My hair is still dry. I close my eyes, hold my breath, and dunk my head. Fighting the panic, I stay under and count to thirty. I come out, clear my lungs and breathe deeply.

I do it again. This time I open my eyes under water, and stare blindly without seeing, it takes all my will to keep the lids from closing. Then I am slowly able to discern the underwater objects. The drain plug looks different, slightly distorted; there is a hair trapped between the hole and the plug, it waves and dances with the movement of the water. I come up, refresh my lungs, examine quickly the overwater world of the washroom, and go in again. I do it several times, over and over. The world outside the water I have seen a lot of, it is now time to see what is inside.

The spring session for adult non-swimmers will begin in a few days at the high school. I must not forget the registration date.

.

The dwindled days of winter are now all but forgotten; they have grown and attained a respectable span. I resume my evening walks, it's spring, and a vigorous thaw is on. The snowbanks are melting, the sound of water on its gushing, gurgling journey to the drains is beautiful. I plan to buy a book of trees, so I can identify more than the maple as they begin to bloom.

When I return to the building, I wipe my feet energetically on the mat because some people are entering behind me, and I want to set a good example. Then I go to the board with its little plastic letters and numbers. The old man's apartment is the one on the corner by the stairway, that makes it number 201. I run down the list, come to 201, but there are no little white plastic letters beside it. Just the empty black rectangle with holes where the letters would be squeezed in. That's strange. Well, I can introduce myself to him, then ask his name.

However, the lobby is empty. I take the elevator, exit at the second floor, wait for the gutang-khutang. It does not come: the door closes noiselessly, smoothly. Berthe has been at work, or has made sure someone else has. PW's cue has been lubricated out of existence.

But she must have the ears of a cockroach. She is waiting for me. I whistle my way down the corridor. She fixes me with an accusing look. She waits till I stop whistling, then says: "You know the old man died last night."

I cease groping for my key. She turns to go and I take a step towards her, my hand still in my trouser pocket. "Did you know his name?" I ask, but she leaves without answering.

Then Mother said, the part I like best in the last story is about Grandpa, where he wonders if Grandpa's spirit is really watching him and blessing him, because you know I really told him that, I told him helping an old suffering person who is near death is the most blessed thing to do, because that person will ever after watch over you from heaven, I told him this when he was disgusted with Grandpa's urine-bottle and would not touch it, would not hand it to him even when I was not at home.

Are you sure, said Father, that you really told him this, or you believe you told him because you like the sound of it, you said yourself the other day that he changes and adds and alters things in the stories but he writes it all so beautifully that it seems true, so how can you be sure; this sounds like an-

other theory, said Mother, but I don't care, he says I told him and I believe now I told him, so even if I did not tell him then it does not matter now.

Don't you see, said Father, that you are confusing fiction with facts, fiction does not create facts, fiction can come from facts, it can grow out of facts by compounding, transposing, augmenting, diminishing, or altering them in any way; but you must not confuse cause and effect, you must not confuse what really happened with what the story says happened, you must not loose your grasp on reality, that way madness lies.

Then Mother stopped listening because, as she told Father so often, she was not very fond of theories, and she took out her writing pad and started a letter to her son; Father looked over her shoulder, telling her to say how proud they were of him and were waiting for his next book, he also said, leave a little space for me at the end, I want to write a few lines when I put the address on the envelope.

R. Bruce Moody

Water

*T*he brilliant stones on which the boy stood burned his feet, giving the rest of his body its cue for excitement. Piling out of the rear seat of the family two-door sedan with his brother, he could barely wait to breathe the air of this new clime, the beach. Now he stood stock-still, his fists clenched, and looked out across the parking lot, hot as a desert, filled with the untouchable, shieldlike flanks of cars. Heat glimmered on their metal tops and sliced through the air toward him from their windows. His white hair blustered about in the hot breeze, and his face squinted into a smile because the air tickled his lungs and because the stones tickled his feet, and because of the light. He closed his eyes, then opened them. Finally, he was here. The long preparations of the morning—the finding of toys, rolling of towels, making of sandwiches, packing of bags—and the long trip from home had finally borne fruit. He had looked forward to coming for the last six days—ever since, in fact, he had been here a week ago. His parents took him often to this beach. He had come here since he was tiny. It was a perfectly ordinary beach, with calm water, but it seemed to him, even though he was now already seven and had been here many, many times, that a trip to the beach was a great holiday that came only once in a great while. He looked forward to each trip with delight, relished the trip almost consciously, savored it without discrimination and to the full, even though ever since he was a tiny child he had feared and hated water.

But now he didn't think of that. The air cooked him. The odor of the sea, the bright sand, the heat that clapped his shoulders filled him with the sure sense of significant arrival, the return to the formalities of pleasures that were well known to him and of which he would never tire. His eyes closed. His feet crinkled in the stones. His anticipation, the anticipation in his flesh, of coming here, back to the beach, was so extreme, so joyous, that he could stand idle, rapt in a calm ecstasy of suspense that was selfish and was all he cared for, thought of, wanted, or possessed, and to which that blazing blue sky, those scalding white stones, and the water were as mirrors.

"Get a move on," his mother would say. "Give your father a hand," she would say, and shove the boy along by the back of the neck, propelling him to the tall, hot trunk of the car.

The boy's father would give his older, more well-behaved, and competent brother, who at the age of eight and a half could "be relied upon," beach bags to carry, but the boy was permitted to carry only the two patched inner tubes they used for floating. The rubber tubes were black-smelling and good, and he cuddled his cheek on them and closed his eyes because they were so cool and yielding.

"Stop dawdling," his mother said.

He turned toward the sea. There it gleamed—out of sight, almost, of his narrowed, happy eyes. It seemed miles away. Miles to get there. He hopped from one foot to the other on the hot stones, thinking of the shivering coolness of it on his feet. The arc of his soul, fixed in delight, sped him through the blue heavens from the hot stones to the touch of the chilly sea. No fear, but only joy, was in him as he began to run toward the water.

"Hold on, me hearty!" his mother said. "Where do you think you're going?"

He stopped, saying nothing, for he had to wait until all the formalities were gone through. The car doors must be locked, the windows turned down a fraction from the top, the impedimenta hauled up and carried over the crippling pebbles, the road between the beach and the parking crossed, the concessionaires' shacks beside it bypassed, the lees of the strand traversed, with its trash, parchmenty paper, bottles, bags, and beer tins. A place had to be found, smoothed down, and settled in. The blanket had to be spread, the umbrella erected, the beach bags deployed, the back rests arranged. But the boy's concerns were elsewhere. Who would there be on the beach, he thought. Would they find a good place to settle? Would the sun stay out? Would the tide be in? Would the water be clean, or cold? Would they stay until six? All these questions were asked and answered one by one, each in turn, with delight, with joy, and without thought, by this boy who had come here with a mortal fear of water. Finally, he pulled off his shorts, tossed off his shirt, and made for the water like mad.

"Hang them up!" his mother would say.

"But the umbrella isn't up yet!"

"Then you'll have to wait for it, won't you?"

He would wait and, when it was up, whip his shorts and shirt over the stays, and turn, this time with his brother, and race toward the shore.

He would fly to the water faster than his feet could carry him. Over the sharp shells and stones he would dance. His brother would be just rushing in ahead of him, splashing up the sunny green and silver water fantastically and then hurling himself under. At eight and a half, his brother was already a prodigious swimmer. The boy himself could not rush in that way. After running wildly toward the water, he would stop and approach it carefully and respectfully, now that nothing stood between it and himself. Where the smooth sand ended and the shelly, stony foreshore began, he would prance on the sides of his feet, jump over the braid of seaweed—a residence of flies—and mince awkwardly over the second shelly rim to where the sand was smooth and wet as it approached the water. This he padded onto comfortably, squeezing it dry where his footprints fell, until he reached the thin strand of live green seaweed floating just at the water's edge. Over this he would step to stand ankle-deep in the water. Cool, sweet, pure, the babylike waves rolled over his feet, soothing them after the sharp, minute bruises of the shells.

The water. Even now that it was finally upon him, he felt no fear and thought of nothing but what lay immediately before his eyes. He would walk into the water up to his calves. He would stand still then and look down at it. He would walk into it up to his knees and look down at it again. He would look at it and through it to see his feet. He would bend over and wipe off the sand that had shifted over his toes under the water. Beneath the water there, they looked like somebody else's toes. He would lower his rear end into the water. It was shockingly cold just then. He would put his head so close to the water that his brow lay on it and peek at his feet, half buried in the sand. Then he would reach down under the water and gather pebbles and stones from the bottom, and these he would allow to sift between his fingers onto his ankles and instep. He would watch with careful relish as they dropped down under the water to fall once more to the bottom with a curious unearthly motion, tickling his feet as they went.

Then he would become frolicsome, even familiar, with the water—touch it, splash it, pat it, treat it roughly. He would splash little splashes, putting his head close to the water and looking sidewise to see the splash shine in the sun. Once done with that, he might, bored and happy, simply stare out ahead of him, not thinking of anything at all.

·

The boy loved the water. He loved it and he hated it. He loved it for much longer than he hated it, but he hated it more intensely than he loved it. He loved it for hours and days. He hated it for half an hour only—the time, always after lunch, when he was made to learn how to swim.

He loved the crisp little waves that expired and expired so unremittingly and tirelessly on the sand. Even at their least, their power was greater than he had expected, they carried farther than he ever thought they could. He had always missed the sea. Even before he had known it he had missed it. He had always been surprised by the sea. It was a spectacle that never faded, never palled on him, because it never repeated itself in quite the same way twice. The sea was strong and showed its strength.

He had thought of death in his bed and knew exactly what it was. His fear of water was part of his knowledge of death, a knowledge he had only when he was young, and which would leave him in time, and although he found the water beautiful, glittering, enticing, he knew something about it—that he could never stand in contention with it. A drop could kill him. Death was moist.

His mother had never learned how to swim. Now she felt that it would not be seemly for her to learn. It was his father who would try to teach him, as he had taught his older brother two summers before. But all this was after lunch. All morning long, he had no thought of it. He would play in the shallow water with a preoccupation into which no fear entered. Then, after lunch and after he and his brother had lain down for an hour, their heads covered by towels, his mother would say, "Time for your swimming lesson." He would wake up from his nap with a start, blinking.

The cloudless skies that until now had given of their blue as an absolutely free gift turned black, as though someone had punched them. The water, too, turned black. He knew before he began that he would not succeed.

His father took his hand in his, and he toddled off next to him down to the water's edge. He ran to keep up with his long stride, but actually he wished to withdraw his hand and himself from his father entirely and vanish in the opposite direction down the beach. His father's hand felt horrible and dangerous, and he wanted to let go of it. To himself he gave the excuse that he wanted to step over the sharp shells at his own pace, but he knew his father might not believe this, for his father, as he knew, was very sensitive to insult by his children. So he did not take his hand away.

As they walked down to the water, he and his father would try to talk together. At these times, and at all other times, he would talk to his father unfamiliarly, as though to a very important stranger. He either tried to be quite natural, which was artificial, or else he tried to be boldly confident, which was also artificial. To neither of these attempts at sociability did his father make any response at all, for his father was even more shy than he himself was. For the boy, however, this silence was part of his father's greatness. For his father was very great indeed—too great, in fact. Walking beside him, the boy was blinded by fear of the coming lesson; the blackness of it was blinding—its endlessness, and its inevitable failure. But what paralyzed him most was the greatness of his father, and when he took his father's hand to be led to the water, he did so with an agony that could not resist that greatness at all. He pretended it was fun, but he knew that his father was too superior a being for him to learn anything from. His stomach churned with the knowledge that he would make a fool of himself before him, appear cowardly, inferior, dull, stupid, and inept.

"First, we'll get wet," his father said, and picked him up high above the beached seaweed, walked with him out into the waves, and lowered him into the shallow icy water.

To forestall a second step, the boy sat down in the water with a sudden plop, laughed in a manner completely unnatural, and looked at his father for approval. The water was painfully cold on his middle at first, and he hoped that his laughter would put his father off the task. He hunched up his shoulders and watched to see what his father would do.

Leaving him, his father waded out into the water with long, sweeping paces, his arms making oaring motions as though they were pushing him forward. When he had got into deep water, he leaned over, pushed forward, and dived under. For a minute, he vanished entirely from view. The boy waited and watched, unable to calculate where his father would appear again. Finally, his father emerged at what seemed a great distance from where he had disappeared and swam a few strokes out to sea. Then he stopped and turned and swam back. Where the water became too shallow to swim, he pulled himself along by the bottom with his hands until he came up face to face with him, his hair dripping down on his brow.

His father's face, so different from his own, was now on a level with his. Its textures, planes, and contours were alien and older and coarser and darker. The boy felt like reaching out and patting it with his hands, but he did not do so. Instead, he dug his hands into the stones, pebbles, and sand under the water in which he sat.

"What do you want to try first?" his father asked.

"I don't know," he said.

"Breathing?"

"Not breathing." He began kicking the water with his feet.

Breathing he disliked very much. In breathing he was obliged to lean over the water and put his face into it and blow bubbles. In addition to this, he was obliged to keep his eyes open. In addition to this, he was obliged to turn his face from side to side to get more air to blow bubbles with. As it was not possible for him to do any one of these things one at a time, to do all of them at once was—was the reason a cold shudder followed his words "Not breathing," and why he began to kick the water abstractedly.

"What, then?" his father said.

He did not answer, placing all his concentration on his feet.

"Kicking?"

He did not answer.

"You have to begin somewhere."

He continued to stare at his feet.

"Upsy-daisy," his father said and seized him and lifted him into the air in his arms again. They began to walk out into the water. He clutched his father tight, wrapping his legs around his chest and flinging his arms around his neck. The deeper they went, the tighter he clung, and he did not look at his father but turned his head in the direction they were going. Slowly and steadily the water came up, lapping over his legs, his hips, his stomach like a sort of unusual clothing in which both he and his father were wrapped and intimate.

"Oooooh," he said.

"Not so tight," his father said.

He looked straight out to sea. He did not lessen his grip.

"Not so tight."

"It's deep," he said.

"Let go," his father said.

"I'm scared."

"I won't let you go," his father said.

But he didn't hear anything. The water was all around him now, and he knew that his father's body was his only support, so he held on even tighter, looking wild-eyed at the water.

"Let go!" his father said.

He looked down. His father's feet touched bottom, but he knew they did not provide any real support at this depth. He hugged his father's neck even tighter.

His father turned his head from side to side to loosen his grip. "If you don't let go, I'm going to be very angry," his father said.

As his father already was very angry, he did not pay any attention to this and he did not let go.

"Do you think I'm going to let you drown? Do you think I brought you all the way out here to drown you?"

Because this was exactly what he thought, and he realized the ignobility of so thinking, he did not answer but only looked at the water with his round eyes and shuddering mouth opened wide.

"Relax!"

"I want to go back."

"Look at me!" His father shook him gently, so that his head bobbed around, and he looked at his father's face timidly and bewilderedly. He looked, but he did not see. A wave splashed against his face, and he shook his head wildly to free his eyes of the water that shrouded them.

"Relax. The whole secret is to relax. Nothing will happen."

His heart beat like a bat in a bottle.

"Don't be scared," his father said.

"I'm cold," he whined.

"Then we'd better start treading water," his father said. "That's what we came out here to do in the first place."

His heart stood still.

"Don't worry, I'll hold you," his father said, holding him out at arm's length in the water.

He stared at his father. He hoped that his father would. He knew the water would not support him at all. The water would only drag him down. All his concentration was placed upon the two arms that connected him to safety. He was petrified lest they leave him, and his legs made frantic, futile running motions in the water to try to get him back to the safety of his father's body, which lay at the end of those arms.

"That's the way," his father said.

But he knew that it wasn't the way, and so did his father. Everything was wrong. The water tickled the back of his neck unbearably and gave him goosepimples. He threw his head back to be free of it. He wanted to scream.

"Breathe through your nose."

He did not do this. He breathed any which way he could. He breathed until he gagged.

"Rest."

He went on kicking. He looked wildly at the sky, his head turning from side to side. He made a little pleading sound.

"Rest, I said."

The water was burning him, licking him like flames. He gasped for air with every drop that touched his face, staring at without seeing the blue sky, which looked down blankly upon him.

"Rest! Rest!" his father said, and stopped him by taking him back into his arms.

"Is it over?" he said.

"Over?" his father said.

He giggled.

"Don't you want to learn how to swim?"

His lip pouted.

"Well, don't you?"

He lowered his eyes. He looked at the nape of his father's neck. He wanted to put his own head there. "Yes," he said. The only way not to cry was to lie.

"Don't you want to swim like the other boys?"

"Yes." He lied again, but this time much less surely, with the only answer he knew to stave off his father's exasperation.

"You're a frog, then," his father said, and held him once again at arm's length out into the water.

"Now watch. This is how frogs do," his father said, and demonstrated how frogs do, kicking his legs under the water. "One, two. One, two. See?"

But he did not see. He could not do it at all, and when he tried, the only thing he could think of was the water itching his back and the sensation of fishes sliding around his ankles and calves. He could feel them bump him, he was sure. He thought of eels and sharks. They seemed to beat against his ankles. Only the water was slicker, slimier, and more sinister than their touch, and all he could think of was that in another moment he would drown in it and die.

"One, two. One, two."

He looked past his father's shoulder into the blue sky above the horizon. A little grunting noise came out of his mouth at each useless thrust of his legs.

"You're not getting it," his father said, and stopped.

His father then drew him into his arms and, holding him with one arm, reached down and manipulated his legs under the water, one by one, like the legs of a paralytic. "One. Two. One. Two," his father said. This demonstration proved too difficult, however, and when his father looked up he saw that he was following it with a fixed concentration that resisted it like stone.

"O.K., we'll stop," his father said.

With this, he came to life, and as though the failure of this portion of the lesson indicated the failure of the lesson as a whole, and as though in response to an invitation that had certainly not been given, he leaped out of the water, skeltered up his father's arms onto his shoulders, wrapped his hands around his brow and his legs around his neck, and hugged his father's head to his chest with his hands over his father's eyes like a dripping-wet, piggyback monkey.

Beneath him, his father sighed.

He stopped hugging and sat up, and his father started moving toward the shore. He let go of his father's brow, feeling it was impertinent to touch him. It was awful. His father's disgust with him was wordless, yet he didn't really care. Being free was worth his father's disappointment with him if it meant that the swimming lesson actually was over. He did not ask his father if this was true, however, for fear he might be given the answer.

Instead, he marched on his father's shoulders toward the shore like a victor. Half of his body was already dry from the sun, and as he rose higher and higher

above the water there came into his eyes a look of incredulous hope for a possibility he did not really dare to entertain—that the lesson actually, finally, and
perhaps forever was over. Slowly, the water swished around them and receded,
and, his relief and excitement increasing with the water's decrease, he looked
with rapt attention toward the shore. The possibility that the lesson was at an
end—this possibility, cancelling out his father's anger with him and completely
outweighing it, this unvoiced longing—grew in his head like a crown, an invisible reward given to him who hadn't deserved it at all. This fantastic dream bur-
geoned into a roselike reality within him, and he breathed more and more
deeply with every step they took. No more swimming. Every step made it more
and more likely.

"I'll teach you the Australian crawl," his father said.

He did not answer.

"How 'bout it?"

He still did not answer.

"Eh?"

"Why is it the Australian crawl?" he said slowly.

"Because once you learn it you can swim all the way to Australia."

A vision of the accomplishment of this unnecessary and undesirable feat
crossed his brain like a snatch from a dirge.

His father reached around and picked him off his shoulders, grabbing him
about the waist so that he was parallel to the water. "You're a seaplane," he said.
"Rrrrrrrrrrr. Rrrrrrrrrrrr." His father zoomed him in short passes back and forth
over the water.

He looked down and saw the water moving darkly below him. It looked as
slick, dangerous, black, and hard as a mussel. When his father made a sweeping
motion toward it, he laughed uncertainly.

"Now we're going to land," his father said. "Rrrrrrrrrrrrrrrrrrrr."

He saw the water coming up at him. His eyes opened wide. He closed his
mouth and stopped breathing. As the water touched his belly, he cringed.

"Kick!" his father said.

He kicked in big, foolish charges from the knee. He jerked his head from
side to side and blew water and air out of his mouth in quick, desperate rasps.
He felt his father's hands under his stomach and realized how completely he
was in their power. The firmer they were, the more powerless was he, the less in
command of his own safety. This thought, which took a vague and therefore
more terrifying form, distracted him from his kicking, so that his left foot struck
out erratically into his father's side, pushing him out of his grasp and down into
the water.

But before he knew what had happened his father snatched him out and
gathered him up into his arms. "Hey," he said. "What're you trying to do, learn

all by yourself?" His father looked at him carefully to see if he was all right. "Before you know it, you're going to be better than Johnny Weissmuller!"

He did not listen to what his father said, but only stared and shivered in his arms. When he heard his father say nothing more, it dawned on him that his father's last words had compared him to Johnny Weissmuller. He began to laugh. His father laughed, too, and when he saw his father laughing, he began to cry, and immediately the crying overcame the laughing, overcame everything, in fact, and he cried loudly, heartfully, and without tears.

"How's this?" his father said. "Crying?"

He did not stop.

"Come on, now," his father said. "It wasn't all that bad. You've got to be brave."

His father accented this last word sentimentally, and although the boy was not really listening to his father's words or drawing any consolation from them, he did hear this word "brave," and he hated it at once as an impossible ideal to which he could never attain and, under the circumstances, an enemy. His father hugged him to his chest to calm him, to comfort him, and especially to quiet him, but this, combined with the word "brave," made him cry even louder, and real tears came.

"There, there," his father said. "Don't cry." His father hugged him and kissed his hair, and since he had run the gamut of his tears, he suddenly stopped crying altogether.

"Don't you want to learn the Australian crawl?"

"No," he said.

"Why?" his father asked.

"Because . . . " he said.

"Because why?"

"Because I can't do it," he said.

"Well, if you give up right away . . . " his father said coaxingly.

"I'm too scared," he said.

"Scared?" his father said. "No. You're not scared. You've got to be a soldier. Then you won't be scared."

A soldier was the last thing in the world he wanted to be. He wanted to be a little girl to whom no one would ever say, "You've got to be a soldier."

"Would you like to learn to float, instead?"

He closed his eyes tight. He wanted to be alone. He wanted his father to leave him alone so that he could sit in the sand by the edge of the water and feel it lap brightly over his legs and recover. He knew that if he said no he would be left alone and would be allowed to do these things, but he felt also that he had better say yes. If he said no, his father and mother might go away without him. If he said no, they might never come here again. If he said no, his mother might beat him. If he said no, his father might be angry and become even quieter than usual. So he said, "Yes."

"Are you sure?"

"Yes," he said. The spacious sea, the azure air, the glittering, shimmering expanse of ever-moving blue water, the ships, the sails, the sunlight, the heat, the dry breeze, the shore, the bathers, the distant sounds upon the sand, the glistering cars, the remote peace that buoyed all around him — all were present and all were meaningless. His eyes closed and his heart constricted as he lay in his father's arms.

His father lifted him up into the air with his back to the water, stiff as a corpse. He gripped his father's arms with his hands as he was lowered slowly down. As he felt the water lap his back and sides, he gripped the flesh of his father's arms tighter, but his hands slipped.

"That isn't so bad, is it?" his father said.

He made a little noise.

"Bring your head forward a bit," his father said. "Move your arms."

He put his arms stiffly into the water and moved them up and down spastically, striking the water with powerful, impotent blows. The water came over his chest and tickled him. Gushing about his ears, it deafened him with hollow, looming sounds.

"Raise your feet," his father said. "Raise your toes."

He tried to do this, but his feet were so far at the end of his now lengthy body and so heavy that he couldn't. But in trying to he looked at them. This brought his head forward and threw the air in his lungs into the center of his body, where it could perform its buoying function properly. He began to float, in fact. And tentatively, finding him floating, his father withdrew his hands and let him go. Instantly, feeling they were gone, he panicked in such a way that his father could not catch him.

Down he went, upside down, backward, head first, a thousand feet. He gasped for air. Water flushed into his lungs. His hair stood on end. His feet pedalled wildly for the bottom. His arms thrashed, reached everywhere, to find the pebbles, to push himself upright, to catch hold of something, to find a purchase somewhere, to beat, strike, kill, drown the water itself, his deadly enemy. Nothing availed. His head sank. His back sank. His arms sank. His legs sank. Everything went down, sank, touched bottom, and he was drowned.

The water was blacker than anything he had ever known. It was blacker than nightmares, blacker than death. Nothing, neither his horror, nor his struggle for breath, nor his furious lashings, made any impression upon that blackness at all. Not even death intervened to relieve it. Nothing relieved it in the aeon between the moment when he fell into it and the next moment, when he realized that he had touched bottom.

When he did touch bottom, his feet and hands immediately sought it out, and he sat, squatted, bent, and then stood up into the air, on his own feet, and he was saved. Water poured off his frame. He was saved. The water was not even up to his chest. He coughed and gagged and coughed again, but as he coughed and gagged and coughed again, he knew that he was not saved. He was alive. But he was not saved.

The sea was black. Glittering black. He saw it with a terrible anger, with a powerful and furious resentment, and, when his lungs were restored to him, he screamed. He screamed in panic and he screamed in hate. He screamed to demand that the gods of the land, whose child he was, save him from the capricious malices of this monster that wished to seize him before his time. He screamed over and over, without modulation, his terrible and inexorable order. The sea was black, and he screamed for the safety of the multitudinous colorations of the land. He screamed with his eyes closed, eyes that he had as yet not dared to open for fear he would see that the sea was still delusively silver and green. It was not. The sea was black.

His father bent down and picked him up in his arms. "Now, now," his father said. "Never mind."

He pushed himself away from his father's chest and continued to scream.

"There, there," his father said. "Never mind, now." His father began to walk with him toward the shore, but before his father had reached the shore he scrambled and kicked in his arms so violently that his father was obliged to put him down in the shallows, where he went on screaming.

His father bent over him solicitously. "I'm sorry," his father said. "It was an accident."

The boy could not believe what had happened. He could not believe it. The worst he had feared had come to pass.

"I didn't mean it," his father said. "I'm sorry."

He screamed on.

His father took his arm to try to turn him around. He wrenched it out of his father's grasp. His father bent around and looked into his face. His eyes were closed. His lips were blue with cold. His father gently took his hands.

He jerked his hands down. "Mummy! Mummy!" he screamed. If his father touched him once again, he would run out into the sea and drown himself.

"There, there," his father said, and took hold of both his arms.

"Mummy! Mummy!" he screamed. His father would not let go of his arms. "Mummy! Mummy!" he screamed, bending over, begging in panic and fear, pulling away from his father's arms, begging to be let go, and did not wait for his entreaty to be granted but twisted his arms out of his father's grasp, opened his eyes, and ran screaming for the shore.

His father watched him run up to where his mother sat on the blanket, but he made no move, except an involuntary one, to stop him. When he saw him reach his destination safely, he turned his back, waded out, bent himself forward over the water, pushed off, dived under, and swam away.

·

"What is it?" the boy's mother said to him.

He tried to throw himself into her arms. She held him off quite firmly and said, "What is it this time?"

"I drowned," he said.

"You didn't drown. You just got a little water on you."

"I drowned!"

He wailed even louder, and when she saw how frightened he was, and knowing it was the quickest way to quiet him, she put her magazine aside and held him to her bosom. He stopped crying at once and threw his arms around her sides and cuddled between her breasts, choking and sobbing in the lulls of his crying.

"There's nothing wrong with the water," she said. "What is there to be frightened of? Look at your brother. Is he frightened? You've got to make sacrifices in this life. The sooner you learn that, the better. You come running to me when you've done wrong. Do you want people to think you're a coward? Is that what you want?"

He nestled his head in her breasts. Although he heard every word, he wasn't really listening to what she said.

She pushed him away from her. "I asked you a question. Do you want people to think you're a coward all your life?"

"No," he said.

"No. Well, then, you've got to learn. All the other boys will know how and you won't. Is that what you want?"

"No."

"You get a little wet, or you swallow a little water, and you think that you drowned. That's ridiculous. Isn't that ridiculous?" She paused. "Answer me."

"Yes."

"What's wrong with you then, if you know?"

"I don't know."

"Well, you'd better find out, me hearty, and pretty quick, too."

"I can't help it."

"You can't help it! You know that nothing is going to happen to you. Isn't that right?"

"Yes."

"Well, what's wrong with you, then?"

"I don't know," he said, and his lip began to tremble and his head filled with tears. "I was frightened," he said, and he began to cry once again.

"You'll never learn," she said. "You'll never learn," she repeated, with a weariness she had done nothing to deserve, and meaning not just swimming but something important about the secret of survival in general, something that she knew but was too wise or too weary to impart, or that he was not worthy to hear. "You'll never learn. You'll always be the same." She picked up her magazine and went on reading where she had left off.

.

In time, the boy did learn to swim. He learned that very summer, in fact, all by himself. His mother had taken him to the beach with her bridge-club girls. It was a weekday, and his father was not there and his brother had stayed at home. His brother did not like the ladies of the bridge club, but he did. Their matronly shapes, their countless cigarettes, their cursing, their wicked, intemperate laughter, their mincing gluttony, their snide and salacious gabbing were a spectacle he enjoyed and one in which he felt at home.

In the late morning of that day, when the ladies had taken themselves out for a dip, he went into the water, and there, with a wild thrill and a brilliant delight, he taught himself how to swim. He dog-paddled. It was not what his father had tried to teach him, but was a tireless and effective dog-paddle.

The tide was low that day, and the ladies had to walk almost a quarter of a mile before the water was even up to their waists. They walked out, swimming a few strokes now and then, and the exercise it took sufficed them. They swam no more but stood about in the water, which came just up to their breasts, gossiping. Eight ladies standing in the water, when out of nowhere a little white-haired boy swam out to greet them.

"Look, Mummy, I can do it. Lookit. Lookit. I can swim!"

"What are you doing out here?" his mother said. "Get back in at once. It's way out of your depth. How did you get out here anyhow?"

"I swam. I can swim!"

"You can not."

"I can!"

"Who taught you?"

"I learned it myself. Just now. Look!"

"What do you mean, you learned it yourself?"

"I did. I learned it. Look!" Victory was keen. Her incredulousness did nothing to dispel it.

"Look at him, girls," she said. "He can swim!"

"I just learned," he said to them. "I taught it to myself." He paddled around in a circle so that he could see all of their faces as they admired him.

They all praised him, ogled him, applauded him. She did, too. He was his mother's brilliant boy.

"Now get into shore at once," she said. "It's way over your head."

"No," he said. "I can do it. I'm not tired."

Whether it was over his head or not didn't matter, because he could swim. He paddled around with his head perched above the water, his hands chopping the waves beneath his chin, his feet kicking along beneath him. He moved at an astonishing pace for one who, until that day, had not moved at all. Around and around he went, paddling through the ladies as though they were pylons of an obstacle course. The women talked to him, jested and laughed with him as he went, cutting across their pleasant chatter as he did so. They would feign, or really experience, surprise as he would paddle up behind them, touch them with a cold finger on the back of their necks, and paddle away with a shriek that would mingle with theirs. The sky was lowering that day, and the water was black and warm—as he, for the first time, noticed it is on dark days. Around and around he paddled, in and among them, back and forth, in to shore and out again, laughing and bobbing, his face dripping with water, so damp and waterlogged it looked as if the next moment would be his last. Sometimes his round white head would sink merrily beneath the waves as he tried to perform some mad and intricate maneuver, but he would emerge spitting and laughing, with a look of hope on his face that had replaced there the look of something else.

Rebecca Morris

The Good Humor Man

All through that hot, slow summer, I lived alone, on ice-cream sandwiches and gin, in a one-room apartment on Carmine Street, waiting while James divorced me. In June he sent a letter saying, "Dear Anne, I have gone West to get the divorce." I was not sure where he meant by "West" and I did not believe he could just do that, without me, until I noticed that he had used the definite article. James was an English instructor at Columbia, and his grammar was always precise. So I knew that he could. The letter arrived two days before graduation. I remember taking it from the mailbox as I left the apartment, stopping just inside the shadow of the doorway to open it. Outside, the sun glanced off Carmine Street and rose in waves of heat, assaulting the unemptied garbage cans by the stoop. For the past week I had been planning to go to graduation. I wanted to see James walk in the academic procession as a member of the faculty, wearing a cap and gown. When the pain struck, I also felt a childish chagrin at having been disappointed.

For the past year, everything had gone badly with us, and James had wanted a separation. He had met someone else. I didn't want him to leave, and for months I alternated between anger and tears. With each new outburst, he became more determined. I never meant to throw his copy of Milton out the window. Finally, just after Christmas, James left, packing his share of our belongings. I didn't know where he had moved to; he wouldn't tell me. I put the rest—one-half of everything—in storage and sublet a small walkup in the South Village. I still wanted to see James, though I knew there was someone else, and I began to search for him. He did not want to encounter me; he hated scenes. That winter and spring, I pursued James through the cold, crowded streets of New York like an incompetent sleuth. What I remember of those sad months merges into one speeded-up sequence, as silent and jumpy as an old movie.

It started one January afternoon, chilly and gray. I was wearing a trench-coat and scarf. Rain blew in on me where I stood, in the doorway of the Chinese laundry on Amsterdam Avenue. My bangs were dripping down onto my dark glasses, so that I could scarcely see who got off the No. 11 bus opposite Columbia. I was coming down with a damn cold. Inside, the Chinaman could be seen talking rapidly to his wife. He pointed repeatedly to me and then to his watch.

In February, I spotted James leaving Butler Library. He glanced nervously over his shoulder. Four girls in scarves and trenchcoats were approaching from various directions of the campus; they were converging on the library. His cheek twitched and he pulled his coat collar high up around his neck.

March, and I sat on a stool looking out the window of the Chock Full O'Nuts at 116th Street and Broadway, watching the subway entrance. The sun burned through the plate glass, and the four cups of coffee I had already drunk were making me so hot that the subway entrance seemed to swim. I ordered an orange drink.

April. James started down the steps of the New York Public Library. Forty-second Street was jammed with marchers. It was a peace demonstration and they were walking—carrying signs, carrying babies—to the U.N. Some were singing. On the other side of Fifth Avenue, a girl in dark glasses and a trench-coat jumped up and down, apparently waving to him. He ducked his head and slipped in among the New Jersey contingent, whose signs proclaimed that they had walked from New Brunswick. Someone handed him a sign. He held it in front of his face and crossed Fifth Avenue. The girl in dark glasses greeted her friend, a woman in tweeds, and they walked off toward Peck & Peck. I stepped out from behind the south lion and joined the march.

And then May. I was baby-sitting for another faculty wife, who supplied me with an infant in yellow overalls and a large aluminum stroller. Under new leaves, cinematically green, we travelled slowly back and forth, bumping over the bricks of Campus Walk, courting sunstroke. It was my most effective disguise. I concentrated my attention on Hamilton Hall, trying to see in the windows. Suddenly there was a rending howl from the stroller. I went rigid with shock; I had forgotten about the baby. James, disguised as a Ph.D., left by a side entrance.

June. Once again I was in that doorway on Carmine Street. I was always standing in that doorway. I was about to cry, and then I walked down the street unable to stop crying. I didn't know where I was going.

·

And so I lived in the one room I had sublet all that summer. I can still see it. There was a couch, a grand piano, and a window that looked out onto a tree and the back of Our Lady of Pompeii School. (The first morning, I was abruptly awakened by a loudspeaker ordering me to wear my hat tomorrow, to Mass. I was confused; I didn't think I had a hat.) The couch, the piano, and I were the three largest objects in the apartment, and we felt a kinship. It was very quiet when the school term ended. I slept on the couch and set my orange-juice glasses on the grand piano. The one or two people whom I knew in New York seemed to have left for the summer. They were faculty people anyway—more James' friends than mine. The part-time job I had in a branch of the Public Library was over; they had gone on summer hours.

I see it so clearly—the window, the couch, the glass on the piano. It is as if I am still there and that endless summer is just beginning. I pour a little more gin in my orange juice. I am drinking orange juice because it has Vitamin C, and I don't like gin straight. Gin is for sleep; it is infallible. I sit on the couch facing the piano and switch the light off behind me. Through the leaves of the tree I can see the lighted back windows of Leroy Street. The dark air coming in my open window is sweet, smelling of night, garbage, and cats. Sounds hover just outside, hesitating to cross the sill. I lean to hear them, and sit in the window, placing my orange juice on the fire escape. Down through the black iron slats I can dimly make out one. . . two, three neighborhood cats stalking each other, brushing through the high weeds, converging toward some lusty surprise. On the top of the piano there is a metronome. I reach over and release its armature. The pendulum swings free—*tock*-over, *tock*-over. I sit looking out across the night. *Tock* in the heavy, slow darkness. *Tock*-over. People framed in the Leroy Street windows are eating at tables, talking soundlessly, passing back and forth. Yellow light filters down in shadows, through the leaves and onto the court, darkly outlining the high wild grass, the rusted cans and gray bottles. I reach over and slide the weight all the way down. The pendulum springs away from my hand, ticking wildly, gathering velocity. Accelerando! In the dark below, the cats dance.

When I awake the next morning, it is already hot and my head hurts. I carefully circle the piano and fill the bathroom basin with cold water. I plunge my face into it, staring down through the cold at the pockmarked porcelain, the gray rubber stopper, until my lungs hurt. After a few minutes, I leave the apartment, bangs dripping, walk through the dark hallway, down a flight of stairs, and out onto the burning pavement of Carmine Street. Pushing against the heat, I cross to the luncheonette on Father Demo Square. This is where I buy my morning ice-cream sandwich. The ice cream is for protein, its cold for my head; the two chocolate-cookie layers merely make it manageable. The sun dries my wet bangs into stiff points over my throbbing forehead. I squint and wish I had my dark glasses. Standing by the corner of Bleecker and Sixth Avenue is a glaring white metal pushcart. A squat man in white pants and rolled shirtsleeves leans a hairy arm on its handle and with the other wipes his brow beneath his white cap. Along the side of the cart, brown letters on a yellow background announce, "Chocolate Malt Good Humor." I walk toward the sign, drawn slowly across Bleecker Street. On the sidewalk chairs at Provenzano's Fish Market two old Italians are slipping clams down their throats, sipping juice from the shells. Dead fish, plumped in barrels of ice, eye me, baleful but cool. The air smells of fish and lemon. I confront the Good Humor man and we squint at each other. "Chocolate Malt Good Humor," I say.

The next week, the Good Humor flavor changes. As I cross Carmine Street, dry-mouthed and stunned in the sunny morning, I read, "Strawberry Shortcake Good Humor." The letters, red against pink, vibrate in the glare. Behind the Good Humor cart, Bleecker Street is in motion. Provenzano's has strung black-and-silver eels in the window. The shop awnings are unrolled, and the canopied vegetable carts form an arcade up toward Seventh Avenue. Italian housewives in black are arguing with the vendors, ruffling lettuces, squeezing the hot flesh of tomatoes, fondling gross, purple eggplants. Ice melts and runs from the fish barrels. I tear the wrapper off my Good Humor—frozen cake crumbs over strawberry-rippled vanilla ice cream—and, tasting its cold, proceed up this noisy galleria. My sandals leak, and I hold my breath passing the clam bar. Loose cabbage leaves scush under my soles, and strawberry sherbet runs down the stick onto my fingers. It is another hot day. At one o'clock, the Department of Parks outdoor swimming pool on the corner of Carmine, where Seventh Avenue becomes Varick Street, is going to open. I have discovered that for thirty-five cents I can stay there until seven in the evening, swimming endless lengths, pastorally shielded from Seventh Avenue by the bathhouse and the two-story Hudson Park branch Public Library. There my neighbors and I lie and tan on the hot city cement, shivering when the late-afternoon shadow of the building creeps over the pale water and turns it dark green. I stay there late every day, until all warmth is gone and evening falls. I no longer cry. I merely wait.

In the last week of June (Coconut Good Humor—a shaggy, all-white confection of shredded coconut frozen on vanilla ice cream), I receive a letter from a Fifth Avenue lawyer telling me that he represents James and that I must consult him in his offices. I find his address formidable. It reminds me that I have not left my safe, low neighborhood for weeks. When I arrive, the lawyer is all smiles and amiability. I sit tensely, feeling strange in white gloves and high heels, while he tells me that James is in Reno, establishing a residence. He asks me if I have a lawyer of my own. I shake my head; I do not want a lawyer. This seems to surprise and annoy him. He shows me a paper that I may sign delegating some Nevada lawyer to represent me. It is only a form, but it is necessary. When it is all over, he says I may have some money, a fair and equable share of our joint assets—if I sign the paper. He offers me a cigarette while I think about it, but I am wearing gloves and I refuse. I do not want to take them off, as if this gesture will somehow make me vulnerable. My gloved hands in my lap look strange, too white below my brown arms. I stare at them and wish I were back on Carmine Street. The lawyer's office is very elegant, with green velvet curtains and an Oriental rug. There is a slim-legged sofa and a low, marble-topped coffee table. All of the walls are panelled in dark oak, and there is a fireplace. I wonder who he is trying to kid. The lawyer pretends to reasonableness. I only want to see James. I do not want to sign anything. I shake my head; I will wait. He looks pained. He does not say so, but he manages to indicate that I am being foolish and unreasonable. I nod yes, and sit mutely. I want to tell this man that when James comes home I am going to be perfect. I wish someone could tell James now that I have stopped crying. The lawyer sighs and takes out a summons, explaining that he is serving me now, if that is all right with me, because he would only have to send someone to serve me with it later. This is saving us both trouble. I nod and hold my hands in my lap. I wonder what would happen if I suddenly jumped up and hid behind the sofa. He extends the paper over his desk, and I watch it come nearer, until it wavers in front of my chest. I reach out and take it. The summons orders me to answer James' complaint in Nevada within twenty days and give reason why I should not be divorced, or be judged by default. I fold the summons in half and put it in my straw handbag. The lawyer smiles, still talking as he walks me to the elevator and shakes my hand. I am glad I am wearing gloves. He is not my friend.

·

On the Fourth of July, the Good Humor company exceeds itself and, in a burst of confectionery patriotism, produces Yankee Doodle Dandy Good Humor. I admire it as I turn it around on its stick. Frozen red, white, and blue coconut on a thin coating of white encasing strawberry-striped vanilla ice cream. I salute the Good Humor man as he hands me my change.

I spend most of my time at the pool now. On hot days, the whole neighborhood lines Seventh Avenue, waiting to get in. We stand outside the brick bathhouse in the sun, smelling chlorine on the city air and eating ice cream to keep cool—children, housewives with babies, retired men, office workers taking their vacations at home. Inside the bathhouse—women's locker room to the left, men's to the right—we hurry into our bathing suits, stuffing our clothes into green metal lockers. The air is steamy from the showers. Children shriek and splash, running through the icy footbath that leads to the pool. Out in the sunlight, we greet the water with shouts, embracing the cold shock, opening our eyes beneath the silent green chill to see distorted legs of swimmers and then breaking the sun-glazed surface again, into the noise and splashing. I wear my old black racing suit from college and slather white cream over my nose. Around the pool edge, four teen-age lifeguards in orange Department of Parks suits rove the cement or take turns sitting astride the high, painted iron guard chair. They are neighborhood heroes and accept admiration from small boys with rough graciousness. The pool cop rolls up his blue shirtsleeves and sits with his cap off in the doorway of the First Aid Room, drinking Coca-Cola. We greet each other and exchange views on the heat. He looks wistfully at the pale-aqua water, but he is on duty. I line up behind the crowd at the diving board. I am working on my one-and-a-half this week, pounding the yellow plank, trying to get some spring out of the stiff wood. My form is good, and the board conceals what I lack in daring. Sometimes Ray Palumbo, Paul Anthony, and Rocky (I never did learn his last name), three of the guards, practice with me. We criticize each other and take turns holding a bamboo pole out in front of the board, high above the water, for the others to try to dive over and enter the water neatly. I am teaching Ray's little sister, Ellen, to back-dive, and her shoulders are rosy from forgetting to arch. We all stand around the board, dripping in the sun, and talk about swimming. The boys are shy with me and respectful of my age, but with their friends they are great wits; they patrol the pool, chests out for the benefit of the teen-age girls, swinging their whistles before them like censers.

I have begun to know the other regular swimmers, too. Only the very young and the very old are as free as I am. There is Paul's grandfather, who is retired; he swims a stately breaststroke the length of the pool, smiling, with his white head held high. And Mama Vincenzio, a dignified sixty, who arrives each evening resplendent in a black dressmaker suit three feet wide. She waits her turn with us at the four-foot board, wobbles to its end, and drops off, *ka-plunk*. She does this over and over, never sinking more than a foot or two below the surface before she bobs up again: *pasta*. I am not sure that she can swim, but, on the other hand, she doesn't sink, and she propels herself to the ladder as if she were sweeping floors. We smile shyly at each other for two weeks. When I finally ask her why she comes so late, she tells me she cooks supper for ten people each evening. I also recognize Mr. Provenzano, who closes the store at four-thirty in the summer and comes swimming. I have taught him to scull feet first, and now when I pass his store in the mornings he offers me a peeled shrimp or—I hold my breath and swallow—a raw clam. I sit in the sun, dangling my feet in the water, and think of James. I try imagining him around a roulette wheel or on a dude ranch, but it doesn't work. My idea of Reno is limited. I know he should be studying, and I am sure there can't be a good library there. I wonder what he is doing, but I cannot visualize a thing. When I try, his face begins to look like a photograph I have of him, but I know he never looked like that photograph. This frightens me, so I don't think at all. I swim, and in the evenings I drink.

.

The thirty-first of July is my birthday. I am twenty-five years old. It is also the day of our trial. I will not know this, however, until the twenty-seventh of August, when the divorce decree arrives in the mail. In this morning's mail I receive a funny card from my mother and one from my aunt. My mother encloses a small check "to buy something you need." I buy a bottle of Gordon's gin. When I announce my birthday to the Good Humor man, he presents me with a Hawaiian Pineapple Good Humor, gratis. It looks like a good day.

My regular friends are already at the pool when I arrive, and we wave to each other. From the two-foot board, Ellen Palumbo shouts for me to watch. She has lost her rubber band, and long black hair streams over her shoulders. Still waving, she turns carefully backward, balancing on her toes, and then, arching perfectly, as I have taught her, falls *splat* on her shoulders in the water. I wince and smile encouragingly as she surfaces. Rocky is in the water doing laps of flutter kick, holding on to a red Styrofoam kickboard. I get another board from the First Aid Room and join him. We race through the green water, maneuvering around small boys playing water tag; our feet church spray. Suddenly my shoulder is grabbed and I am ducked from behind by Rocky's ten-year-old brother, Tony. My kickboard bobs away, and Rocky and I go after Tony, who is swimming quickly to the deep end. He escapes up the ladder and races to the diving board. Thumbing his nose, he executes a comic dive in jackknife position, one leg extended, ending in a high, satisfying splash. It is the signal for follow-the-leader. With shouts, children arrive from all sides of the pool, throwing themselves off the yellow board in imitation.

On the deck, Paul's grandfather is sunning himself, eyes closed, smiling upward toward heaven. I pull myself out of the water and join him. He squints and grins toothlessly, delighted to have someone to talk to. The night before, he has been to see a free, outdoor Shakespeare performance. A mobile theatre unit is performing in our neighborhood this week, in Walker Park Playground. We sit together in puddles on the cement, leaning against the hot bathhouse wall, and he tells me the story of "King Lear." He has been going to the free Shakespeare performances every summer since they began and has seen each play two or three times, except for "Richard II"; he saw that one six times. We watch the boys diving, and he proudly lists all the plays he has seen. When I admit that I have never seen one of the open-air performances, he says I must. He thinks for a minute, then shyly offers to escort me. He will wait in the ticket line at Walker Park this evening and save me a place. I protest, but he says he has nothing at all to do in the evening and he probably will go again. I tell him it is my birthday. He smiles; July is a good month to be born. See?—he holds up his wrinkled, brown hands and turns them over in the sun; on the second of July he was seventy.

When I arrive at the playground that evening, the line seems endless. It stretches along Hudson Street, and I pass whole families seated on the cement, eating supper out of paper bags, reading books, playing cards. Ice-cream vendors wheel carts up and down. I recognize my Good Humor man, and we wave to each other. He is selling sherbet sticks to two girls. Frost steams up from the cold depths when he opens his cart. Mr. Anthony is at the front of the line; he must have been waiting for hours. He is wearing a good black wool suit, of an old-fashioned cut. It is a little too big, as if he has shrunk within it. I suspect that it is the suit he wears to weddings and funerals, and I am glad that I have put on my green linen dress, even if it will go limp in the heat. I have braided my wet hair and wound it round my head in a damp coronet. I look like a lady. We smile shyly, proud of our finery.

At eight, the line begins moving into the playground, where the Parks Department has put up wooden bleachers. They form a semicircle around the mobile stage; folding chairs are ranged in rows in front of the bleachers. We surge through the entrance with the crowd and find seats quite close to the apron. Behind the gray scaffolding of the stage I can see the wall of the handball court and the trees on Leroy Street; to the south, the old Food and Maritime Trades High School. Trumpets and recorded Elizabethan music herald our arrival. The crowd fills the playground, and the sky gradually darkens. Floodlights dim, and light falls upon the scaffolding. Onstage, Lear summons his three daughters; the play begins. Mr. Anthony and I lean forward from our folding chairs, drawn into the court of Britain. Under the calm, blinking stars, Lear runs mad, contending with the far-off rumble of traffic on Hudson Street. High above, an airplane passes.

During intermission, I tell Mr. Anthony all I can remember about the Elizabethan stage, of the theatre that was a wooden O. We eat ice cream out of Dixie cups with miniature wooden paddles, and he compliments me. I would be a good teacher; in this city they need teachers. Later, as the final act closes, we sit and weep, on our folding chairs, for Lear, for Cordelia, for ourselves. "Never, never, never, never, never." Floodlights open over the playground; it is over. We crowd out with a thousand others onto Clarkson Street, past the dark swimming pool that is reflecting the street lights, to Seventh Avenue. On the way home, Mr. Anthony buys me a glass of red wine at Emilio's to celebrate.

We walk by the dark steps of Our Lady of Pompeii, and on my doorstep we smile at each other and shake hands.

.

On August 27th, the decree arrives—four pieces of typed paper stapled to heavy blue backing, with two gold seals. It looks like a diploma. I read it in the doorway, then walk back upstairs and drop it inside the lid of the grand piano. It is all over, but just now I am late. I eat my Toasted Almond Good Humor hurriedly, on my way to the pool. The Parks Department has been giving free swimming lessons to beginners, from ten o'clock to twelve o'clock in the mornings, and I help teach. When I get there, there are at least thirty children waiting for me around the pool edge, kicking their feet in the water.

That summer, Labor Day Weekend comes early. Few people in my neighborhood are leaving town, and the pool is crowded; everyone goes swimming. The pool will be closing soon. It is my last swim. Tomorrow I begin at P.S. 84 as a substitute teacher; I want to find out if Mr. Anthony is right. The day is hot, making the water icy by contrast. My bathing suit has bleached to a sooty gray now, and my wet hair drips in a long braid down my back. Children shout and splash, and the tarred seams on the pool bottom leap and break in refracted patterns on the moving water. At the far end, in the playground, old men throw boccie. My dark glasses begin sliding down the white cream on my nose. I push them up and join my friends sunning beyond the diving boards. The Good Humor man has parked his truck in the street, just beyond the wire fence. Children range the fence, handing dimes and nickels through, carefully drawing ice-cream sticks in. Mama Vincenzio has come early today, and she buys this week's special, Seven Layer Cake Super Humor, for her two noisy grandchildren and me. We eat them carefully, backs to the sun, counting to make sure we get seven different layers of ice cream and alternating chocolate. The children's faces smear with melted chocolate, and ice cream runs down my arm to the elbow. I toss my stick in the trash can and dive into the water. The green chill slides over me, and I move in long strokes toward the bottom, cool and weightless. Ellen Palumbo passes me and we bubble faces at each other. When my air runs out, I pick up a stray bobby pin as my civic duty (it would leave a rust mark on the bottom) and, flexing, push to the surface. Oooh.

From the guard chair, Ray beckons to me, and I swim over. For weeks, Rocky and Ray have been working on flips, somersaulting in tucked position. They have reached a point where they have perfected a double flip—two of them, arms linked, somersaulting in unison. All of the younger boys have been imitating them, working variations—forward, backward, spinning in twos above the green water. We have had one broken leg. Now Ray thinks that a triple flip can be done. No one has tried it yet, but if they can do a double—

why not? It will be dangerous, of course. If anyone is off, everyone may get hurt. You have to have reliable buddies. He and Rocky wonder if I will try it with them. I'm not as daring as their friends, but my form is better. I won't open at the wrong time. They tell me that I always keep my head. I swallow, standing there in the sun, and wonder if they have ever seen me weeping up a fit over on the Gansevoort Pier, crying into the Hudson as I angrily skip stones. I nod and promise not to crack us up. I am apprehensive.

Rocky grins and chases everyone off the board. Children stand around, dripping puddles, watching us as we carefully pace to the end. The sun burns our shoulders, and the board wavers and dips as our combined weight passes the fulcrum. Above, the sky is bright blue. We link upper arms tightly to make a pivot of our shoulders, and at Rocky's signal we begin flexing for spring, playing the board. "Now!" We are lifted and thrown upward, tucking into the air. The pool turns upside down, sky spins over our knees, the bathhouse revolves. We turn, holding together like monkeys, high above the glazed water. I have a snapshot Mr. Provenzano took of that historic moment. In it, we hang, crouched against the sky, backsides to heaven; one second later we will cut the water together, perfectly straight, to shouts and cheering. We break apart underwater and surface separately, mouths open, to the applause of our small pupils, who rim the deep end and now flop into the water like seals. On the deck, we congratulate each other, shaking hands. Then Rocky climbs the playground wall and high-dives, just missing the cement, into the deep end. It is the traditional signal to close the pool. He surfaces, puts on his orange Department of Parks poncho, and the guards begin blowing their whistles; everybody out of the pool. Summer is over.

When I leave the bathhouse, the sun is slanting. Walking up Carmine Street, I buy myself a Chocolate Eclair Good Humor as a reward. The long summer is over at last. Summer is over, and I have kept my head.

Diana Nyad

Mind over Water

I have been working on swimming since I was ten, four hours a day or more, every day, skipping the greater part of my social life, not a huge sacrifice, but something. I have put more grueling hours into it than someone like Jimmy Connors will ever know in a lifetime. I don't begrudge him his talent in that particular sport. There is simply no way he could comprehend the *work* that goes into marathon swimming.

What I do is analogous to other long-distance competitions: running, cycling, rowing, those sports where training time far exceeds actual competition time. But swimming burns more calories per minute than anything else. The lungs, heart and muscles must all be working at peak efficiency for this sport, which doesn't require brute strength but rather the strength of endurance. I can do a thousand sit-ups in the wink of an eye—and I never do sit-ups on a regular basis. I've run the mile in 5:15, not exactly Olympic caliber, but better than most women can do. My lung capacity is six point one liters, greater than a lot of football players. My heartbeat is forty-seven or forty-eight when I am at rest, this is compared to the normal seventy-two for other people. A conditioned athlete usually has a heartbeat of sixty plus. These characteristics are not due to genetics—I attained them by swimming hour after hour, year after year.

My first marathon, the ten-miler at Hamilton, Ontario, scared me to death. Judith De Nijs, the best in the world throughout the Sixties, was there, saying that if a woman ever beat her she would retire from the sport. She came over to me and said, "Vell, I hear you're a very good svimmer. Vell, you are not going to beat me." She put on her cap and walked away. I thought, whew. I swam the race and beat her by about fifteen minutes, which is a lot for a ten-miler. Judith De Nijs never swam again.

Greta Andersen was the same way. She swam the Channel I don't know how many times, as well as the Juan de Fuca Strait, and sixty miles across Lake Michigan. She beat every man she swam against at least once. She could have gone on forever. But she said that if another woman ever beat her, she'd quit. When Marty Sinn beat her, Andersen kept her word.

I'm not like that. Sandra Bucha has beaten me a couple of times in individual swims. I've been beaten by Corrie Dixon. They were better than me on those days.

·

Because I'm interested in people who are involved in exploring their potential, there is no one group I can respect more than marathon swimmers. When I'm in a hospital bed in La Tuque, for instance, after swimming in a twenty-four-hour team race, weak from exposure and nearly having frozen to death, and next to me is the guy I passed at three in the morning, we look at each other as if we're kings of the mountain. We have a love for each other, a close camaraderie.

There is considerable anxiety before a swim. I don't know until the day of the race whether the wind will be whipping up fifteen-foot waves or whether the surface will be glass. On the morning of a swim, our trainers wake us at around three a.m. for breakfast. We see the press, we eat. Nobody talks. The tension in the room is amazing. I never look at the swimmers; I look out at the lake and wonder what it will do to me, whether I'll be able to cross it. The race is more than me versus my competition. There is always the risk that I may not conquer the water.

At breakfast I have five or six raw eggs, a lot of cereal, toast and jam, juice. For my feedings during the race from the boat, I drink a hot powdered liquid that provides me with thirteen hundred calories and more protein per tablespoon than a four-ounce steak. It gets my blood sugar back up. In a race my blood sugar drops below metabolism level in three minutes. A cup of this stuff every hour barely helps. Before the hour's up my sugar is way down. I can feel it. I feel depressed. But if my protein level stays high, I'm not really in trouble.

I would say that eighty percent of success in a race is due to mind. Before starting, all natural reserves are working for me, my adrenaline, everything.

Once out there, it's a matter of mental guts. After twelve hours in cold water, my blood sugar down, I'm seventeen pounds lighter, exhausted, it takes more than knowing I've trained hard for this. I have to dig down deep.

I've done some marathon running, but the isolation in long-distance swimming is more extreme. I'm cut off physically from communication. The water sloshing over my cap leaves me virtually deaf. I wear tiny goggles that fit just over my eyes—they're always foggy, so I can't see very well. I turn my head to breathe on every stroke, sixty times a minute, six hundred strokes every mile for hours and hours. As I turn my head I see the blur of the boat and some people on it.

These countless rhythmic hours make marathon swimming unique. John Lilly, the dolphin experimenter, has found that a subject floating in a tank with eyes and ears covered becomes disoriented, slipping into a near dream state. During a long swim I'm left with my own thoughts. My mind drifts in a mesmerized world. It's hypnotic. My subconscious comes to the fore. I have sexual fantasies and sometimes flashbacks to my childhood. It's dreaming hours on end. All I hear is the water slapping and my arms whishing through water. All I see is fog. It is extremely lonely.

I'm strong at the beginning of a swim, then I have low points. I know the pain in my shoulders will be bad all the way. I've rolled over on my back, thinking this body will not do another stroke. Sometimes at a low point a swimmer will get out. In ten minutes he's saying to himself, "Why didn't I stick it out? I could have made it. I could have come back around." That's happened to me, too, when I couldn't get back into it.

In rough ocean, I have thrown up from beginning to end of a thirteen-hour swim, swishing around like a cork, violently sick to my stomach. I would do anything to stop this feeling—and the only thing that will is to be on dry land. But I can put up with it—I have to. In my first year of marathon swimming, I got out because of seasickness. Now I get just as seasick and stick it.

Fatigue, pain, and huge waves are manageable. The toughest condition is cold water. Cliff Lumsdon, my trainer since 1972, swam in the Canadian Nationals in 1955. Lake Ontario was forty-five degrees. The life expectancy for a normal-weight person in forty-five-degree water is something like forty minutes. A marathon swimmer has only a film of grease for insulation, which wears off after a little while. After one hour, everyone was out of the water but Lumsdon. The temperature simply couldn't be handled. But Cliff stayed in for the entire fifteen miles, finishing in nineteen hours, eighteen minutes. He went through a substantial recovery period but was never hospitalized.

My coldest time was training on Ontario for the Capri to Naples race in 1974. I was supposed to leave later that day for Europe, but thought, why waste the time? Why not swim for an hour, just to loosen up? I did a thousand strokes out, then stopped to turn around, empty my goggles, get a sighting onshore. But I realized I hadn't been feeling my legs. I couldn't bring them to the surface. My skin was lobster red. My breath stuck in my throat. I tried to scream to some boys onshore, but nothing came out. I started to swim a slow breaststroke. My hands were so cold I couldn't close my fingers. People onshore finally saw I was in trouble. By now I was onto shallow rocks. A man waded out and grabbed me under my arms to lift me out of the water. His hand, his ninety-eight-point-six-degree hands, burned my skin. They took me to the hospital and put me in a warmer. I had severe burns all the way through the Capri-Naples race.

The temperature that day in Ontario was forty. I'd been in the water an hour. It freaks me out when I think Cliff lasted nineteen hours in forty-five-degree water. I just couldn't do it. My body weight is less than his, but still. . . . I really have to psych myself up for cold water.

.

There are still a few bodies of water I want to conquer. I'm considering all of the five Great Lakes in the summer of '76. Each lake is a different challenge.

The lakes are pretty cold. Superior is so cold I'd have to cross it at the shortest point. A legal marathon may be undertaken only in a regular racing suit, cap, goggles, and grease—no flotation devices, no insulating suit. Even at the shortest crossing, Superior may be impossible, given these requirements.

I've found suitable start and finish options for each lake. I could swim from Michigan City to Chicago, for instance, which is thirty miles; or from Benton Harbor to Chicago, which is sixty. My route will depend on how cold the water is. Distance doesn't mean anything to me; it's the condition of the water that counts.

Marathon swimming will never be as popular as other sports for obvious reasons. Spectators can only watch the finish, not the whole process. It's like the Tour de France—the most popular cycling race in the country and you can't see anything. But there is empathy among the spectators when the contestants stop for the night. You see their huge legs, muscular bodies dust-covered and sweaty, their power exhausted.

There is the same empathy at the end of a marathon swim. People have spent the whole day waiting. From a mile out I can hear clapping and screaming. The people realize I swam from a place they couldn't see on the clearest day. They know I may faint when I arrive. They share with me the most extreme moment of all—for after the pain, the cold, the hours, the distance, after the fatigue and the loneliness, after all this comes my emergence. And my emergence is what it's all about.

Sharon Olds

The Motel

When I hear it's torn down I can hardly believe it,
I can see the square O of adobe
facing in, onto the inner
courtyard, and the pool, and the flowers, it feels
permanent as a Platonic idea,
as far beyond destruction as the Garden of Eden.
When I visited them I would stay there the last
night, next to the airport, get up
at six, put on my bathing suit
in the dark, open the glass and cross
the cold garden to the pool. Curls of
steam wandered up from the surface,
the birds in the palms awoke, I slid in
and sank and I was at home, in the green
breathless liquid world where I had often
gone with my father. The sicker he got,
those last months, the more I felt
this is where I would always find him —
underwater, body squeezed
in the water's airless hug.
I would pad back to my room, past
the bush with its stray camellia, the love
I longed for from him,
I'd turn on the hot, put my head under
as if it were upright Jordan, and I could
baptize myself his daughter, and now
it's a pile of rubbish — the tile surround,
palm-nuts, gardenia buds,
dirt, nests, girders. They will have
sold the beds, set aside the triple-milled
amber fluted soaps — and did they
save the pool, unsuction it up and
leave a hole like a grave, or did they
cave it in, Pompeiian. Anyway,

every trace of everything
that held me
holding him
will be removed from the planet. Only this small
oasis—sparrows and pittosporum,
a woman down inside the water, and
down inside her heart her snoring
father, and in his snore his daughter,
the pool, the courtyard, the city, the earth,
the universe, expanding blossom of wreckage.

Sharon Olds

The Swimmer

The way the seed that made me raced
ahead of the others, arms held to her sides,
round head humming, spine
whipping, I love to throw myself
into the sea—cold fresh
enormous palm around my scalp,
I open my eyes, and drift through the water that lies
heavy on the earth, I am suspended in it
like a sperm. Then I love to swim slowly,
I feel I am at the center of life, I am
inside God, there is sourweed in skeins like
blood beside my head. From the beach
you would see only the ocean, the swell
curling—so I am like a real being,
invisible, an amoeba that rides in spit,
I am like those elements my father turned into,
smoke, bone, salt. It is one of
the only things I like to do
anymore, get down inside the horizon
and feel what his new life is like, how
clean, how blank, how griefless, how without error—
the trance of matter.

Mary Oliver

The Swimmer

All winter the water
　　has crashed over
　　　　the cold sand. Now
　　　　　　it breaks over the thin

branch of your body.
　　You plunge down, you swim
　　　　two or three strokes, you dream
　　　　　　of lingering

in the luminous undertow
　　but can't; you splash
　　　　through the bursting
　　　　　　white blossoms,

the silk sheets — gasping,
　　you rise and struggle
　　　　lightward, finding your way
　　　　　　through the blue ribs back

to the sun, and emerge
　　as though for the first time.
　　　　Poor fish,
　　　　　　poor flesh,

you can never forget.
　　Once every wall was water,
　　　　the soft strings filled
　　　　　　with a perfect nourishment,

pumping your body full
　　of appetite, elaborating
　　　　your stubby bones, tucking in,
　　　　　　like stars,

the seeds of restlessness
    that made you, finally,
        swim toward the world,
            kicking and shouting

but trailing a mossy darkness—
    a dream that would never breathe air
        and was hinged to your wildest joy
            like a shadow.

Dick Powell

Channel Swimming Association Report

*T*ed Erikson, the world's fastest two-way conqueror of the English Channel, told how he won the battle of the jelly fish and of the roses that grow in the sea.

The 37-year-old swimmer from Chicago had to cleave his way through a shoal of jelly fish on his way to France.

The roses were an illusion, as he struggled over the last few miles of the return trip to England.

Ted completed the two-way swim in 30 hours, 3 minutes.

"I had about two miles to go and everything started to go black," Erikson said.

"My pilot boat faded into a black smear. Then it turned into a rose bush. Suddenly there were roses growing all around me.

"I just closed my eyes and swam on. I guess that was the moment of crisis."

Erikson, a research chemist who started long distance swimming only five years ago, plotted to lower Abertondo's time with the help of a computer, operated by his Chicago scientist colleague Tony Dundzilla.

Dundzilla fed the computer Erikson's swimming speed and the complicated tidal currents which make the channel a nightmare for swimmers.

Ted attempted the swim in 1964 but gave up after 23 hours, defeated by the cold weather conditions on the second leg. Twice in the last two weeks he attempted the crossing but was swept off course and gave up. These two attempts were planned by computer.

"This time I decided not to stick rigidly to the computer, although the point of start was a computer working and formed the basis of my plan," Erikson said.

"I relied on my pilot Peter Winter, to amend our course as we went along. I had perfect weather and it worked out fine."

After the swim Ted took four hours sleep and then got up to read the messages of congratulations.

Facts: Point of Start. 1 mile West of St. Margarets Bay
Point of Finish. Within ¼ mile of Starting Point.

Ted Erikson   America

Report of Swims 1965

PILOT	PETER WINTERS & ARTHUR LIDDEN
BOAT	VEGA

12th September 1965

POINT OF COMMENCEMENT	20 yds. EAST OF THE EASTERN ARM DOVER
POINT OF FINISH	APPROX. 10 MILES FROM ENGLISH COAST
TOTAL TIME	5 HOURS 20 MINUTES

14th September 1965

POINT OF COMMENCEMENT	20 yds. EAST OF THE EASTERN ARM DOVER
POINT OF FINISH	3 MILES OFF WISSANT
TOTAL TIME	10 HOURS 2 MINUTES

19th September 1965

TWO-WAY NON STOP

POINT OF START	1 MILE WEST OF ST. MARGARETS BAY
POINT OF FINISH	¼ MILE EAST OF STARTING POINT (¼ mile off St. Margarets Bay, England)
ENGLAND TO FRANCE	
TIME	14 HOURS 15 MINUTES
FRANCE TO ENGLAND	
TIME (return)	15 HOURS 48 MINUTES

TOTAL TIME   30 *HOURS 3 MINUTES*
                                          RECORD

OLD RECORD: ANTONIO ABERTONDO 1961—
43 HOURS 10 MINUTES
13 HOURS 7 MINUTES OFF
TED ERIKSON   AMERICA
RECORD BREAKING ENGLISH CHANNEL DOUBLE SWIM—
30 HOURS 3 MINUTES

The motor yacht "Vega" left the inner harbour at Dover on 19th September 1965 at 7.15 P.M. and proceeded to St. Margarets Bay some 3 miles to the East, on board were the Capt. P. Winter, the pilot A. Lydden, the engineer Miss C. Sharp, and the Channel Swimming Association Officials Miss N. Martin and myself. The Vega cruised some ½ mile off shore, it was very dark. Capt. Winter, Miss Martin and myself went ashore in the dingy clad in swim-suits to verify the time of starting, and to see that the rules of the C.S.A. were carried out.

The pilot gave me instructions as to the time of starting and to take the swimmer about one mile from the bay Westwards and to start from the rocks, the starting time, 8.15 P.M.

.

At about 7.50 P.M. we struck the beach with our punt in an awkward swell to give us our first "ducking," there we found Reg Barrett our Assistant Secretary of the C.S.A. busy greasing up the swimmer; the swimmer entered the punt after another ducking, and the Capt. started the outboard. It was not long before we reached our starting point; we got Ted into the water some 20 yards off the rocky shore, in a few minutes he was standing on the rocks; I shouted him in at 8.10 P.M. There was no sense in making him wait another 5 minutes in the cold. Ted then followed us to the Vega where the pilot took over, and we dried off and put on our warm clothing.

9.10 P.M. We now have St. Margarets about 1 mile astern with a starlight sky, but very dark; the water temperature is 59°F., lights on sea fronts of Deal and Ramsgate very clear, as all those at Dover, the South Goodwin lightship is on our port bow some 2 miles away, as the remainder of the flood tide takes us to the East, we are steering 135°.

10.15 P.M. Passing South Goodwin lightship 300 yards on starboard beam, land side. Ostende ferry passed ½ mile ahead, sea calm, air temperature 54°F., sea 59°F., stroking 60.

11.30 P.M. Steering 140°, water slack, very dark but clear for all light houses and vessels.

12.18 A.M. South Goodwin lightship dead astern and Calais dead ahead.

12.30 A.M. First feed, coffee and glucose warm.

1.30 A.M. Second feed, yoke of egg, milk and glucose, hot, he requests bigger feed next time.

2.40 A.M. Ran through shoal of jelly fish, Ted flew across to the starboard side for 10 mins. no complaints about being stung, but rotten feeling against his body, we could see the white patches quite plainly, Ted now back on port side.

3.15 A.M. Ted has another feed of corn syrup and mashed peaches. I estimate the South Goodwin lightship some 6 miles astern. Cap Gris Nez some 8 miles to the South, the ebb tide is taking us away to the West now, steering 135°.

4.45 A.M. Another feed as before, we appear to be about 5 miles from France.

5.45 A.M. Our position is not too good, we are not far enough to the West, now the flood starts to set.

6.30 A.M. Ted has good feed, peaches mashed, corn syrup and carton brown sugar. We are about 3 miles off Sangatte, the pilot has asked Ted for a spurt for an hour, to get inside of the next flood tide, & now probably make Calais.

7.30 A.M. We are now closing with the memorial of the French Dover patrol on top of the cliffs looking at us.

7.45 A.M. The pilot and I have just had breakfast; cereal, 2 eggs, 2 rashers bacon, 2 sausages, 2 tomatoes, 2 slices of toast, marmalade and coffee. Thanks to our engineer.

8.00 A.M. Now only 2 miles from Sangatte, steering 165°. Ted takes coffee and glucose.

8.05 A.M. Enterprise II slows down and passes 300 yards on port beam.

8.10 A.M. No complaints from Ted after 12 hours, his stroke has dropped to 58, and I tell him I want the other two.

9.10 A.M. Ted full of beans now, 1 mile from Calais Harbour with any luck, we should start back with about 7 hours ebb, could not be better, hope the weather holds out.

10.10 A.M. After 14 hours we are now running in on West side of Calais Harbour some ¼ mile in slack water steering 160°.

10.17 A.M. Enterprise I entering Calais Harbour on our port side.

10.17 A.M. Peter Winters, Miss Martin and myself leave in the punt for another ducking and to receive Ted on the sands, before leaving I instructed all not to touch him (Ted) during his stay of 10 minutes, if he wanted grease on his back, I would put it on.

10.20 A.M. We are welcomed ashore by a dozen ladies and men and a shrimper, Peter's French tells them to keep clear and we are swimming back.

10.25 A.M. Ted leaves the water, falling once only, then coming straight in, he was very cold, he asked for grease on his stomach and back. I put on about 3 lbs. lanolin, Ted takes hot coffee, I then escorted him back in the water.

10.35 A.M. Ted restarts his swim back to England, the sea away from the shore is dead calm but we take the usual ducking before getting into the punt to return to the Vega laying off shore some ¼ mile, I took a whole sea in my lap. We reach Vega all aboard except "one." and we set course 310° for home.

10.45 A.M. Compagne leaving Calais.

11.40 A.M. Enterprise II car ferry passing ¼ mile port beam going to Calais.

11.50 A.M. Enterprise I car ferry passing ¼ mile port beam going to Dover.

12.25 P.M. Air temp. now 78°F. in the sun, sea dead calm 60°F. steering 310°, leaving war memorial in France 4 miles on port beam.

1.00 P.M. Wind increasing to force 3 with swell and chop, we all pray this will not increase.

1.15 P.M. Wind now force ¾ W.N.W., nasty chop boat rolling unable to write, only between rolls, steering 310°. Ted feeding every 75 minutes, tomato soup, corn syrup, coffee and glucose, mashed peaches.

1.40 P.M. Normania passes 2 miles to starboard to Calais.

2.00 P.M. Just received Shipping Forecast over the air. S.W. force 3 or less, this is good news which we quickly pass on to Ted as at the moment it is quite rough, and we ask him to come round on the lee side.

2.20 P.M. Enterprise II passing on starboard beam 2 miles; heading to Dover.

3.30 P.M. We have the French Patrol Memorial dead astern 6 miles, the ebb is not very strong, and we want to go West. Ted has another feed of tomato soup, corn syrup, he is now feeling the cold, and showing signs of fatigue.

4.35 P.M. Ted stiff, feeling the cold and asks for hot coffee often, we are about halfway back, and he wants to know how long it will take.

5.00 P.M. We estimate he will require another 8 hours, which will mean some 15 hours or more, this added to the 14 hours 15 minutes in water at 59°F. is pretty terrible. Now white lies start, we cannot tell him the truth.

5.45 P.M. We can now see Dover Castle and the Harbour, our fix gives us about 10 miles out from Dover, the flood tide starts shortly, this should, we hope, bring us inside the South Goodwin Lightship, we gave Ted the news, told him if he kept going we should be home by Midnight, that is another 6 hours, what a hope! but we must keep him going, he says he is so cold, All lies told on Channel swims are not entered in the big "Book" above, there is no book big enough.

6.35 P.M. More food, steering 310°, we grumble at him every time he stops, our position is 9 miles S.E. of Dover.

8.30 P.M. We are rolling so badly I cannot write and take the temperature.

8.35 P.M. Another shoal of jelly fish, Ted shouts, he wonders in the dark what are hitting his body. Ted has been swimming 10 hours back to England and so very tired and cold. We have to start going for him, we cannot show pity, he has now been swimming for 24 hours 15 minutes, it is very dark, and out come the torches again, partly for company, and partly so that we do not lose him, we will have got some fifteen hours holding torches, cold job! but we know he is watching us 25 feet away.

12.35 A.M. We are now about ½ mile from St. Margarets Bay, he is very tired, we have told him a thousand lies, this ½ mile is getting to be murder, it is a good job we are in slack water, we tried very hard to get him on the land side of the South Goodwin Lightship earlier, but he was stopping so often, we passed the Lightship on the East side, then the Lightship buoy, after which we knew, we had only to keep him in the water to WIN.

Between 1 A.M. and 2.20 A.M. we had to fight all the way, Peter, Nioma and I got into the punt and tried to get him along, what we called him, is nobody's business. The Vega left us to continue with the swimmer for the last 400 yards, it was very dark and required two torches to keep him in view, we dared not get too close for he would have grabbed the boat, we shouted him all the way in, we lied so often he rumbled us, we could see our friends and their lights on the beach at St Margarets Bay, now only 200 yards away.

We were unable to make it into St Margarets Bay, and took him in to the rocks straight ahead, we heard a woman's voice shouting from the cliff 200 feet above, it was Mrs. Martin. We finally made the rocks, not more than 300 yards from the spot where he started some 30 hours before. Ted soon recovered lying on a hung rock attached to the base of the cliffs with about a foot deep in seaweed as a cushion. After a few minutes rest we got Ted into the boat which was bumping into the rocks, we were about to leave for the Vega when two photographers who had been clambering over the rocks somehow, called us back 20 yards and took many flashlight photos. We then started back to the Vega getting Ted aboard to warm him up. The Vega then made off for Dover where we arrived about 3 A.M. to be met by all our friends and many photographers and press representatives. By now Ted was full of beans, and was taken home for a nice bath to remove the grease, and so ended a swim of 30 hours 3 minutes that will probably last for many years, having beaten the record by 13 hours 7 minutes.

Signed: Dick Powell
CSA Observer

Don Schollander with Duke Savage

from Deep Water

*I*n top competition a whole new ingredient enters swimming, one that you never know until you reach this level—pain. You learn the pain in practice and you will know it in every race. As you approach the limit of your endurance it begins, coming on gradually, hitting your stomach first. Then your arms grow heavy and your legs tighten—thighs first, then knees. You sink lower in the water because you can't hold yourself up; you are actually swimming deeper in the water, as though someone were pushing down on your back. You experience perception changes. The sounds of the pool blend together and become a crashing roar in your ears. The water takes on a pinkish tinge. Your stomach feels as though it's going to fall out—every kick hurts like hell—and then suddenly you hear a shrill, internal scream.

In a race, at the threshold of pain, you have a choice. You can back off—or you can force yourself to drive to the finish, knowing that this pain will become agony. It is right there, at the pain barrier, that the great competitors separate from the rest. Most swimmers back away from the pain; a champion pushes himself on into agony. Is it masochistic? In a way, yes. When it comes it is oddly satisfying because you know it had to come and now it is there, because you are meeting it, taking it without backing down—because you enjoy the triumph of going through it, knowing it is the only way you can win. It's those last few meters of the race, while you're in agony, that count. If you can push yourself through that pain barrier into real agony, you're a champion.

Anne Sexton

The Nude Swim

On the southwest side of Capri
we found a little unknown grotto
where no people were and we
entered it completely
and let our bodies lose all
their loneliness.

All the fish in us
had escaped for a minute.
The real fish did not mind.
We did not disturb their personal life.
We calmly trailed over them
and under them, shedding
air bubbles, little white
balloons that drifted up
into the sun by the boat
where the Italian boatman slept
with his hat over his face.

Water so clear you could
read a book through it.
Water so buoyant you could
float on your elbow.
I lay on it as on a divan.
I lay on it just like
Matisse's *Red Odalisque.*
Water was my strange flower.
One must picture a woman
without a toga or a scarf
on a couch as deep as a tomb.

The walls of that grotto
were everycolor blue and
you said, "Look! Your eyes

are seacolor. Look! Your eyes
are skycolor." And my eyes
shut down as if they were
suddenly ashamed.

Charlotte Watson Sherman

Swimming Lesson

I like to sit on this big old mossy pillow and lay my head back on one of them twisted red oak roots that look like arms comin up outta the ground, arms that feel like the satin of Aunt Leatha's skin when she stoops down to gather me up and swing me round, and I lay in the roots like I'm layin in my mama's lap, listenin to her hum them old old songs, sound like folks bottled up with sorrow so sweet it turn to sugar.

This tree's right next to the old black pond where sometimes we get out in the water that covers our skinny arms with sparklin oil and we splash and kick and laugh.

I member the day somebody got the crazy idea to throw Neethie in the water and try to make her swim, and we all knew it was the wrong thing to do and didn't think bout what grown folks always say bout if you know better do better. We didn't think bout that when we was way out in all that green by the black water neath that big old red sun, but we shoulda, like I told everybody what would listen later. But nobody listened, not Egghead Sammy Ray Yarbrough, not even C.C. Beauregard whose daddy runs the funeral parlor and everybody is scairt of him cause he might get mad and get his daddy to come for ya in the middle of the night and put ya in that old hearse look like a big fat shiny beetle and take ya to the funeral parlor and put ya in a casket. So nobody, not me, not

Elmo, not Ruby, not nobody said a word when Egghead Sammy Ray Yarbrough and C.C. Beauregard decided they was gonna make Neethie swim.

Now, anybody got half a piece of sense know Neethie can't swim, don't like the water, can't even walk right on land on accounta one leg bein shorter than the other and don't nobody usually say nothin bout it one way or nuther cause that just the way she come into the world, lookin kinda like a crookedy upside-down wishbone. But some folks be laughin bout that big-sole shoe she gotta wear on her short leg so she don't walk lopsided. But she still limp a little even with that big shoe on. I like Neethie even though she do live in the Bible most of the time.

Mama always say ain't nothin wrong with Neethie livin in the Bible and wrinkle up her face and tell me I need to live in it too and ask me don't I want to enter the Golden Gates of Righteousness? I say I only wanna enter the golden arches of that shiny new hamburger stand they got there in Jackson and she won't even let me do that.

But we probably wouldn'ta thought to put Neethie in the water if Ruby hadn'ta been talkin bout how Jesus could walk on water. C.C. Beauregard said: No he can't, can't nobody walk on water. But I told em what my playuncle Eaton told me bout the slaves in the old days who left beatins and hoein and cotton and cleanin and set out cross the fields and headed north where they thought they could be free, and how some of em come to that yellow river that flow not too far from here and thought they had come to the end of they journey cause they couldn't swim and didn't know what all was in that water. Then they'd stoop at the edge and wet they faces and start moanin pieces of words they member from when we was all free, sound like: *hmmhmm o-o o-o-o-o mlongo.* And the wind would start to blow and the trees on the edge of the riverbank would start to sway and the air would feel like how my mama say it feel sometime when Reverend Samuel hit a high note in the middle of his preachin, and the women start to tremble and the deacons start to shake and everybody's eyes start to water with tears rollin down. That's how my playuncle Eaton say it feel when the runaways bent down at the edge of the yellow river thinkin bout freedom and how they couldn't swim and hummin: *mlongo mlongo hmmhmmhmmhmm o-o.* They knew they couldn't turn back so they kept on hummin that song and then they feet sank in the red mud at the edge of the river and come up covered with green sprouts climbin on they ankles and circlin round and tiny wings grew from each ankle and started flappin back and forth and back and forth, gentle at first and then faster and faster. And they could feel the cold of them chains deep in the wet earth and the wings beatin harder and then they took a step into the yellow water but they first foot didn't go down. It stayed right on top of the waves, and they put they other foot in the water and the same thing happened, it didn't go down, and they look over they shoulder for they last look at the land that tried to turn em into mules. They know they wouldn't never turn back, so they kept on walkin and the tiny wings kept beatin and they glided on cross the yellow river and only got the bottom of they pants and dresses wet.

But then Sammy Ray Yarbrough, whose head's big as a jug of water, broke in with his silly self and said, "Can't no slaves or nobody else walk cross no water, not even with wings on they back," and he don't believe Jesus did it neither. Ruby said she's gone tell his mama he said that, so he said o.k., if Neethie can walk on water, then anybody can cause Neethie was the closest thing to Jesus any of us knew bout. C.C. Beauregard said he'd go and get Neethie and bring her to the pond.

Now me and Ruby and Elmo tried to shift round and act like we wasn't scairt, but I knew we all musta been thinkin bout the whuppin we was gonna get when our mamas found out we'd pushed Neethie in the water, specially since she had a short leg and had to wear that big old shoe. I wasn't sure but it sound to me like this was cruelty and mama always say cruelty's one of the worst things in the world. Anyway, after a little while here come C.C. Beauregard holding Neethie by the hand and pullin her through bushes the color of bloodstone.

Soon as they got up to where we was standin near the edge of the pond Elmo started cryin, but didn't nobody pay him no mind cause Elmo always start cryin whenever somethin's bout to happen, good or bad. Mama say that boy just like to cry.

But when C.C. Beauregard brought Neethie to the edge of the pond I could feel tears wellin up in my own eyes, cause I knew it was gonna be one of them whuppins what hurts for a long, long time, probably one with a switch, cause Neethie was dressed up in a white ruffly dress that looked like it was for Sunday school, had her hair curled all over her head and had on some black patent leather buckle up shoes that was shinin like a mirror. I could see the trees and the sun when I looked down in them shoes.

Now Neethie's eyes was full of all of that kindness from livin in the Bible. And folks never made much over her short leg in front of her. She looked like some kind of brown angel standin there by the pond holdin C.C. Beauregard's hand.

"See, I told you I'd tell you what I brought you to the pond for, didn't I?" C.C. Beauregard asked.

"Uh huh," said Neethie.

Nobody else said a mumblin word. It was pretty quiet cept for the crickets whistlin and a few birds talkin in the trees and frogs croakin. We wasn't gonna say nothin and I was hopin Neethie have sense enough to turn round and go on back home, but C.C. Beauregard told her he was gonna teach her how to swim so she could come out and play with us at the pond every day steada goin and sittin up with the Bible and all them old folks all the time. Then he asked her wouldn't she like that?

"Uh huh," Neethie said.

So then C.C. Beauregard told her the onliest way for him to teach her how to swim was for him to see if her body was heavy in the water and the only way he could tell that was if she stepped out on that log and walked clear back to us. Egghead Sammy Ray Yarbrough'd found a short log and pushed it up to the edge of the pond where it lay in the water lookin like a big fat link sausage.

Neethie said, "You want me to walk out on that log and walk back on the water like Jesus?"

And C.C. Beauregard said, "Yeah, I want you to walk back just like Jesus."

Well, what he go and say that for? I didn't know whether to laugh or cry so I just started hummin that sound my playuncle Eaton told me was magic: *mlongo mlongo hmmhmmhmm o-o.*

Neethie started to get out on the log and Elmo started to holler. Ruby started cryin real soft-like where you almost couldn't hear her, what with Elmo's screamin and the wind whistlin in the trees.

C.C. Beauregard said, "Neethie, you think you better take that big shoe off?"

Neethie didn't say nothin, just looked kinda sweet and pitiful with her big black eyes lookin out on the water.

Now we all knew she couldn't swim a lick so if she fell in, there was gonna be hell to pay as my daddy say when I'm in double trouble. My legs started to itch and I could already feel that switch, but I just kept on singin: *hmm-hmmhmm o-o mlongo.* When Neethie was at the end of the log, she dropped her head back and looked up into the sky and said, "I believe." That was it. Just "I believe," and me and Ruby and Elmo with his cryin self all held hands and stood in a kinda circle at the end of the log, and C.C. Beauregard and Egghead Sammy Ray Yarbrough started movin back to the trees slow and easy. And then Neethie turned round and looked at C.C. Beauregard and asked, "You ready?" And that crazy boy just looked at Neethie with his eyes poppin out and didn't say nothin. So me and Ruby started singin them old magic words and Elmo was so scairt he stopped cryin and started singin em too: *mlongo mlongo hmm-hmmhmm o-o.* The words that was old magic went deep inside Neethie, deep inside, and Neethie stepped off the log into the air and put her foot down on that black water and she stayed up even with that big shoe on. Me and Ruby and Elmo squeezed our hands tighter and pressed our eyes shut, and sang the words louder and louder: *mlongo mlongo hmmhmmhmm o-o.* And the words pulled Neethie on cross the water and when we opened our eyes, Neethie was standin right there with us, her smile big as Egghead Sammy Ray Yarbrough's head, cept he wasn't there to see it.

Well, I thought that woulda fixed C.C. Beauregard and Egghead Sammy Ray Yarbrough good, but they didn't even get to see Neethie walk on water cause they slipped through the trees and run off soon as she stepped off the log.

We told Neethie it was good they was gone, cause they probably wouldn't'a knowed what they was lookin at anyway.

Then Ruby said, "Let's go over to the Sunflower Ice Cream Shop and get us some sodas to celebrate."

"Celebrate what?" Neethie asked.

"Us all not getting the whuppin of our lives," I said, and naturally Elmo started cryin.

Alix Kates Shulman

from In Every Woman's Life

*I*n every woman's life a time must come to think about marriage. And now it has come for Daisy Streeter. Though she often secretly thinks of herself as still a child (her friends are *girls*, not *women*, and the males she knows have progressed from *boys* only up as far as *guys*), her second trimester is rapidly approaching.

Lately she's begun to read her dreams as portents, and this morning she woke in the grip of an anxiety dream. She was swimming in deep water when someone, a man, began ducking her under. . . . And then? . . . She can't quite remember the rest. But she knows that whatever her dream, very soon, before the second trimester, she must decide what to do.

Like everyone, Daisy wants everything, all the pleasures and rewards of existence: safety and freedom, trust and passion, family and work and love. Who wouldn't? But how can she pull it off?

Most people marry. Some do it blindly: they step out to the end of the rocks, hold their noses, squeeze their eyes closed, count to three and leap. Others go slowly, one step at a time—the courtship, the affair, the shared apartment, the engagement, perhaps a pregnancy—until they feel they have no choice left. Some make flamboyant promises, pretending they'll do it just as soon as they graduate, get the promotion, placate the family, finish analysis, sign their divorce—then temporize for up to a lifetime. Some choose chastity, some fidelity, some adultery, some polygamy. But all settle for less than all.

Once, the choice seemed simple. No question of *if*, only *who*. When your time came to marry, you searched the available waters for the strongest swimmer and then you plunged in as if you had fallen, crying to be saved. He saved you or you sank: simple. But now the rules have changed. It's free swim for everyone. No guards blowing whistles. It's shameful to need a savior, but the water's as deep as ever, and if you're reckless you can drown.

Daisy is unprepared for these waters, despite all the advantages life has showered on her. Anxiously, she sits on the beach at Santa Cruz watching her choices fan out around her like the branchings of a complicated seaweed newly risen from the depths. Mysterious and strange they appear, with sinister nodules and fronds and blades. Are they nourishing or poisonous? How shall she choose? She lets the sand sift through her fingers as the child inside her turns and dreams.

Though Daisy's conscientious mother tried to teach her children the facts of life, she has confused them with abundant possibilities. Renouncing the strict, censorious ways of her own mother, Rosemary tried to condemn nothing. Instead, she discreetly concealed her shames, tucking her secrets in the crevices of her life, hoping they would not, like winter ice, tear treacherous holes in the surface of things. Now, those very secrets, shocking and real, are what Daisy most needs to know. She needs a map of the potholes. And her father's secrets too, the secrets of men, in place of his fusty advice. Without them, how can she surmount the confusions and hypocrisies of her own generation, who disparage marriage as ardently as they seek it? She watches the surfers spin flashy wakes as she tries to divine what to do.

She can marry like her mother and her mother's mother and all her ancestors. (No, not all: not dashing Aunt Sarah, her mother's favorite, whom Grandpa denied from the day she left home—and how many more?) There, in that comfortable house with the good kitchen and the good Michael returning every night, she could be a good, could be the best of mothers. But one child of hers, her own unbounded spirit, born out of wedlock, would be missing. And after a sufficient time, declared dead. A hero, but dead. A dead hero. And then every time she gazed out a certain window of her cozy life she'd see the gold star hanging there and remember her missing child—daring, dashing, dead. But, for the sake of the living children, she would not permit herself to mourn.

Or she can refuse the bondage of the past and go her own way, making of herself an exception, an example. (A spectacle, her father would call it, shaking his head and counseling prudence, as she stood naked in the window flagging her ears at the neighbors' sons.) But then she'd have only one child, whom she'd carry through the world in a pack on her back. Gypsies together, they'd sing for their supper. Anesthetized, she'd tie her tubes to be free.

Or she could marry Michael in every sense but the legal. Have a party to prove it, clap three times to undo it. A fairy tale. (But who would believe it?) Daisy piles little heaps of sand around her like reasons, but try as she may, she can't figure out if such an arrangement would have the benefits of marriage without the penalties, or the penalties without the benefits. She thinks she'd enjoy having people look at them like a married couple as long as they're not, but if they really were, she probably couldn't stand it. She will *not* be addressed as *Mrs.* or described as *wife!* Her mother would say you were tied forever to the father of your children, legally or not; but her father would make a great to-do about the documents. (Whatever they said on the matter, Daisy noted, they'd made sure to have the document themselves—and she was glad.)

But there was another, a fourth, possibility. Born of prudence coupled with defiance, it seemed to Daisy to embody her birthright: her patrimony and her matrimony. She sensed that it was no less absurd than her other choices, but it appealed to her sense of drama (and there was the baby to consider):

A secret marriage, then, like Romeo and Juliet's. She'll marry Michael—for the baby's sake—but only in the strictest secrecy. No one, not even their parents, will know.

Daisy pulls off her sweatshirt, drops her jeans, and walks down to the water. How quickly everything changes. Even in this new loose swimsuit her belly no longer looks flat, and does she only imagine as she plunges into the ocean that her body is more buoyant?

Dreamily she floats on her back, watching the huge blue sky. Suddenly she remembers her morning dream. She was swimming. Then a man began pushing her head under water. Terrified, she began to struggle—until she gradually discovered she was able to breathe under water.

Yes, like her parents and ancestors before her, she will marry; and no one, she consoles herself, need ever be the wiser.

Stevie Smith

Not Waving but Drowning

Nobody heard him, the dead man,
But still he lay moaning:
I was much further out than you thought
And not waving but drowning.

Poor chap, he always loved larking
And now he's dead
It must have been too cold for him his heart gave way,
They said.

Oh, no no no, it was too cold always
(Still the dead one lay moaning)
I was much too far out all my life
And not waving but drowning.

Maureen Stanton

Water

I see that old woman every now and then at the Y, the one who is not a lunch
meat lover. She swims, as I do. She swims in a pair of black shorts and a
black shirt. She is ashamed to show her loose, curdled flesh in front of the old
men in the hot tub, with their big bellies and skinny legs, red faced, eyeing the
teen-age girls splashing each other.

She's been coming here every day for 17 years. She swims a half-mile, I
heard her tell someone. Her swimming is more like walking and treading than
swimming, so slow I pass her three times before she reaches the end of the pool.
Underwater, blurry and dark, she is like a manatee, slow and graceful, as if her
ancestors dwelled in the water, like the water is her voice.

I, on the other hand, am fast. I am faster than any of the other swimmers.
My arms are long and they easily pull the water to me. My legs are pure muscle
and they push me along. I glide through the water like a slippery fish. The water flows in and out of my mouth, like a filter, separating air from water, like
gills, and I feel like a fish. I am a fish.

I do a turn at the end of each length, a neat, tucked somersault, efficient
and powerful, propelled by my fins. I submerge and glide, scissor kick and go
deeper, rise for air. I swim back and forth, one end to the other like the neon
tetras in my tank at home. And each time I pass over a bobby pin at the bottom

of the pool, or a Band-Aid, a rubber band. It makes me feel lonely. I stare down at the one-inch-square, dirty blue and white tiles at the bottom of the pool. Some are missing. It reminds me of when I was a child, scared of driving through Callahan Tunnel in Boston because little squares of tiles had fallen out. Water dripped from the ceiling, and I imagined more tiles popping off from the pressure and then water from Boston Harbor bursting through, rushing in, drowning us. Like a tidal wave.

I was never afraid of the ocean until I thought I could swim so well that I owned it, until once in California when I was a fearless teen-ager I swam out to some pelicans and couldn't get back in. No matter how hard I swam I still was being dragged farther and farther out to sea. I panicked. I put my face in the water and paddled my arms as hard as I could, and finally stepped down and touched soft sand on the ocean floor. I was never the same in the ocean. Never again let myself be seaweed and let the waves tumble me about until my bathing suit is full of sand, and weak and chilled fall onto the warmth of my towel to let the sun bake me.

On top of the water I am fast, like a water bug. But underneath, to myself, swimming, everything is in slow motion, dreamy. Underwater I am honest. I am left with myself. My lungs, my heart, my thoughts. When I swim I fantasize. I invent my life. Scenes are acted out in my mind. I am confident. I am witty. I am sleek and smart, and sophisticated. I am a poet of the sea. I am a painter, an athlete, a walker, a hermit on a mountain. I am dreaming. Fish water water water. I talked in my sleep once, and my friend told me I said that. Fish water water water. It has become my mantra.

After our laps, we sit in the hot tub, I and the old woman and others I don't know. Once she said to anyone, "We're blessed, ain't we?" And no one answered her. They just stared at each other. I stare too. It's because we are afraid. We are exposed. We come waddling out of the locker room. Fat hangs off our arms and legs and necks. Nipples and penises are outlined in wet bathing suits. Makeup is washed away. Hair is flattened. Baldness shows. People look like they were just born, wet and slick and ugly. They are honest.

There is a man I see often at the Y. He has broad shoulders and takes bold strokes. He has distinguished, graying hair and looks like a corporate executive. I thought he was, until one day I recognized a man in the airport and placed him as the corporate executive swimmer at the Y. His uniform pulled his shoulders down, he seemed too tall for his job, barely fit under the electronic metal detector, as he took a woman's belongings and put them in a Tupperware container, asked her to pass through again. And after that, when I saw him at the Y, I thought he could see right through me, because I can see through him. I know him now, know he is not a corporate executive, but a man who stands in the airport all day, watching people come and go, looking inside their bags and purses. But still he swims fast with strong, powerful arms that make him seem like a giant, like a great white.

There was another man who I only saw in the hot tub once. He struck up a conversation like he was lighting a cigar and puffing until he got it going, asking me if I ever listened to the radio, liked that new jazz station. I said no.

"I'm tired of listening to country, all they ever do is cry about a broken heart. I know enough about that, my wife left me two weeks ago after 18 years. She was 20 years younger than me."

"That's too bad," I said. I am not good at small talk.

"How old do you think I look?" he asked. I thought he looked 60 so I said, "55?"

He said proudly, "61."

"Nice talking to you," he said and shook my hand like we were in a business meeting, and he stepped out of the hot tub in his bathing trunks and I felt like I was acting in a movie.

It happens a lot to me, on buses and in supermarkets. Once a woman at the grocery store told me about her life, taking all the time she wanted to ring up my items, hesitating, holding my canned ham in her hand, shaking it at me when she wanted to make a point, throwing my tomatoes into the bag because she was angry about her boyfriend cheating on her and leaving her. I said, "Maybe you could start over," and she said, "Nah, too many broken promises, too many shattered dreams." And she gave me my change and picked up the tabloid she was reading with Sarah Ferguson and Lady Diana on the cover.

.

I take a shower after sitting in the hot tub, and the old woman is there too. Her belly falls below her pubic area so you can't see her hair there, and her skin is gathered together, stretched out from so much use, years and years of movement. Her legs are like logs, her ankles and knees are lost. She puts her dripping clothes into the new machine in the women's locker room which dries them out through centrifugal force. She turns to a lady behind her. "Ain't that wonderful?"

After her shower, she asks someone to rub lotion on her back. Her wide, white, curved back. She asks anyone who happens to be around. I've seen her. A kind stranger softens her back with lotion and she talks.

"My son and his wife are coming over today so I am making my special casserole with tomatoes and green peppers and rice and cheese."

And the other woman said, "I have a wonderful casserole that I make with peas and noodles and deli loaf."

"Oh, I'm not a lunch meat lover," the old woman says. It sounded to me like a sad poem. They talk about leftovers, what keeps, what doesn't, as the stranger kneads the old woman's back. She closes her eyes and says, "You don't know how much I appreciate that."

.

One day I see the woman who is not a lunch meat lover with a gadget, a towel thing with handles that lets her rub her own back, which she uses when no one is around. Some days I want to see her, with her short cropped hair, that yarn yellow of blondes when they get old, not gray or silver but like the color of her teeth. Other days I don't want to see her, cheerful and happy because we have a bathing suit dryer or a hot tub.

She looks at me and I glance away. But our eyes touch, enough for her to ask me if I would mind rubbing lotion on her back. Slowly, I put some cold lotion in my hand and touch her soft, ashy skin and she begins to talk. She says she used to be a dancer and worked on Broadway and then taught dance lessons.

"You like to swim," I said to her.

"Oh, that's not swimming," she said. "That's ballet."

I rub the lotion into her skin, and add more, basting, and coating and moving my hand all over her back without taking it off, like her back was a Ouija board and my hand, moving mysteriously, would reveal something to me. I start to cry, silently, tears streaming down my face, and she reaches around and touches my arm and says, "There, there."

And I swim. I remember my life and it seems to me, underwater, what has happened was purposeful. I go back to childhood and I remember my birth, hypnotized. I am a fish, swimming from my little stream out into the big ocean, and sometimes, I am scared.

Linda Svendsen

Up Late

*W*e were going for a moonlight swim. It was just us. She parked by Trout
Lake and said take off your pedal-pushers, panties will be O.K. Who will
see? Her dress was over her head and gone. She wore girdle, garters, a white bra
with fat straps. She rolled the windows down, turned the radio on, up, and the
song said *you say potato and I say potahto*. I kept my sneakers; between us and
water were rocks and evergreen needles, and then in the lake, invisible nipping
fish. My mother took my hand. She said, "Come on, small fry."

That lake had no bottom. Every summer a boy fishing fell backward out of
a canoe and it was curtains. None were found. I didn't think about drowning: I
was six, could kick and float, held Mum's hand, would never die until God
needed a new angel. We followed the flashlight beam until the moon took
over—down the little hill to the dock. Then she remembered the emergency.
She had parked on an incline and the car might roll down the hill to sink in the
lake. We would have to sleep on the dock until sunup or the lifeguard. People—
my father, who was dead—would wonder. She headed back to the road.

I climbed the big water slide and sat up top. No breeze. Across the lake
were houses with sundecks, porch lights, wind chimes and pools, and I could
hear people living a late August life, and the ruckus of grasshoppers rubbing
themselves, and the radio host in our car say, "Speak up, you're on the air."

I was forbidden to slide in the dark, in the deep part. I stayed still and sang "Kookaburra," and when the door hadn't slammed, and I didn't see her light, "Policeman, policeman, do your duty, here comes Adele, the bathing beauty, she can do the rumba, she can do the splits," etc., and then stuck in my mother's name, June, and then her middle name, Ruth.

·

I was the baby and Mum had taken me with her to the Elks Club. This was how she kept steak in our mouths, barrettes in my hair. I usually sat at the staff table with my coloring book and crayons and soft drink, guarding everybody's smokes. This time I had waited in the coat check. It was empty in hot weather. In the heat all the women were bare shoulders and napes and loud splashed cologne. A cocktail waitress named Cindy brought me a big glass of ice cubes with a pink straw and let me look at the photos in her wallet and read the backs. I wanted her for my sister.

When my mother touched the piano, the crowd shut up. They squeezed each other and slowed down. The men stood tall and swayed a little this way, a little that. Ladies closed their eyes and just didn't care. It was *"Que Sera, Sera."* Lights went off. I was lying on the cold linoleum under hundreds of thin wire coat hangers. This was where we were before the lake.

·

She walked back to the dock keeping the beam barely ahead of her next step. I saw a face in her knee. Without clothes on, my mother looked like somebody else and I didn't know who. She put towels down by the slide and raised her arms. I let myself into them. "Ready, mermaid?" she said. Behind her the lake loomed like a trick. Light glinted off safety pins fastened below.

She clung to the rope ladder and lowered her body bit by bit. She said it burned. She was only waist-deep when I jumped. I liked getting things over with. I could hold my breath for seconds. My mother couldn't even swim. She hated getting her hair wet and losing her style. She wouldn't even duck her head underwater to see what was what. She found a warm spot and didn't budge.

When I asked, she spread her legs wide to let me swim between. The first time I couldn't find her. The lake was ink. Once I got the knack I couldn't get tired of this. I made it harder. If my hand brushed, if I bumped into, if the smooth rubber sole of my sneaker nicked, she would die. She would die before Christmas. I touched her. I changed the rule. She would die after I skipped grade two, before 1961, whenever I wanted. I kept touching. She stayed living. Her life stretched long, longer than mine. It was up to me. She was goosebumps. She was just a shadow I passed through to get to the other side.

．

She heard it first, of course. I was diving. I was beneath her. I was being pickled by the lake. I thought it was a speedboat—a fisherman trolling for breakfast with a bright hook. The motor was rude; it was a lawn mower chopping away at the water. Whether to stay under, I wasn't sure. If I came up, someone might see my no top, our hardly anything on. A little later, and I didn't hear it anymore.

After that I lost track: lost track of how long I'd skimmed bottom, of when she would be kaput, lost track of fun and was I good. I was more water than girl. I was on your mark, get set, go, keep going or else. The lake spilled up my nose. My mother was still my arch. This may have taken one sheer minute.

．

Her face wasn't like an ice cube, a crack, the flame of a match, or the moon. It didn't keep you looking. Sometimes the hook of her nose scared me and I could not hug her. I had to glance behind, around her waist, as if somebody surprising us had just walked in a door. Then she would turn around, turn back and say, "What did you see?" and forget we were going to touch.

We were lying on towels on the dock and I was looking at her. She was looking up at the night. I shut off my flashlight and twinned her. I bent my knees, making my legs steep hills. I crossed myself. I tried to think about everything she could think of and this was too easy so I tried to look like I was thinking. I put her soft voice in mine and said *Look both ways* and *Did you have enough? There's more.*

"Who are you whispering to?" She rolled over. "Do you have a secret friend?"

The stars were still out. Each star was part of a family picture, each family of light had a name. It all fit. People said stars told stories if you stared. I did this for a long time, different times, and I could not see a spoon spilling cough syrup or the dog lifting a hind leg or an arrow aimed at us. When I looked, each star was already gone. I was only seeing old light left behind. This was science. I stared at the space between two stars then shut my eyes to see which was darkest. It was darkest inside. I heard her go by, each plank making a new noise under her foot. "Where are you going?" I said.

"I don't know." She stopped by the ladder of the slide and grabbed the bars. "I don't want to go home yet," she said. She leaned back letting her arms do the work, hold her, and then climbed up. She looked down on me from the top of the slide. "I think you took a nap," she said.

I shook my head. I never slept, I was never not awake, I had never had a dream. In the middle of the night, if she woke thirsty, she was out of bed after me, after water ran cool and hit the glass bottom. When my father was sick, I sat big and close by his side and watched the life drip clear into him. He could not die if I was watching. We both knew it.

"I'm going to let go," she said. "I'm letting go."

I slid the switch on the flashlight and buttered her in its cone. Her arms surrendered over her head. Her legs were crooked, straight when she slipped in. She was here, then gone. Her whoop, mouth wide open, was eaten by the lake. The splash—noisy, tall, a surprise, a lily shaking—made stars leap out of the lake and gleam where she had hung.

.

The night did not stop being hot. It kept getting warmer. Across the lake, the people in those houses were lying on top of beds listening to fans like big bugs. The trees were slack and bored, and the ones wearing leaves gave some up. They rode the water. When my mother tried to float, her face stayed above the water and the rest of her sank. She did not believe me when I told her. I had done breath bobs beside her. "You're sinking," I said and she said, "I am not."

I left. I could tell when she wanted to be alone. I leaned forward onto the lap of the water and kicked once. I didn't need her; I kept my chin down in the water and turned into a crocodile: all eyes, silence, might.

I looked up when the man walked out of the bush and onto the dock. He saw us and kept coming. He sat on the edge of the dock and undid his sandals. The moon lit us all. He looked older than her. He was seeing her in her brassiere. She saw him seeing and ran a hand through her hair, then hung onto a strand and twisted. He looked at me. Without blinking I looked back. He eased off a sandal, a black sock, and tucked the sock under the sandal straps, watching me. He did the same to the other foot. The socks weren't all black. There were stripes of lightning on the sides. He stood up and started taking off his shirt.

My mother glanced back where our car was parked like she had a kink in her neck or had to be somewhere by a certain time. The radio in our car gave the report. It would be the same again tomorrow and that was hot. Her face said she had lost something. I wondered where he had come from and when he would go. I wondered if he would be naked soon. "Guess what I am," I said to her. I spun in the lake. My sneakers slapped and raised mud. I tapped her. "Guess." "Not now," she said and tried to take my hand. "Swizzlestick," I said. "In a drink." He folded his shirt. I kept whirling. I refused to let go and be dizzy. I looked at the dock, her, the dark yards on the other side, the tongue of the slide, the dock, to keep my bearings. I wondered if he lived in a cave in the woods. "Guess now. Guess what I am now," I said. "You're very loud," she whispered. "Do you want to wake up the fish?" He was pulling down his pants. I could see the shiny rim of swim trunks. "I'm a swizzlestick in Orange Crush," I said. I was exhausted. They were both tilting.

The man looked down on us. He was so strong, he looked like he could throw me high up in the air and catch me and keep doing it. He nodded at her, then me, and said, "Ladies." His hands made a prayer. He fixed upon a point and then sprang off the dock and flew over me. For a moment he made another kind of night, pale, closer to day. For a second I smelled his hair and under his arms and breath. He smiled back at me. I wasn't afraid. He entered the lake like a stone thrown sideways, skimming, and broke into a crawl. He swam without a splash, his stroke and kick caught no light. I watched until she clapped. "Out," she said. "It's late. It's time to go."

We got out and she wrapped me in a damp towel. I lost my balance and almost fell back in; she made me lie down and pulled me across and over her legs like a cape. Before Dad died, he could not hold me on his knees. I was too heavy. "Keep your head down," she said. "Close these," she said and kissed above my eyes. Her garter biting into my cheek would make a mark gone by morning.

I felt much better. When I asked who he was, in her story voice she said she didn't know. Maybe his wife read long books in bed and kept the light burning. Maybe he was on a team and had to practice to beat everybody. Maybe he was a man who could never fall asleep in August, or after midnight. Maybe he was king of the lake. She said he could have been anybody.

In my mother's arms, I looked for him. I couldn't tell if he was coming or going. He was a tear, a tiny rip in the white scarf tossed down by that moon. He could have been an angel.

Charles Tomlinson

Swimming Chenango Lake

Winter will bar the swimmer soon.
   He reads the water's autumnal hesitations
A wealth of ways: it is jarred,
   It is astir already despite its steadiness,
Where the first leaves at the first
   Tremor of the morning air have dropped
Anticipating him, launching their imprints
   Outwards in eccentric, overlapping circles.
There is a geometry of water, for this
   Squares off the clouds' redundances
And sets them floating in a nether atmosphere
   All angles and elongations: every tree
Appears a cypress as it stretches there
   And every bush that shows the season,
A shaft of fire. It is a geometry and not
   A fantasia of distorting forms, but each
Liquid variation answerable to the theme
   It makes away from, plays before:
It is a consistency, the grain of the pulsating flow.
   But he has looked long enough, and now
Body must recall the eye to its dependence
   As he scissors the waterscape apart
And sways it to tatters. Its coldness
   Holding him to itself, he grants the grasp,
For to swim is also to take hold
   On water's meaning, to move in its embrace
And to be, between grasp and grasping, free.
   He reaches in-and-through to that space
The body is heir to, making a where
   In water, a possession to be relinquished
Willingly at each stroke. The image he has torn
   Flows-to behind him, healing itself,
Lifting and lengthening, splayed like the feathers
   Down an immense wing whose darkening spread

Shadows his solitariness: alone, he is unnamed
    By this baptism, where only Chenango bears a name
In a lost language he begins to construe—
    A speech of densities and derisions, of half-
Replies to the questions his body must frame
    Frogwise across the all but penetrable element.
Human, he fronts it and, human, he draws back
    From the interior cold, the mercilessness
That yet shows a kind of mercy sustaining him.
    The last sun of the year is drying his skin
Above a surface a mere mosaic of tiny shatterings,
    Where a wind is unscaping all images in the flowing obsidian,
The going-elsewhere of ripples incessantly shaping.

Damp in the Afternoon

*W*hen I began trying to describe *taureaux piscine* to people in America, I was struck by how many of them had precisely the same response: "You have to be kidding!" I'll admit that I might have been tempted to use that phrase myself when *taureaux piscine* first came to my attention, except that my French wouldn't have been up to it. My French isn't up to a lot, although I know a number of nouns. I probably just shook my head in amazement, or did my imperfect imitation of that look Frenchmen in cafés use to indicate without a word that what has just been said may well be true for the simple reason that so many other silly things are.

This happened one Saturday, market day, in Uzès. I was sitting with Alice and Abigail and Sarah in an outdoor café we favored on Saturdays for its proximity to our market-day *pommes frites* specialist, a thorough craftsman who would not consider offering a customer a sackful of French fries until he had fried them at least twice. On a tree next to our table, a handwritten sign announced an event that would take place in the local arena at nine that night: TAUREAUX PISCINE. I do not have to be kidding.

I had been under the impression that both *taureaux* and *piscine* were among my nouns, but I couldn't think of any way to translate them except as "bulls" and "swimming pool." The next time our table was visited by the café's proprietress, a woman who had already demonstrated her good nature by a tolerant view of carried-in *pommes frites*, I tried to get some more information. "*Taureaux comme taureaux?*" I asked, using my fingers as horns to do a passable imitation of a fighting bull. (I know several conjunctions; it's verbs I don't do.)

"*Oui, monsieur*," she said.

"*Piscine comme piscine?*" I went on, demonstrating with an Esther Williams breaststroke that I happen to do almost flawlessly as long as I'm out of the water.

"*Oui, monsieur.*"

She bustled off to see to her other customers, leaving me with a lot of questions unexpressed and, for me in French, unexpressible. I knew that the South of France, particularly the area toward the mouth of the Rhône, had its own tradition of Provençal tauromachy. I suppose you could say that the South of France, particularly the Côte d'Azur, has its own tradition of swimming pools. But how would the two go together? Why would the two go together?

The answers were not immediately forthcoming. As it happened, we were unable to attend the *taureaux piscine* being held in the arena that evening. We did have a couple of English-speaking acquaintances who had lived in Uzès for some time, but they had never heard of *taureaux piscine*. I made a careful survey of wall posters in Uzès and in any other town we happened to drive through that next week. No *taureaux piscine*. I began to think that I had missed the opportunity to see a unique coupling of bulls and swimming pool. It occurred to me that I might be left with only that astounding name—*taureaux piscine*. Aside from the energy it produced with its jarring juxtaposition, it had struck me from the start as a name of great euphony. It was clearly at its best when used as something like a war cry, with all four syllables plainly and loudly enunciated—"TAU-REAUX-PI-SCINE!" In fact, as we drove through the countryside around Uzès, I occasionally found myself shouting "TAU-REAUX-PI-SCINE" out the car window into the wind, as if to announce to the residents of the next village what my quest was. The next Saturday was our last Saturday in Uzès. We went to the same café. I saw the same sign on the same tree: TAUREAUX PISCINE.

We arrived at the arena late. By chance, we had guests that weekend, and some of them were reluctant to rush through dinner, even though I kept telling them that, for all we knew about *taureaux piscine*, the best part might be right at the beginning. The arena looked like the bullfight arena of a Spanish provincial town except, of course, that in the middle of the ring there was a swimming pool—a rather small swimming pool, with only a couple of feet of water in it, but still a swimming pool. From the stands it looked like one of those plastic swimming pools that people in the suburbs buy at the discount store and stick out in the back yard for the smaller kids to splash around in. There were a few dozen teenage boys in the ring. There was also a bull—a small bull, with blunts on the points of his horns, but still a bull. In other words, the bull in *taureaux piscine* was a bull, and the swimming pool was a swimming pool. Upon my oath.

Within a few minutes it was clear that *taureaux piscine* has an extraordinary aspect that I had not anticipated during the week I'd spent simply amazed at its existence and enamored of its name. It is the only sport I have ever encountered that has only one rule: If you and the bull are in the pool at the same time, you win. If you do it again, you win again; a limitation of the rule would require a second rule.

The boys in the ring that night seemed to be having trouble winning. An announcer talked constantly over a public address system—exhorting the boys, taunting the boys, praising the bull, increasing the number of francs that would go to anybody who managed to share the pool with the bull. The boys, most of whom were dressed in blue jeans and T-shirts, spent a lot of time jumping up and down to attract the bull's attention and a lot of time running from the bull once they had it—usually ending the run by leaping over the inner fence that separates the ring from the stands in a bullfight arena. Occasionally, two or three of them would simply stand in the pool waiting for the bull to join them—like those towering but ungainly centers in the earlier days of basketball who planted themselves under the basket—and would have second thoughts about the strategy once the bull actually approached.

Suddenly, one boy, realizing that he had attracted the bull's attention from just the right angle, started his run toward the *piscine* simultaneously with the bull's charge and dived in head first just as the bull rumbled through the water. I thought it was a brilliant, daring move—something I might have been tempted to describe, if I had been a fan of longer duration, as "what *taureaux piscine* is all about."

I have to say that it was not enough to make *taureaux piscine* enthusiasts out of my companions. Alice and Abigail agreed that *taureaux piscine* was at least boring and maybe cruel. Sarah gazed upon the goings-on as she might have gazed upon a mixed-vegetable plate. One of our guests said that *taureaux piscine* was a mess. Somebody in our party, I am obligated to report, said to me, "You have to be kidding!" even after he had seen *taureaux piscine* with his own eyes.

I liked it. Of course, as someone who had spent a week in a state of excitement over the very existence of *taureaux piscine*, I might have been expected to have a certain proprietary feeling about it. That did not blind me to its faults. "I'll admit it lacks finesse," I said after the head-first hero had shaken himself off, collected forty francs from the announcer, and rejoined his fellows. Still, how could anybody fail to be engaged by it? It provoked so many questions. How, for instance, had *taureaux piscine* come about? It was as if a game had been invented by the wild man in the old-fashioned Hollywood story conference—the one who's there to come up with something like "I've got it! Her long-lost father is the King of England," so that someone else is jogged into saying, "Well, not the King of England, but some sort of English aristocrat might not be a bad idea." The wild man says, "Here it is—a bull and a swimming pool," and for some reason nobody says, "Not a swimming pool, Harry, but we could have a nice little obstacle course or something like that." Why had Americans spent so much time and energy analyzing the Spanish bullfight while completely ignoring *taureaux piscine?* I intended to take care of that oversight the following summer. During the winter, while driving along turnpikes, I occasionally opened the window and shouted, "TAU-REAUX-PI-SCINE," just to keep my hand in.

·

It's not as if you could just call up the United Taureaux Piscine League and ask for the summer schedule. We were back in France the next June, but I couldn't seem to find any *taureaux piscine.* We were staying in a town just east of the Rhône, still in the part of Provence where any good-sized village is likely to have both a bullfight arena and a café that serves as headquarters for the local *club taurin.* There was no shortage of posters with pictures of bulls on them. It was already high season for the Provençal version of bullfighting, which is often called La Course Camarguaise—after the Camargue, a vast salt marsh in the Rhône delta, where most of the bulls are raised. A French bullfight isn't exactly a fight. There are no swords or capes or elaborate costumes. In the variety that has become an organized professional sport, the bull has a sort of rosette, called a *cocarde,* attached to his horns; the participants—men who are dressed in white pants and white T-shirts and white sneakers—run in a long arc that passes in front of the bull, try to snatch off the *cocarde* with what amounts to a comb, and then try to get themselves over the barrier before the bull can demonstrate his displeasure.

The participants, called *rasateurs,* are competing against one another rather than against the bull; they amass point totals that are listed regularly in the newspapers, like the winnings of professional golfers. The leading *rasateurs* become famous in Provence, as do the leading bulls. *Rasateurs* are not in the least embarrassed by having to leap over the barrier all the time. A Spanish matador who ran out of the ring, of course, might as well just keep going, but for a French *rasateur,* carrying only a four-inch comb by way of protection, a *coup de barrière* is the logical exit. In the magazines devoted to La Course Camarguaise—I read a number of them, looking for notices of *taureaux piscine*—nearly every picture seems to be of a *rasateur* leaping over the barrier toward the stands, followed at a distance of an inch or two by an angry bull. It would be gratifying, I suppose, to report that the French version of tauromachy—sporting, nonlethal, good-humored, relatively unpretentious—is more exciting than the Spanish *corrida.* But I found that a little of it goes a long way.

For my money, I thought as I watched some celebrated *rasateurs* go through their paces one afternoon, the performance could be improved greatly by the simple addition of a swimming pool.

In my search for *taureaux piscine*, I found that the French, not being locked into bullfighting as a ritual, had developed all sorts of variations on the theme of La Course Camarguaise. Particularly during a festival, a Provençal town is likely to complement the performance of the *rasateurs* with less formal events, which are designed to include anyone who feels like having a go. In the simplest form, a small bull or cow is let out into the ring, and the local boys swerve in front of it on their way to the barrier—trying to pick off a *cocarde*, or, in the more common version, simply trying to show how close they can get. A number of games take off from there. Lydie Marshall, a French-born friend of ours who had volunteered to act as a provider of verbs for my quest while she was visiting us in Provence, tracked down a friend of hers who had participated in a game called *taureaux pastèque*, or *taureaux* watermelon. It's one of those games that sound simple but turn out to be complicated. Every contestant is given a piece of watermelon to eat, and the one who finishes first wins. That's the simple part. The complicating factors are that the watermelon can be eaten only while the contestant is seated on a bench, the bench is in the bullring, and so is a bull. One of the games I heard about sounded almost as ingeniously simple as *taureaux piscine*. It's called *taureaux football*. Two teams engage in a game of soccer. The only difference from conventional soccer is that there's a bull in the ring.

I had a certain amount of curiosity about *taureaux football*. It was obviously a game that could include some subtle strategic wrinkles. For instance, would the best strategy be simply to play soccer, glancing over your shoulder regularly for the bull, or would the best strategy be to have one man stand behind the opposing goalie and try to attract the bull's attention?

I did not let my curiosity about *taureaux football* deflect me from the thrust of my research—*taureaux piscine*. Where was it? I got some guidance from a woman we fell into conversation with in a town called Eyragues while watching an *abrivado*—an entertainment in which a bull is run up and down a street within a phalanx of Camarguaise horsemen while the brave lads of the town try to pry him from his blockers, sometimes by the tail. She said that *taureaux piscine* was much more common toward July, when the evenings could be counted on to be warm. Of course! I should have realized that a sport requiring its successful participants to run around in soaking-wet clothing had to be played in warm weather. It was clear that I could not yet be described as a true student of the game.

·

I had never thought of looking for *taureaux piscine* at the Nîmes Feria. Nîmes, along with a few other places in Provence, regularly stages absolutely traditional Spanish *corridas*—its Roman arena is even better suited to that than to the acrobatics of Le Chicago—and the Feria is a festive week of Spanish bullfighting that can inspire some citizens to talk about how much the people of Nîmes have in common with the people of Seville. The Feria always presents leading Spanish matadors. The bulls are from illustrious Andalusian bull ranches. The press coverage is marked by the sort of purple *corrida* prose I have treasured ever since I read, many years ago in Seville, that a matador named Diego Puerta had in his fight the previous day "written brilliant pages in the book of valor." During the Feria, we read in the local newspaper that "the presentation of Curro Caro was a sonnet of artistic success" and that "in the space of an instant, no more, but an instant that seemed an eternity, with the fourth bull Emilio Muñoz created a masterpiece of purity." I couldn't see where *taureaux piscine* would fit in with talk like that. Then, toward the end of the Feria, I happened to glance through the schedule of events and saw that there was a *taureaux piscine* that very evening at eight o'clock. We headed for Nîmes.

The *taureaux piscine* was not being held in the Roman arena. It was in a small arena that belonged to the Nîmes bullfighting school. During the Feria, the bullfight-school arena was the last stop along a sort of midway of food booths and carnival rides and a bandstand that featured, the evening we were there, Alain May et les Mod Beats. Lydie quickly found the man in charge—Lucien Moulin, who worked for the city of Alès, twenty-five miles or so north of Nîmes, and staged *taureaux piscines* on the side. Moulin said that for the Feria he had arranged and announced five *taureaux piscines* a day, each with six bulls—a pace so grueling that he had abandoned his normal practice of introducing each bull with his own trumpet fanfare and settled for a taped rendition over the public address system. The *taureaux piscine* we saw him put on was squarely in the tradition of what I remembered from Uzès, although with a closer look I realized that the swimming pool was made not of plastic but of hay bales and a canvas tarp. Moulin spoke constantly over the public address system, providing play-by-play and offers of great rewards from various sponsors and taunts for the brave young men and jokes that tended to dwell on mothers-in-law or on the potential consequences of being followed very closely by a bull. Occasionally, a triumphant young man would stand before Moulin, dripping wet, to be tossed fifty or sixty francs in coins. I thought that one tall boy wearing blue jeans but no shirt might be said to have written brilliant pages in the book of valor if he hadn't slipped a bit in the mud that forms from the splashing just outside the pool. A boy wearing a T-shirt that said ÉCOUTEZ RADIO 102 made a leap toward the pool that I would consider at least a rhyming couplet of artistic success.

After the last bull had left the ring, we had a chat with Moulin. I was hoping to learn something of how *taureaux piscine* had developed—from a chance puddle at a Camarguaise bull ranch, maybe, or through some old Provençal connection between bulls and rivers that I hadn't yet put together. When I asked if special bulls were required, Moulin said he always got his bulls from Jean-Marie Bilhau, whose father, Émile, had invented *taureaux piscine*.

"Did he say 'invented *taureaux piscine*'?" I asked Lydie.

"That's what he said," Lydie replied.

Invented *taureaux piscine!* There was an inventor of *taureaux piscine!* I asked Moulin if Émile Bilhau was still alive. Moulin said that the elder Bilhau was up in years but still quite active. I could presumably drive down to his place, near Saint-Gilles, and have a chat with him. I felt like a baseball nut who had just been told that it wouldn't be any problem to have a beer with Abner Doubleday.

•

Saint-Gilles turned out to be a town whose signs identified it as Gateway to the Camargue and City of Roman Art. I found Émile Bilhau a few miles outside of town in a place called Mas d'Estagel—a place that began as a medieval monastery, was converted into a hotel, and was then converted by Bilhau and his wife into a kind of rural catering hall for parties and special events. The buildings were surrounded by fields and vineyards. Next to a sort of picnic ground for outdoor parties was a roughly made bullring. Émile Bilhau turned out to be a small, straightforward country man who looked something like a Camarguaise version of Barry Fitzgerald. He said he had been interested in horses and bulls all his life; as a young man, he told us, he became the only rider in France who could leap from a horse onto the back of a bull, a trick he picked up from watching a visiting American rodeo. He acknowledged that he was indeed the inventor of *taureaux piscine*. While I was taking that in, he added that he had invented *taureaux football* as well. He had nothing to do with *taureaux* watermelon.

It all came about, he said, while he was managing the arenas at Saint-Gilles and Les Saintes-Maries-de-la-Mer, a Camarguaise seaside resort that is particularly well known for taurine events. He had decided that the *courses de nuit*—the amateur events held in the evening during the festivals—were boring. A lot of young men just ran around with bulls; nobody in the stands knew exactly what was going on. The solution he came up with, in 1957 or 1958, was *taureaux piscine*. In other words, *taureaux piscine* had come about for the same reason that, say, Ladies' Day in baseball had come about—as a way to build the gate. I liked that. It did not lack finesse.

Bilhau had decided that any of the games could be improved by an announcer. The announcer, he said, was the key to *taureaux piscine*—the person who involved both the participants and the audience. Bilhau, of course, had been the first announcer. One of his trademarks, he told us, was picking out young men in the ring and giving them heroic names—Napoleon, maybe, or Charlemagne. He said he still announced occasionally, but ordinarily he contented himself with renting out bulls to other *taureaux piscine* promoters. He could also furnish the hay bales and the specially designed tarp for the pool—a contraption that, it almost goes without saying, he invented.

But how, I asked, had he come up with his greatest stroke of invention, the combination of bulls and swimming pool?

"I wanted to find the comical point of view," Bilhau said. "What is there that's comical? There's water. There's a custard pie."

If Abner Doubleday could have expressed himself that succinctly, I suspect, baseball would not be so difficult for foreigners to understand. I was definitely in the presence of the inventor, a man who could have tossed off *taureaux* custard pie if he had been in the mood. I decided that Saint-Gilles should add to its sobriquets. It was not simply Gateway to the Camargue and City of Roman Art. It was also Birthplace of Taureaux Piscine.

·

I met Jean-Marie Bilhau, Émile's son, the next Sunday. A local *club taurin* was holding a *ferrade* at Mas d'Estagel, and the elder Bilhau had invited our whole family to attend. A *ferrade* is a sort of informal rodeo and picnic; in the principal event, calves run across a large field toward a branding fire, and horsemen try to push them over with long poles that look like jousters' lances. Jean-Marie told me that *taureaux piscine* had been a great hit in Barcelona and that he had plans to take it to Germany and Italy. He asked me how I thought it would go over in America. It was not a question I had considered. "You have bulls there, right?" Jean-Marie asked.

I told him our bulls were less the sort that charged young men than the sort whose back you jumped onto from a horse. He said that bringing along his own bulls would be no problem; the Spanish had invented a sort of box to carry bulls on airplanes. I suppose the second generation is always more technologically oriented.

"America is ready for *taureaux piscine*," he said.

"You may be right," I said.

I was just being polite. But the more I thought about it, as we drove through the vineyards away from Mas d'Estagel, the more clearly I could see *taureaux piscine* in America—the analytical stories in the sports section, the opening night at some place like Madison Square Garden, the interview on local TV with some soaking-wet hero from the Bronx. I opened the window of the car. I shouted into the wind, "TAU-REAUX-PI-SCINE!"

John Updike

Lifeguard

*B*eyond doubt, I am a splendid fellow. In the autumn, winter, and spring, I execute the duties of a student of divinity; in the summer I disguise myself in my skin and become a lifeguard. My slightly narrow and gingerly hirsute but not necessarily unmanly chest becomes brown. My smooth back turns the color of caramel, which, in conjunction with the whipped cream of my white pith helmet, gives me, some of my teen-age satellites assure me, a delightfully edible appearance. My legs, which I myself can study, cocked as they are before me while I repose on my elevated wooden throne, are dyed a lustreless maple walnut that accentuates their articulate strength. Correspondingly, the hairs of my body are bleached blond, so that my legs have the pointed elegance of, within the flower, umber anthers dusted with pollen.

For nine months of the year, I pace my pale hands and burning eyes through immense pages of Biblical text barnacled with fudging commentary; through multivolumed apologetics couched in a falsely friendly Victorian voice and bound in subtly abrasive boards of finely ridged, prefaded red; through handbooks of liturgy and histories of dogma; through the bewildering duplicities of Tillich's divine politicking; through the suave table talk of Father D'Arcy, Etienne Gilson, Jacques Maritain, and other such moderns mistakenly put at their ease by the exquisite antique furniture and overstuffed larder of the hospitable St. Thomas; through the terrifying attempts of Kierkegaard, Berdyaev, and Barth to scourge God into being. I sway appalled on the ladder of minus signs by which theologians would surmount the void. I tiptoe like a burglar into the house of naturalism to steal the silver. An acrobat, I swing from wisp to wisp. Newman's iridescent cobwebs crush in my hands. Pascal's blackboard mathematics are erased by a passing shoulder. The cave drawings, astoundingly vital by candlelight, of those aboriginal magicians, Paul and Augustine, in daylight fade into mere anthropology. The diverting productions of literary flirts like Chesterton, Eliot, Auden, and Greene—whether they regard Christianity as a pastel forest designed for a fairyland romp or a deliciously miasmic pit from which chiaroscuro can be mined with mechanical buckets—in the end all infallibly strike, despite the comic variety of gongs and mallets, the note of the rich young man who on the coast of Judaea refused in dismay to sell all that he had.

Then, for the remaining quarter of the solar revolution, I rest my eyes on a sheet of brilliant sand printed with the runes of naked human bodies. That there is no discrepancy between my studies, that the texts of the flesh complement those of the mind, is the easy burden of my sermon.

On the back rest of my lifeguard's chair is painted a cross—true, a red cross, signifying bandages, splints, spirits of ammonia, and sunburn unguents. Nevertheless, it comforts me. Each morning, as I mount into my chair, my athletic and youthfully fuzzy toes expertly gripping the slats that make a ladder, it is as if I am climbing into an immense, rigid, loosely fitting vestment.

Again, in each of my roles I sit attentively perched on the edge of an immensity. That the sea, with its multiform and mysterious hosts, its savage and senseless rages, no longer comfortably serves as a divine metaphor indicates how severely humanism has corrupted the apples of our creed. We seek God now in flowers and good deeds, and the immensities of blue that surround the little scabs of land upon which we draw our lives to their unsatisfactory conclusions are suffused by science with vacuous horror. I myself can hardly bear the thought of stars, or begin to count the mortalities of coral. But from my chair the sea, slightly distended by my higher perspective, seems a misty old gentleman stretched at his ease in an immense armchair which has for arms the arms of this bay and for an antimacassar the freshly laundered sky. Sailboats float on his surface like idle and unrelated but benevolent thoughts. The soughing of the surf is the rhythmic lifting of his ripple-stitched vest as he breathes. Consider. We enter the sea with a shock; our skin and blood shout in protest. But, that instant, that leap, past, what do we find? Ecstasy and buoyance. Swimming offers a parable. We struggle and thrash, and drown; we succumb, even in despair, and float, and are saved.

With what timidity, with what a sense of trespass, do I set forward even this obliquely a thought so official! Forgive me. I am not yet ordained; I am too disordered to deal with the main text. My competence is marginal, and I will confine myself to the gloss of flesh with which this particular margin, this one beach, is annotated each day.

Here the cinema of life is run backwards. The old are the first to arrive. They are idle, and have lost the gift of sleep. Each of our bodies is a clock that loses time. Young as I am, I can hear in myself the protein acids ticking; I wake at odd hours and in the shuddering darkness and silence feel my death rushing toward me like an express train. The older we get, and the fewer the mornings left to us, the more deeply dawn stabs us awake. The old ladies wear wide straw hats and, in their hats' shadows, smiles as wide, which they bestow upon each other, upon salty shells they discover in the morning-smooth sand, and even upon me, downy-eyed from my night of dissipation. The gentlemen are often incongruous; withered white legs support brazen barrel chests, absurdly potent, bustling with white froth. How these old roosters preen on their "condition"! With what fatuous expertness they swim in the icy water—always, however, prudently parallel to the shore, at a depth no greater than their height.

Then come the middle-aged, burdened with children and aluminum chairs. The men are scarred with the marks of their vocation—the red forearms of the gasoline-station attendant, the pale X on the back of the overall-wearing mason or carpenter, the clammer's nicked ankles. The hair on their bodies has as many patterns as matted grass. The women are wrinkled but fertile, like the Iraqi rivers that cradled the seeds of our civilization. Their children are odious. From their gaunt faces leer all the vices, the greeds, the grating urgencies of the adult, unsoftened by maturity's reticence and fatigue. Except that here and there, a girl, the eldest daughter, wearing a knit suit striped horizontally with green, purple, and brown, walks slowly, carefully, puzzled by the dawn enveloping her thick smooth body, her waist not yet nipped but her throat elongated.

Finally come the young. The young matrons bring fat and fussing infants who gobble the sand like sugar, who toddle blissfully into the surf and bring me bolt upright on my throne. My whistle tweets. The mothers rouse. Many of these women are pregnant again, and sluggishly lie in their loose suits like cows tranced in a meadow. They gossip politics, and smoke incessantly, and lift their troubled eyes in wonder as a trio of flat-stomached nymphs parades past. These maidens take all our eyes. The vivacious redhead, freckled and white-footed, pushing against her boy and begging to be ducked; the solemn brunette, transporting the vase of herself with held breath; the dimpled blonde in the bib and diapers of her Bikini, the lambent fuzz of her midriff shimmering like a cat's belly. Lust stuns me like the sun.

·

You are offended that a divinity student lusts? What prigs the unchurched are. Are not our assaults on the supernatural lascivious, a kind of indecency? If only you knew what de Sadian degradations, what frightful psychological spelunking, our gentle transcendentalist professors set us to, as preparation for our work, which is to shine in the darkness.

I feel that my lust makes me glow; I grow cold in my chair, like a torch of ice, as I study beauty. I have studied much of it, wearing all styles of bathing suit and facial expression, and have come to this conclusion: a woman's beauty lies, not in any exaggeration of the specialized zones, nor in any general harmony that could be worked out by means of the *sectio aurea* or a similar aesthetic superstition; but in the arabesque of the spine. The curve by which the back modulates into the buttocks. It is here that grace sits and rides a woman's body.

I watch from my white throne and pity women, deplore the demented judgment that drives them toward the braggart muscularity of the mesomorph and the prosperous complacence of the endomorph when it is we ectomorphs who pack in our scrawny sinews and exacerbated nerves the most intense gift, the most generous shelter, of love. To desire a woman is to desire to save her. Anyone who has endured intercourse that was neither predatory nor hurried knows how through it we descend, with a partner, into the grotesque and delicate shadows that until then have remained locked in the most guarded recess of our soul: into this harbor we bring her. A vague and twisted terrain becomes inhabited; each shadow, touched by the exploration, blooms into a flower of act. As if we are an island upon which a woman, tossed by her laboring vanity and blind self-seeking, is blown, and there finds security, until, an instant before the anticlimax, Nature with a smile thumps down her trump, and the island sinks beneath the sea.

There is great truth in those motion pictures which are slandered as true neither to the Bible nor to life. They are—written though they are by demons and drunks—true to both. We are all Solomons lusting for Sheba's salvation. The God-filled man is filled with a wilderness that cries to be populated. The stony chambers need jewels, furs, tints of cloth and flesh, even though, as in Samson's case, the temple comes tumbling. Women are an alien race of pagans set down among us. Every seduction is a conversion.

Who has loved and not experienced that sense of rescue? It is not true that our biological impulses are tricked out with ribands of chivalry; rather, our chivalric impulses go clanking in encumbering biological armor. Eunuchs love. Children love. I would love.

My chief exercise, as I sit above the crowds, is to lift the whole mass into immortality. It is not a light task; the throng is so huge, and its members so individually unworthy. No *memento mori* is so clinching as a photograph of a vanished crowd. Cheering Roosevelt, celebrating the Armistice, there it is, wearing its ten thousand straw hats and stiff collars, a fearless and wooden-faced bustle of life: it is gone. A crowd dies in the street like a derelict; it leaves no heir, no trace, no name. My own persistence beyond the last rim of time is easy to imagine; indeed, the effort of imagination lies the other way—to conceive of my ceasing. But when I study the vast tangle of humanity that blackens the beach as far as the sand stretches, absurdities crowd in on me. Is it as maiden, matron, or crone that the females will be eternalized? What will they do without children to watch and gossip to exchange? What of the thousand deaths of memory and bodily change we endure—can each be redeemed at a final Adjustments Counter? The sheer numbers involved make the mind scream. The race is no longer a tiny clan of simian aristocrats lording it over an ocean of grass; mankind is a plague racing like fire across the exhausted continents. This immense clot gathered on the beach, a fraction of a fraction—can we not say that this breeding swarm is its own immortality and end the suspense? The beehive in a sense survives; and is each of us not proved to be a hive, a galaxy of cells each of whom is doubtless praying, from its pew in our thumbnail or esophagus, for personal resurrection? Indeed, to the cells themselves cancer may seem a revival of faith. No, in relation to other people oblivion is sensible and sanitary.

This sea of others exasperates and fatigues me most on Sunday mornings. I don't know why people no longer go to church—whether they have lost the ability to sing or the willingness to listen. From eight-thirty onward they crowd in from the parking lot, ants each carrying its crumb of baggage, until by noon, when the remote churches are releasing their gallant and gaily dressed minority, the sea itself is jammed with hollow heads and thrashing arms like a great bobbing backwash of rubbish. A transistor radio somewhere in the sand releases in a thin, apologetic gust the closing peal of a transcribed service. And right here, here at the very height of torpor and confusion, I slump, my eyes slit, and the blurred forms of Protestantism's errant herd seem gathered by the water's edge in impassioned poses of devotion. I seem to be lying dreaming in the infinite rock of space before Creation, and the actual scene I see is a vision of impossibility: a Paradise. For had we existed before the gesture that split the firmament, could we have conceived of our most obvious possession, our most platitudinous blessing, the moment, the single ever-present moment that we perpetually bring to our lips brimful?

So: be joyful. Be joyful is my commandment. It is the message I read in your jiggle. Stretch your skins like pegged hides curing in the miracle of the sun's moment. Exult in your legs' scissoring, your waist's swivel. Romp; eat the froth; be children. I am here above you; I have given my youth that you may do this. I wait. The tides of time have treacherous undercurrents. You are borne continually toward the horizon. I have prepared myself; my muscles are in-stilled with everything that must be done. Someday my alertness will bear fruit; from near the horizon there will arise, delicious, translucent, like a green bell above the water, the call for help, the call, a call, it saddens me to confess, that I have yet to hear.

Monica Wood

Disappearing

When he starts in, I don't look anymore, I know what it looks like, what he looks like, tobacco on his teeth. I just lie in the deep sheets and shut my eyes. I make noises that make it go faster and when he's done he's as far from me as he gets. He could be dead he's so far away.

Lettie says leave then stupid but who would want me. Three hundred pounds anyway but I never check. Skin like tapioca pudding, I wouldn't show anyone. A man.

So we go to the pool at the junior high, swimming lessons. First it's blow bubbles and breathe, blow and breathe. Awful, hot nosefuls of chlorine. My eyes stinging red and patches on my skin. I look worse. We'll get caps and goggles and earplugs and body cream Lettie says. It's better.

There are girls there, what bodies. Looking at me and Lettie out the side of their eyes. Gold hair, skin like milk, chlorine or no.

They thought when I first lowered into the pool, that fat one parting the Red Sea. I didn't care. Something happened when I floated. Good said the little instructor. A little redhead in an emerald suit, no stomach, a depression almost, and white wet skin. Good she said you float just great. Now we're getting somewhere. The whistle around her neck blinded my eyes. And the water under the fluorescent lights. I got scared and couldn't float again. The bottom of the pool was scarred, drops of gray shadow rippling. Without the water I would crack open my head, my dry flesh would sound like a splash on the tiles.

At home I ate a cake and a bottle of milk. No wonder you look like that he said. How can you stand yourself. You're no Cary Grant I told him and he laughed and laughed until I threw up.

When this happens I want to throw up again and again until my heart flops out wet and writhing on the kitchen floor. Then he would know I have one and it moves.

So I went back. And floated again. My arms came around and the groan of the water made the tight blondes smirk but I heard Good that's the crawl that's it in fragments from the redhead when I lifted my face. Through the earplugs I heard her skinny voice. She was happy that I was floating and moving too.

Lettie stopped the lessons and read to me things out of magazines. You have to swim a lot to lose weight. You have to stop eating too. Forget cake and ice cream. Doritos are out. I'm not doing it for that I told her but she wouldn't believe me. She could imagine.

Looking down that shaft of water I know I won't fall. The water shimmers and eases up and down, the heft of me doesn't matter I float anyway.

He says it makes no difference I look the same. But I'm not the same. I can hold myself up in deep water. I can move my arms and feet and the water goes behind me, the wall comes closer. I can look down twelve feet to a cold slab of tile and not be afraid. It makes a difference I tell him. Better believe it mister.

Then this other part happens. Other men interest me. I look at them, real ones, not the ones on TV that's something else entirely. These are real. The one with the white milkweed hair who delivers the mail. The meter man from the light company, heavy thick feet in boots. A smile. Teeth. I drop something out of the cart in the supermarket to see who will pick it up. Sometimes a man. One had yellow short hair and called me ma'am. Young. Thin legs and an accent. One was older. Looked me in the eyes. Heavy, but not like me. My eyes are nice. I color the lids. In the pool it runs off in blue tears. When I come out my face is naked.

The lessons are over, I'm certified. A little certificate signed by the redhead. She says I can swim and I can. I'd do better with her body, thin calves hard as granite.

I get a lane to myself, no one shares. The blondes ignore me now that I don't splash the water, know how to lower myself silently. And when I swim I cut the water cleanly.

For one hour every day I am thin, thin as water, transparent, invisible, steam or smoke.

The redhead is gone, they put her at a different pool and I miss the glare of the whistle dangling between her emerald breasts. Lettie won't come over at all now that she is fatter than me. You're so uppity she says. All this talk about water and who do you think you are.

He says I'm looking all right, so at night it is worse but sometimes now when he starts in I say no. On Sundays the pool is closed I can't say no. I haven't been invisible. Even on days when I don't say no it's all right, he's better.

One night he says it won't last, what about the freezer full of low-cal dinners and that machine in the basement. I'm not doing it for that and he doesn't believe me either. But this time there is another part. There are other men in the water I tell him. Fish he says. Fish in the sea. Good luck.

Ma you've lost says my daughter-in-law, the one who didn't want me in the wedding pictures. One with the whole family, she couldn't help that. I learned how to swim I tell her. You should try it, it might help your ugly disposition.

They closed the pool for two weeks and I went crazy. Repairing the tiles. I went there anyway, drove by in the car. I drank water all day.

Then they opened again and I went every day sometimes four times until the green paint and new stripes looked familiar as a face. At first the water was heavy as blood but I kept on until it was thinner and thinner, just enough to hold me up. That was when I stopped with the goggles and cap and plugs, things that kept the water out of me.

There was a time I went the day before a holiday and no one was there. It was echoey silence just me and the soundless empty pool and a lifeguard behind the glass. I lowered myself so slow it hurt every muscle but not a blip of water not a ripple not one sound and I was under in that other quiet, so quiet some tears got out, I saw their blue trail swirling.

The redhead is back and nods, she has seen me somewhere. I tell her I took lessons and she still doesn't remember.

This has gone too far he says I'm putting you in the hospital. He calls them at the pool and they pay no attention. He doesn't touch me and I smile into my pillow, a secret smile in my own square of the dark.

Oh my God Lettie says what the hell are you doing what the hell do you think you're doing. I'm disappearing I tell her and what can you do about it not a blessed thing.

For a long time in the middle of it people looked at me. Men. And I thought about it. Believe it, I thought. And now they don't look at me again. And it's better.

I'm almost there. Almost water.

The redhead taught me how to dive, how to tuck my head and vanish like a needle into skin, and every time it happens, my feet leaving the board, I think, this will be the time.

Contributors' Notes

Carol Anshaw is a swimmer and the author of *They Do It All With Mirrors* and *Aquamarine*, winner of the 1992 Carl Sandburg and Society of Midland Authors awards for fiction, and finalist for the Lambda Literary Award. She is on the faculty of the MFA in Writing program at Vermont College. She has been awarded a 1995 National Endowment for the Arts Fellowship.

Philip Booth has published ten books of poetry, the most recent of which is *Pairs*. He has won numerous prizes and fellowships, including two Guggenheim Fellowships, a National Endowment for the Arts Fellowship, the Theodore Roethke Prize and the Maurice English Poetry Award. Until his retirement in 1985, he taught at Syracuse University. *Trying to Say It, Outlooks and Insights on How Poems Happen* will be published in spring, 1996.

Ray Bradbury is a prolific poet, playwright, screenwriter, and science fiction writer. He is the author of countless short stories, including "Fahrenheit 451," and many novels for children and adults.

Daniel Chambliss is chairman of the Sociology Department at Hamilton College in Clinton, New York. He coached swimming throughout the 1980s. His book is called *Champions*.

John Cheever, one of the great American short story writers of the twentieth century, is also known for his Wapshot novels, *The Wapshot Chronicle*, *The Wapshot Scandal*, and *Bullet Park*. *The Stories of John Cheever* was published in 1978. "The Swimmer" was made into the 1968 movie of the same name, starring Burt Lancaster.

John Ciardi, poet and poetry editor of *The Saturday Review*, translated Dante's *The Divine Comedy*. He edited *Mid-Century American Poets* and *How Does a Poem Mean?*, which is still used as a college text.

Laurie Colwin is the author of several novels, including *Goodbye Without Leaving* and *A Big Storm Knocked It Over*, short story collections including *Passion and Affect* and *The Lone Pilgrim*, a collection of essays, and two cookbooks, *Home Cooking* and *More Home Cooking*.

James Dickey is a poet and the author of the novel *Deliverance*, for which he also wrote the screenplay. *The Whole Motion: Collected Poems of James Dickey* was published in 1992. He teaches at the University of South Carolina.

M. Coleman Easton is the author of *Masters of Glass*, *Isklir*, *Spirits of Cavern and Hearth*, and *The Fisherman's Curse*.

David Allan Evans is a poet, fiction writer, and essayist. His poems on sports have appeared in *Aethon: The Journal of Sports Literature* and in the anthologies *American Sports Poems* and *The Sporting Spirit*; a short story was included in *The Norton Book of Sports*, edited by George Plimpton. His latest book of poems is *Hanging Out With the Cross*. He and his wife Jan have written a memoir of their Fulbright year in China, *Double Happiness: Two Lives in China*. Evans teaches at South Dakota State University.

John Fox is the author of four short stories and the novel *The Boys on the Rock*.

Dawn Fraser won the gold medal in the 100-meter freestyle at three successive Olympics, Melbourne (1956), Rome (1960), and Tokyo (1964). She was the first woman to break a minute for the 100-meter freestyle. Her story, written with Harry Gordon, is told in *Below the Surface: Confessions of an Olympic Champion.*

Jewelle Gomez is an activist, teacher, administrator, and literary critic. She is also the author of the black vampire lesbian novel, *The Gilda Stories*, winner of two Lambda Literary Awards, and *Forty-three Septembers*, a book of essays.

Polly Rose Gottlieb is the sister of famous show business impresario Billy Rose, about whom, in part, the movie *Funny Lady* was written. In the movie, the part of Eleanor Holm is played by swimmer Heidi O'Rourke. The Aquabelles are played by the Oak Park Marionettes, supervised by Marion Kane.

Richard Halliburton was a young American adventurer whose books and lectures made him famous in the twenties and thirties. He died prematurely while crossing the Pacific in a Chinese junk specially designed and built for him in Hong Kong.

Jonathan Holden's most recent poetry collection, *The Sublime*, was winner of the 1995 Vassar Miller Prize. He is University Distinguished Professor and poet-in-residence at Kansas State University.

A. E. Housman is the author of *A Shropshire Lad* and *Last Poems*. "Tarry, delight . . . " is taken from his *Collected Poems*, published in 1940. It retells the Greek myth of Hero and Leander, in which the young Leander swims the Hellespont nightly to be with Hero, the Greek priestess of Venus with whom he is in love. Each morning, before dawn, he swims back to Asia Minor. One night he drowns, his body washes ashore below Hero's tower, and she throws herself, heartbroken, into the sea.

Barney Hutchinson's poem appeared in *Sports Illustrated*.

Edmond Jabès, who supplies the epigraph, was born into a French-speaking community of Jews in Egypt. His poetry was influenced by the French surrealists and by Hebrew Biblical and legal commentary. The translation is by Rosemarie Waldrop.

Annette Kellerman, an Australian swimmer, overcame a crippling childhood disease to become one of the greatest swimmers and most popular celebrities of her day. Her book, *How to Swim*, was published in 1918. She made several movies, including *Neptune's Daughter*, later remade with Esther Williams, who also starred in a movie of Kellerman's life, *Million Dollar Mermaid*.

A. M. Klein was a Canadian short story writer, essayist, and poet of Ukrainian origin. *The Complete Poems* was published posthumously in 1990.

Maxine Kumin won the Pulitzer Prize for *Up Country* in 1972. Her latest book of poetry is *Looking for Luck*. In addition to her numerous books of poetry, she is the author of novels, essays, and children's books.

Doris Lessing was born of British parents in Persia in 1919 and moved with her family to Rhodesia at the age of five. She has lived in London since 1949. She is the author of more than twenty books—novels, stories, reportage, poems, and plays. Her latest book is a memoir, *Under My Skin*.

Jenifer Levin is the author of four novels, two of which are about swimming: *Water Dancer*, reissued in 1994, which won the PEN/Hemingway Best First Novel Award when originally published; and *The Sea of Light*.

Jack London wrote *The Call of the Wild* and other romantic adventure stories of the Arctic and the South Seas.

Thomas Lux teaches at Sarah Lawrence College. He is the author of five books of poetry, the most recent of which is *The Drowned River*.

Colleen J. McElroy lives in Seattle, Washington where she is on the faculty of the Department of English at the University of Washington. She has published collections of poetry and short stories, and writes for stage and television. Her two latest publications are a short story collection, *Driving Under the Cardboard Pines*, and *What Madness Brought Me Here: Selected Poems, 1968–88*. Winner of the Before Columbus American Book Award, she also has received two Fulbright Fellowships, two National Endowment for the Arts Fellowships, and a Rockefeller Fellowship. Her work has been translated into Russian, German, Malay, and Serbo-Croatian.

Walter Russell Mead is a political economist who serves as President's Fellow at the World Policy Institute at the New School for Social Research in New York City. He is the author of *Mortal Splendor: The American Empire in Transition*. In addition to his articles, essays, and reviews in political economy, he is well-known for his feature and travel writing.

Rohinton Mistry was born in Bombay in 1952, and has lived in Canada since 1975. He is the author of a collection of linked stories, *Swimming Lessons and Other Stories from Firozsha Baag*, and two novels, *A Fine Balance* and *Such a Lonely Journey*, which won the 1991 Commonwealth Writers Prize for Best Book of the Year, the Governor General's Award, and the W. H. Smith/Books in Canada First Novel Award. He is the recipient of the 1995 Canada-Australia Literary Prize.

R. Bruce Moody published a second story, "Repertory in New York," in the *National Review*.

Rebecca Morris published another story, "Bellevue Circus," in *The Saturday Evening Post*.

Diana Nyad is probably the most famous contemporary American long-distance swimmer. Her book, *Other Shores*, tells the story of her extraordinary career.

Sharon Olds is the author of five books of poetry, the most recent of which is *The Wellspring*. Her second book, *The Dead and the Living*, won the Lamont Poetry Prize and the National Book Critics' Circle Award.

Mary Oliver has won both the National Book Award and the Pulitzer Prize. Her latest books are *New and Selected Poems* and *A Poetry Handbook*.

Dick Powell was the official observer of Ted Erikson's two-way swim across the English Channel. He wrote the official report for the Channel Swimming Association.

Don Schollander won four gold medals at the 1964 Tokyo Olympics, the most medals ever won in a single Olympics at that time; only Mark Spitz, who won seven gold medals in Munich in 1972, has outdone him. Schollander wrote his swimming story with Duke Savage in *Deep Water*.

Anne Sexton wrote seven books of poetry during her lifetime, including the groundbreaking *To Bedlam and Part Way Back*, *All My Pretty Ones*, and the Pulitzer Prize–winning *Live or Die*.

Charlotte Watson Sherman is the author of a book of short stories, *Killing Color*, and several novels, including *One Dark Body* and *Touch*. She is the editor of *Sisterfire: Black Womanist Fiction and Poetry*.

Alix Kates Shulman's most recent book is a memoir, *Drinking the Rain*. She is the author of four novels, starting with the bestselling *Memoirs of an Ex-Prom Queen*, several works of nonfiction, children's books, stories, and essays. She has been Visiting Writer at the American Academy in Rome and has received grants from the NEA and the Lila Wallace/Reader's Digest Foundation.

Stevie Smith established her reputation with the publication of a novel, *Novel on Yellow Paper*, and her first book of poems, *A Good Time Was Had By All*. Her *Collected Poems* was published in the United States in 1976.

Maureen Stanton lives and swims and works in Portland, Maine.

Linda Svendsen is a fiction- and screenwriter living in Vancouver. Her first collection of short stories, *Marine Life*, was published in 1992.

Charles Tomlinson is an artist as well as a poet, critic, and translator. His most recent poetry collection is *The Door in the Wall*.

Calvin Trillin is a reporter, syndicated columnist, travel writer, and humorist. His latest books include *American Stories, Remembering Denny*, and *Deadline Poet*, a collection of his weekly verse from *The Nation*. "Damp in the Afternoon" is reprinted from *Travels with Alice*.

John Updike, prolific novelist, poet, short story writer, and critic, is perhaps best known for his series of Rabbit novels, two of which, *Rabbit is Rich* and *Rabbit at Rest* won the Pulitzer Prize and the National Book Critics' Circle Award. His *Collected Poems* was published in 1993.

Monica Wood published a novel, *Secret Language*, in 1993. Her stories have appeared most recently in *Redbook, North American Review*, and *Manoa*. Her work has been read on Public Radio International, awarded special mention in the 1992 Pushcart Prize anthology, and nominated for a National Magazine Award. She lives in Maine.

Copyright Acknowledgments

About the Editor

Laurel Blossom is the author of three volumes of poetry: *Any Minute, What's Wrong,* and *The Papers Said.* She has received grants from the National Endowment for the Arts, the New York Foundation for the Arts, and the Ohio Arts Council. She is co-founder of the writing workshop and residency program, The Writers Community, which is now part of the National Writer's Voice Project of the YMCA of the USA.